Early Modern Europe

**Recent Titles in
Historical Facts and Fictions**

The Victorian World: Facts and Fictions
Ginger S. Frost

The Vikings: Facts and Fictions
Kirsten Wolf and Tristan Mueller-Vollmer

American Civil War: Facts and Fictions
James R. Hedtke

The Middle Ages: Facts and Fictions
Winston Black

The History of Christianity: Facts and Fictions
Dyron B. Daughrity

The History of Buddhism: Facts and Fictions
Geoffrey C. Goble

Ancient Egypt: Facts and Fictions
Stephen E. Thompson

Ancient Rome: Facts and Fictions
Monica M. Bontty

William Shakespeare: Facts and Fictions
Douglas J. King

Colonial America: Facts and Fictions
K. David Goss and A. A. Grishin

The 1960s Cultural Revolution: Facts and Fictions
Joel P. Rhodes

Early Modern Europe

Facts and Fictions

Brian Jeffrey Maxson

Historical Facts and Fictions

BLOOMSBURY ACADEMIC
NEW YORK • LONDON • OXFORD • NEW DELHI • SYDNEY

BLOOMSBURY ACADEMIC
Bloomsbury Publishing Inc, 1359 Broadway, New York, NY 10018, USA
Bloomsbury Publishing Plc, 50 Bedford Square, London, WC1B 3DP, UK
Bloomsbury Publishing Ireland, 29 Earlsfort Terrace, Dublin 2, D02 AY28, Ireland

BLOOMSBURY, BLOOMSBURY ACADEMIC and the Diana logo
are trademarks of Bloomsbury Publishing Plc

First published in the United States of America by ABC-CLIO 2023
Paperback edition published by Bloomsbury Academic 2026

Library of Congress Cataloging-in-Publication Data
Names: Maxson, Brian, 1978- author.
Title: Early modern Europe : facts and fictions / Brian Jeffrey Maxson.
Description: New York : Bloomsbury, [2023] |
Series: Historical facts and fictions | Includes bibliographical references and index.
Identifiers: LCCN 2022049308 | ISBN 9781440867453 (hardcover) |
ISBN 9798216171324 (ebook) | ISBN 9781440867460 (epdf)
Subjects: LCSH: Europe—History—1492-1648—Errors, inventions, etc. |
Europe—History—1648-1789—Errors, inventions, etc.
Classification: LCC D210 .M36 2023 | DDC 940.2—dc23/eng/20221019
LC record available at https://lccn.loc.gov/2022049308

ISBN: HB: 978-1-4408-6745-3
PB: 979-8-2164-6052-7
ePDF: 978-1-4408-6746-0
eBook: 979-8-2161-7132-4

Series: Historical Facts and Fictions

For product safety related questions contact productsafety@bloomsbury.com

To find out more about our authors and books visit www.bloomsbury.com
and sign up for our newsletters.

Contents

Preface

This book explores nine common myths about the history and culture of early modern Europe, defined as roughly the period between 1350 and 1700. The aim of each chapter is to either dispel or complicate popular assumptions about a topic. I have written and compiled this book with a curious layperson or college undergraduate in mind. As a professor of late medieval history and early modern history, I encounter many of these myths both in my classrooms and in popular culture. I remember that before I became a specialist in this topic, I too held many of the same assumptions! Many of the myths discussed in the following chapters have their origins in the nineteenth and twentieth centuries. In the first decades of the twenty-first century, popular documentaries and television shows about historical families have tended to reinforce what we think we know about the world before the French Revolution. The success of shows like *Game of Thrones* has opened visual, fantastical, and entertaining worlds for viewers, even as what we think we know about the early modern past does not always match what experts have figured out over the past decades.

In selecting nine myths for this book, I have tried to focus on areas that I thought most readers would find familiar and that possessed many different scholarly studies, especially in English, so readers could pursue their curiosity further. For this reason, the topics focus—with a few exceptions—primarily on western Europe. The book begins chronologically, with chapter 1 debunking the idea that a Renaissance inaugurated the early modern world—or even the modern world—after a period of darkness. Chapter 2 tries to dispel ideas such as the early modern belief in a flat earth or the belief that Europeans arrived in mostly depopulated American continents.

In chapter 3, the significance of women comes to the forefront, with an emphasis upon the variety of lives that women led long before the Industrial Age. From women, the book turns to the myth of secularism (in chapter 4), for the early modern period remained just as religious as the medieval period before it. Two myths about Catholicism in this period follow. In chapter 5, I try to recontextualize the pope as a much more limited political ruler than the popular view of unlimited papal power in past times. Chapter 6 complicates the common narrative that the Protestant Reformations were an inevitable response to the failures of the Catholic Church. In the next chapter, the European witch hunts take center stage. The story that emerges is at times dark, but it is also quite different from what many modern readers might expect. Chapter 8 turns to science. Science did not immediately sweep the belief in witches to the dustbin of history; and the Scientific Revolution happened very differently than readers might assume. Rather than a series of great triumphs by scientific geniuses, early modern science tended to be piecemeal, collaborative, and included all sorts of people. In the final chapter, the book turns to the Crusades, a topic ordinarily associated with the medieval period. The chapter shows that the Crusades continued throughout the early modern period. Along the way, the chapter also challenges the myth that the Crusades overlay a stark division between a unified western Christian Europe and an eastern Islamic Ottoman Empire.

Acknowledgments

This book has allowed me to think about how to bridge the gap between current scholarship and popular conceptions about early modern Europe. I am grateful to my editors at ABC-CLIO, especially George Butler, Robin Tutt, and Saville Bloxham, each of whom provided guidance, patience, and encouragement throughout the extended time it took to write this book. I also want to thank Kimberly Woodring and Alexis Doutrich, who read and commented on chapter drafts. My family has provided their support throughout the years it took to put this book together. I would like to thank David and Linda Maxson, Kathy Van Zuuk, Vivian Roach, Michael Schmidt, and Ronald and Cathy Maxson. I would also like to, especially, thank my wife Jennifer and daughter Alex: Much of this book was drafted during the COVID-19 pandemic in 2020 and 2021, and their support provided a level of normalcy to life that made it possible to continue progressing on projects like this.

Introduction

Long ago, the fall of Rome shackled all of Europe with chains of super-stition, violence, poverty, and general despair. After nearly 1,000 years of hopeless Dark Ages, the Renaissance finally brought a new dawn to the bleak landscape. As the Renaissance spread from Italy, the "Early Modern" period was born. It was an age when explorers like Columbus defeated the superstitions of the past and discovered the untapped American wil-derness. It was an age when men discovered secularism. The cumulative experiments of a series of geniuses laid the foundations for modern sci-ence. Science allowed society to progress, to move away from accusa-tions of witchcraft and the machinations of powerful popes. Europeans embarked on a new period of prosperity. They obtained global power by conquering far-off lands and finally defeated the Islamic Ottoman Empire closer to home.

The previous paragraph repeats many different myths about early mod-ern Europe that this book tries to complicate and, in some cases, dispel altogether. The first chapter of the book begins with the idea of periods in history, such as "medieval," "Renaissance," and "early modern." Since the turn of the twentieth century, historians have been trying to break loose the idea of a "Dark Age" from popular culture. As the first chapter of this book shows, people in the 1800s and 1900s looked back at Italians in the 1300s and 1400s and saw bits of themselves. Those Italians had argued that their new Latin studies were different from the academic foci of pre-vious thinkers. Thus, those Latin scholars believed that they were living in a new and better age. Nineteenth- and twentieth-century writers agreed with them. Not only that, but those writers in the 1800s and 1900s also claimed that, over time, the writings and cultures of the Italian Renaissance spread across Europe. They called the new Europe that emerged "early modern" to distinguish the centuries imbued with Renaissance culture from the medieval centuries before them. Specialists today think differently. Historians continue to disagree about what defined "medieval," "Renaissance," and "early modern," yet they all agree that no Dark Age existed and that any links between pre-1700 Europe and the present are extremely complicated and challenging to draw. For ease of understanding, I have defined "early modern" in this book as encompassing Europe from around 1350 until around 1700.

Popular myths about early modern Europe point to a variety of changes to separate that period from earlier centuries. One central myth about Europe during the period hinges upon ideas about the Columbian Exchange after 1492. It is true that the early modern world began global exchanges that continue to this day. Yet, several myths accompany these exchanges. Very few, if any, people believed that the world was flat before Columbus, the subject of chapter 2. Medieval and early modern people knew that the world was round, even as they disagreed about its size and assumed that most of the planet was covered by land rather than water. Columbus arrived in heavily populated islands in the Caribbean that lay near the also-heavily-populated, diverse, and sophisticated American continents. The motivations of Columbus, his patrons, and other sailors were complex. They sought access to spices and gold and desired to spread the Christian faith. Columbus also sought profits by enslaving people and seizing lands for the Spanish crown. Scholars have only recently begun unpacking questions about racism and slavery in Europe during Columbus's day. But it is clear even from initial studies that Columbus and his contemporaries viewed different kinds of people through racial lenses, including prejudices about skin color.

Another myth about "early modern Europe" is that the lives of most Europeans were fairly similar during that time. Yet, early modern Europe was full of different kinds of people: non-elites, people of different faiths, people from different places, people with different skin complexions, people who spoke different languages, people with different sexual orientations, people with disabilities, and many others. Although scholars have only just begun to unpack the experiences of many of these groups in early modern Europe, the history of women has been one area that has challenged a uniform view of early modern Europe. Chapter 3 introduces the myth that women in early modern Europe played an entirely passive, unchanging, and secondary role. There certainly is evidence that that description fits the lives of some women from the early modern period and that some of those women lived full and satisfying lives. But the lives of women from this period were just as diverse as that of men. Early modern Europe witnessed an explosion of women writers and thinkers, many of whom gained universal respect in their fields. Women served as rulers. They commissioned art. They ran businesses. Of course, early modern Europe was not a society in which women and men enjoyed equal status. However, the range of experiences in the lives of women from this period—despite the social and cultural challenges placed before them—defies the myth of their historical unimportance or basic banality.

Religion often is the focus of myths about early modern Europe. For a long time, people used to think that Europe became a more secular place after the 1300s. The myth that Europeans moved away from religion after the medieval world is the focus of chapter 4. This idea took its stubborn roots in the writings of people in the 1800s, writers who were searching the past for the origins of their own increasingly secular views of the world. Writers during the 1800s claimed that the culture of the Renaissance in Italy rejected medieval religion and turned their energies to the here and now. From Italy, this point of view spread to the rest of Europe during the early modern period. That secularism, those nineteenth-century writers claimed, slowly prevailed over superstition. Yet, this view of early modern society ignores the continued centrality of religion in almost all aspects of early modern Europe, from politics to culture to economics to society and all topics in between. It also ignores the constant religious violence and persecution that plagued Europe during the early modern period. There were changes in religion and general views about life and death during this period, but those changes did not remove the centrality of religion and religious faith from the lives of almost all Europeans.

One of the most common religious myths about early modern Europe relates to the figure of the pope. Chapter 5 explores the common idea that the pope was an exceptionally powerful figure during that period. It is accurate to discuss the popes of the 1100s and early 1200s as among the most powerful political entities in Europe. However, from the 1300s at the latest the papacy lost much of its ability to make other rulers do its bidding. By the early modern period, the papal court had established itself as a news center of Europe—a place where diplomats and courtiers gathered to collect and report information. Rulers continued to court the papacy to form political alliances. But, by that time, the most powerful rulers on the continent were not based in Rome. Even other Italian powers agreed or disagreed with the pope based upon current considerations rather than some existential fear of papal power. As the chapter explains, our ideas about papal power are largely rooted in religious debates that took place during the early modern period itself, from which emerged an image of exaggerated papal power that has endured down to the present.

The book then turns to a third common religious myth—the idea that the Protestant Reformations were the inevitable consequence of the failures of the Catholic Church. In Protestant parts of the world especially, but not exclusively, the common assumption is that people had become so fed up with the moral failures of the Catholic Church that Martin Luther and the Protestantism of the 1500s were more or less inevitable. Chapter 6 seeks to show a more complicated view of the past. It is clear that early modern people, and medieval people for that matter, repeatedly voiced their criticisms and frustrations about the behaviors of priests, cardinals, popes, and other religious figures in and outside their communities. But they rarely criticized the central teachings of the Catholic faith itself. Rather, most people seem to have accepted the role of the Church in their salvation. Some people from the 1300s and 1400s led exceptionally pious lives. Those who didn't were criticized for their worldliness. Perceptions of the Catholic Church, therefore, are only one part of a very complicated story. Another part of the story is that Martin Luther, after 1517, offered a new sort of attack against many aspects of the faith itself. He benefited from historical developments such as the advent of more powerful political rulers and the printing press and cultural developments like humanism.

Another key development of the early modern period was the so-called Scientific Revolution. This is also another area where myths are very common. The term "Scientific Revolution" is usually used to describe the increasing fascination of Europeans with the natural world, experimentation, and empiricism during the early modern period. One common myth claims that early modern science finally began to brush away medieval superstitions. However, once again, this myth about early modern Europe oversimplifies the past. For example, chapter 7 discusses the European witch hunts. A variety of myths exist about early modern witches, the accusations made against them, and their prosecution. Alongside those myths is the belief that the development of science ended the whole sordid affair. However, the reality is that the worst decades of the early-modern witch hunts directly coincided with the years often associated with the Scientific Revolution.

Scientific developments coincide with the witch hunts because many myths inaccurately depict the history of science in early modern Europe.

For example, scientific disciplines sometimes trace their histories through a series of great discoveries made by past geniuses. In those narratives, the work of individual geniuses over time led to more accurate results, and those results improved technology, medicine, and offered better explanations for natural phenomena. Yet, rather than a series of progressively better experiments conducted by solitary geniuses, early modern science was characterized by collaborations, a range of different participants, explorations of topics that are both relevant and irrelevant today, successes and failures, and, of course, the broader historical contexts of early modern Europe. In addition, our modern idea about how science leads to progress over time is inherited from the very end of the early modern period. When we think about time today, we often assume that things, with the benefits of science, will get better as the decades pass. But that assumption dates to thinkers during the 1700s. During the 1400s, 1500s, and 1600s, other assumptions about the passage of time existed: many early modern people, for example, assumed that things were getting progressively worse because the world was moving toward the end described in the Christian Bible.

Another common myth about the Scientific Revolution is that the Renaissance coincided with a newfound interest in the natural world after centuries of medieval neglect. However, it would be more accurate to point to medieval precedents for later developments in the natural sciences than to scholars in the 1300s or 1400s. Early modern science, as chapter 8 seeks to show, was so complex as to defy modern myths about it.

From science, the final chapter of the book turns to the idea of Europe itself. Modern myths tend to accept that Europe is a clearly defined continent with discernible boundaries. However, the history of Europe and geography itself make it very hard to support this claim: Where, exactly, for example, does Europe begin or end? Is Turkey, home to ancient Troy but also long-time capital of the Islamic Ottoman Empire, a part of Europe? Both the Islamic Ottoman sultan and the later Russian tsars claimed that their titles derived from the ancient Romans. Most of the Ottoman Empire had once been a part of the old Roman Empire. The history of early modern Europe also complicates the myth that Europe can neatly be separated from its neighbors into a West—generally associated with places like Germany, France, Italy, Spain, and England—versus a distinct East—usually associated with places like Turkey and the Middle East. The Crusades, the focus of chapter 9, bring these sorts of issues to the forefront. It is a myth that the Crusades ended in the medieval period. In fact, European crusading efforts extended throughout the early modern period. Crusades could be launched against people from different religions, like the Ottomans. Crusades could also be launched within Europe itself, against other Christians. The Islamic Ottoman Empire maintained a continuous presence in early modern European war, diplomacy, and politics. It allied with powers like France and fought against powers like Spain in the context of a broader early modern world. The Ottomans, like other powers, slowly lost significance as the Mediterranean Sea yielded to the Atlantic Ocean as a key economic center. But the Crusades and the role of the Ottomans in early modern Europe complicate our myths about an easily defined Europe or a "West" versus an "East."

These nine myths reflect a small sampling of the places where popular conceptions of early modern Europe oversimplify or differ from historical fact. Many other myths could also have been included. However, ultimately, the nine myths chosen for this book reflect a mixture of popular conceptions of early modern Europe, current scholarship on the period, and my biases as an author. I have tried to select myths that many readers will find familiar. I have then, in many cases, tried to use those myths as an introduction to current scholarly approaches to related topics. Taken together, my goal for the book is that it should provide a basic introduction to the period for readers with ample leads for more in-depth studies in areas of interest. Perhaps the biggest myth of all, not just about early modern Europe but for the study of history in general, is that the past is written in stone; and thus, historians memorize dates and names that they, in turn, expect their students to also memorize. Like all modern academic disciplines, the view of the past, including the early modern past, changes as people discover new documents or think of new ways to tease out new information from older ones. The study of early modern history is everchanging, exciting, influential, important, alive, and well.

1

The Italian Renaissance Ended the Dark Ages and Ushered in the Modern World

What People Think Happened

One of the most common myths about early modern Europe is that the period started after a "Renaissance" ended the "Dark Ages" and then sowed the seeds of the new modern world. The myth claims that people only wanted to learn about devotedly Christian topics after the fall of Rome during the 400s. Technological innovations stopped. Disease and starvation took hold of the European continent. Bearded barbarians only set their mugs of ale aside long enough to burn and pillage helpless peasants. Wealthy kings cared little for their subjects and instead spent their days feasting in marvelous castles, jousting, and rescuing damsels in distress.

The myth contends that these dark days were finally ended by the rediscovery of curiosity, the individual, and prosperity during the Renaissance. It says this Renaissance of learning began in Italy before the rays of its rising intellectual sun banished the darkness from the bleak European landscape. Vernacular poets like Dante, Petrarch, and, to the north, Chaucer broke the stranglehold with which Latin had gripped the throats of European intellectuals. New books from ancient Rome and Greece were discovered that offered a welcome new way to think about the world. People no longer needed to take recourse to the oppressive dictates of the

Church. Money began to be made again, and people finally emerged from their small, dreary hovels. It was as if the Renaissance not only banished ignorance but did so with a washcloth and antiseptic soap.

Out of the Renaissance came the first examples of good art after centuries of amateur doodles designed more to scare the faithful than to be admired. Giotto began the process by adding more naturalistic details to his paintings. A century later, Masaccio introduced perspective into his works and thus reached previously undreamed-of heights of naturalism. In sculpture, Donatello's study of surviving ancient examples led to new-found realism. Artists progressively built upon these successes during the 1400s. By the early 1500s, art had reached new degrees of perfection in the painting, sculpture, and architecture of Michelangelo.

Italy was invaded in 1494 and the armies of France and the Holy Roman emperor brought the new Renaissance styles with them when they returned home. Previously oblivious to the freedom afforded by Renaissance culture, northern writers, artists, and other people immediately benefited from the transfer. After the Counter-Reformation suppressed curiosity in Italy, these northerners took up the cultural torches and lit fires in multiple innovative directions. The Enlightenment, the Scientific Revolution, the revival of republican-based governments, and so many other aspects of progress all marched forward, especially in tolerant, protestant states like the Dutch Republic and England.

How the Story Became Popular

The myth of a Renaissance sweeping away a Dark Age is as old as the 1300s itself. The Italian Francesco Petrarch sought to promote himself and his preferred area of study by attacking opponents and ridiculing traditional scholarly pursuits like theology and scholasticism. Petrarch claimed that, after Rome, worthwhile culture had ceased to be produced. As he looked around the mid-1300s, he claimed that he continued to live and write in a period of cultural darkness. He even wrote letters to long-dead ancient Romans, bemoaning the lack of letters in his own day.

Other writers from the Renaissance agreed with Petrarch. For example, in the early 1400s, the Italian historian Leonardo Bruni set out to write a history of his city, Florence, from its foundations to his time. Bruni praised the knowledge of people during the period of the Roman Republic and argued that a shadow had fallen over Europe with the rise of Julius Caesar. He bemoaned the lack of sources to help write the history for the centuries preceding his own. Bruni's contemporary and acquaintance

Depiction of the Annunciation. Popular myth holds that the revival of interest in the classical world, as seen in the architectural details of an image like this, brought an end to the Middle Ages and the beginning of a new period. However, the past is much more complicated. Note, for example, how things like classicism and perspective are used to heighten the effect of the religious story in this image. (The Metropolitan Museum of Art, Robert Lehman Collection, 1975)

Biondo Flavio also thought that a golden era of culture had ended with Rome. However, Biondo, unlike Bruni, took a more positive view of the millennium between the years ca. 400 and ca. 1400 and focused much of his work on reconstructing the history of those centuries. For Biondo, ancient Rome had ended and ushered in a different period. But he also argued that the efforts of the Church and learned men could possibly bring about a new greatness, this time centered less upon pagan antiquity and more upon a revived papal Rome.

The myth of a Renaissance shining its light upon the Dark Ages persisted after the 1400s. During the 1500s, some Italians were already certain that some areas of their society were better than they had been since Antiquity and, in some cases, better than they had ever been. The painter and biographer Giorgio Vasari wrote dozens of biographies of artists from the thirteenth, fourteenth, fifteenth, and sixteenth centuries. He claimed that Cimabue and Giotto had revived art from the crude darkness of the late 1200s. Vasari argued that artists gradually improved upon their forms until, in Vasari's day, Michelangelo Buonarroti perfected the art of painting, sculpting, and architecture. In the 1700s, the popular writer Voltaire claimed that the city of Florence under the Medici family created a society that paralleled the greatness of ancient Greece.

These opinions continued to gain traction into the nineteenth century, and it is to these more recent writings that our own myths find their most direct ancestry. In the mid-1800s, Jacob Burckhardt argued that the modern world was invented during the Italian Renaissance. Burckhardt claimed that fifteenth-century Italians, especially Florentines, rejected the hyper-religious, hierarchical groupthink of the medieval period. Instead, those trendsetting men and women valued the individual, promoted equality, and embraced a form of secularism. Meanwhile, nineteenth-century art historians adopted the triumphant narrative of Vasari to contend that good art had begun with Giotto before reaching its peak during the "high" Renaissance of Leonardo da Vinci, Raphael, and Michelangelo. Historians and popular writers continued to propagate these myths—or slightly revised versions of them—in the 1800s.

The popular image of the Italian Renaissance shedding its light upon an age of darkness appears in many other places. For example, since the 1980s, many children have first heard names like "Raphael" and "Michelangelo" from the popular *Teenage Mutant Ninja Turtles*, in which the names of the turtle characters derive from notable Italian artists. However, the brutality of shows like *Game of Thrones* is taken as a more realistic view of the medieval period. The natural sciences are thought to have started with the early empirical studies of Renaissance writers, suggesting the foolish backwardness of earlier writers who are best forgotten. Images like Michelangelo's *David* or Botticelli's *The Birth of Venus*, even when not known by name, are associated with high culture and elegance, while medieval art is deemed more primitive. Perhaps the most striking example of the continued legacy of the Renaissance myth is the sale in 2018 of a small, little-known, devotional piece probably—not certainly, but likely—by Leonardo da Vinci to a prince from Saudi Arabia for $450 million.

PRIMARY SOURCE DOCUMENTS

In this letter to future readers, Petrarch describes his greatest interests and how the pursuit of letters has enabled him to temporarily escape the crudeness of his own time. The letter is often used to argue that Petrarch, unlike earlier thinkers, possessed a basic idea that his day was different—much worse, in fact— than the glory days of Antiquity. Petrarch and writers like him are where we get our conception of a major change around 1350 from the "Middle Ages" to a "Renaissance."

Greeting. It is possible that some word of me may have come to you, though even this is doubtful, since an insignificant and obscure name will scarcely penetrate far in either time or space. If, however, you should have heard of me, you may desire to know what manner of man I was, or what was the outcome of my labours, especially those of which some description or, at any rate, the bare titles may have reached you.

To begin with myself, then, the utterances of men concerning me will differ widely, since in passing judgment almost everyone is influenced not so much by truth as by preference, and good and evil report alike know no bounds. I was, in truth, a poor mortal like yourself, neither very exalted in my origin, nor, on the other hand, of the most humble birth, but belonging, as Augustus Caesar says of himself, to an ancient family. As to my disposition, I was not naturally perverse or wanting in modesty, however the contagion of evil associations may have corrupted me. My youth was gone before I realised it; I was carried away by the strength of manhood; but a riper age brought me to my senses and taught me by experience the truth I had long before read in books, that youth and pleasure are vanity . . .

. . . I possessed a well-balanced rather than a keen intellect, one prone to all kinds of good and whole-some study, but especially inclined to moral philosophy and the art of poetry. The latter, indeed, I neglected as time went on, and took delight in sacred literature. Finding in that a hidden sweetness which I had once esteemed but lightly, I came to regard the works of the poets as only amenities. Among the many subjects which interested me, I dwelt especially upon antiquity, for our own age has always repelled me, so that, had it not been for the love of those dear to me, I should have preferred to have been born in any other period than our own. In order to forget my own time, I have constantly striven to place myself in spirit in other ages, and consequently I delighted in history; not that the conflicting statements did not offend me, but when in doubt I accepted what appeared to me most probable, or yielded to the authority of the writer . . .

Francesco Petrarch, excerpts from "To Posterity," in *Petrarch, the First Modern Scholar and Man of Letters*, edited by James Harvey Robinson and Henry Winchester Rolfe (New York: G.P. Putnam's Sons, 1907), 59–60 and 64.

In these brief excerpts from Vasari's massive collection of biographies, Vasari describes the—in his view—rebirth of art under Cimabue, after the dark preceding period, and then the culminating perfection of art 300 years later under Michelangelo. Vasari's arguments about art and periodization have

*proven stubbornly difficult to dislodge from popular assumptions about art
and this period in European history.*

Excerpt from *Life of Cimabue*

The endless flood of misfortunes which overwhelmed unhappy Italy
not only ruined everything worthy of the name of a building, but completely extinguished the race of artists, a far more serious matter. Then, as
it pleased God, there was born in the year 1240 in the city of Florence,
Giovanni, surnamed Cimabue, of the noble family of the Cimabue, to
shed the first light on the art of painting . . .

Excerpt from the *Life of Michelangelo*

While industrious and choice spirits, aided by the light afforded by Giotto and his followers, strove to show the world the talent with which their
happy stars and well-balanced humours had endowed them, and endeavoured to attain to the height of knowledge by imitating the greatness of
nature in all things, the great Ruler of Heaven looked down and seeing
these vain and fruitless efforts and the presumptuous opinion of man more
removed from truth than light from darkness, resolved, in order to rid
him of these errors, to send to earth a genius universal in each art, to show
single-handed the perfection of line and shadow, and who should give relief
to his paintings, show a sound judgment in sculpture, and in architecture
should render habitations convenient, safe, healthy, pleasant, in proportion, and enriched with various ornaments. He further endowed him with
true moral philosophy and a sweet poetic spirit, so that the world should
marvel at the singular eminence of his life and works and all his actions,
seeming rather divine than earthly. In the arts of painting, sculpture, and
architecture the Tuscans have always been among the best, and Florence
was the city in Italy most worthy to be the birthplace of such a citizen to
crown her perfections. Thus in 1474 the true and noble wife of Ludovico
di Lionardo Buonarotti, said to be the ancient and noble family of the
counts of Canossa, gave birth to a son at Casentino, under a lucky star . . .

Giorgio Vasari, excerpts from the *Lives of the Painters, Sculptors, and Architects,*
translated by A. B. Hinds (London: J. M. Dent, 1900), vol. 1, p. 3; vol. 8, pp. 3–4.

*In this excerpt, Voltaire compares the golden age of Florentine history under
Cosimo and Lorenzo de' Medici to a similar peak in history in ancient Greece.
Voltaire's work reinforced earlier writers who had also viewed fifteenth-century
Florence in particular as ushering in an age of progress over the preceding
centuries.*

Tuscany, a country less beholden to the gifts of nature, was to Milan what the ancient Attica was to Boeotia; for within the last century Florence had signalized itself, as we have already seen, by its attention to commerce and the liberal arts. The family of Medici was at the head of this polite nation, than whom no house ever acquired supreme power by a more just title. It obtained it by mere dint of beneficence and virtue. Cosmo de Medici, born in 1389, was a private citizen of Florence, who lived without seeking for titles; but acquired by commerce a fortune equal to the greatest monarchs of his time. He employed his great wealth in relieving the poor, in making himself friends among the rich by lending money to them, in adorning his country with superb edifices, and in inviting to Florence the men of learning among the Greeks who were driven from Constantinople. His advice was for the space of thirty years the law of the republic. His only arts were his good deeds, which are of all others the most just. After his death his papers showed that he had lent immense sums to his countrymen, of which he had never demanded the least payment, and he died, in 1464, universally regretted by his very enemies. The people of Florence with one consent adorned his tomb with the glorious epitaph of father of his country, a title which not one of the many kings we have seen pass in review were ever able to obtain.

His reputation procured his descendants the chief authority in Tuscany. His son took the administration under the name of Gonfalonier. His two grandsons, Lorenzo and Julian, who were masters of the republic, were set up on in the church by a band of conspirators at the time of the elevation of the host. Julian died, in 1478, of the wounds he received, but Lorenzo made his escape. Florence resembled Athens, but in government and genius. It was at one time aristocratic, and at another popular, and dreaded nothing so much as tyranny.

Cosmo de Medici might be compared to Pisistratus, who, not withstanding his great power, was ranked in the number of sages. The sons of this Cosmo resembled those of Pisistratus, who were assassinated by Harmodius and Aristogiton. Lorenzo escaped from his murders, and so did one of the sons of Pisistratus, and both of them lived to avenge the death of his brother: but that happened in Florence which did not at Athens; the chiefs of religion were concerned in this bloody conspiracy. Pope Sixtus IV planned it, and the archbishop of Pisa set it on foot.

The people of Florence avenged this cruel act on those who were found guilty; and the archbishop himself was hanged at one of the windows of the public palace. Lorenzo, thus avenged by his fellow citizens, made himself beloved by them during the rest of his life. He was surnamed the father of the muses, a title not equal indeed to that of father of his country, but which showed that he was so in fact. It was a thing no less admirable than foreign to our manners to see this citizen, who always addicted himself to commerce, selling with one hand the produce of the Levant, and with the other supporting the weight of the republic entertaining factors and ambassadors; opposing an artful and powerful pope, making peace and war, standing forth the oracle of princes, and the cultivator of the belles-lettres, furnishing amusements for the people, and giving a reception to the learned Greeks of Constantinople. His son Peter held the supreme authority in Florence, at the time that the French made their expedition to Naples; but with much less credit than either his predecessors or descendants.

Voltaire, excerpts from *Ancient and Modern History*, translated by William F. Fleming (New York: St. Hubert Guild, 1901), vol. 14, part 1, pp. 186–8.

In these excerpts from his influential book, Burckhardt describes several of the—in his view—major advancements of Renaissance Italy during the period before it. Burckhardt claimed that the Renaissance gave birth to the modern individual, to the rudiments of secularism and equality, and to many other positive changes. For over 150 years, scholars have shown that most of Burckhardt's arguments were overly simplistic or even wrong. Nevertheless, Burckhardt's views continue to influence popular conceptions of medieval, Renaissance, and early modern history.

. . . The struggle between the popes and the Hohenstaufen left Italy in a political condition which differed essentially from that of other countries of the West. While in France, Spain and England the feudal system was so organised that, at the close of its existence, it was naturally transformed into a unified monarchy, and while in Germany it helped to maintain, at least outwardly, the unity of the empire, Italy had shaken it off almost entirely. The Emperors of the fourteenth century, even in the most favorable case, were no longer received and respected as feudal lords, but as possible leaders and supporters of powers already in existence; while the Papacy, with its creatures and allies, was strong enough to hinder national unity in the future, but not strong enough itself to bring about that unity. Between the two lay a multitude of political units—republics and despots—in part of long standing, in part of recent origin, whose existence was founded simply on their power to maintain it. In them for the first time we detect the modern political spirit of Europe, surrendered freely to its own instincts, often displaying the worse features of an unbridled egotism, outraging every right, and killing every germ of a healthier culture. But, wherever this vicious tendency is overcome or in any way compensated, a new fact appears in history—the state as the outcome of reflection and calculation, the state as a work of art . . .

. . . In the character of these states, whether republics or despotisms, lies not the only but the chief reason for the early development of the Italian. To this it is due that he was the first-born among the sons of modern Europe.

In the Middle Ages both sides of human consciousness—that which was turned within as that which was turned without—lay dreaming or half awake beneath a common veil. The veil was woven of faith, illusion and childish prepossession, through which the world and history were seen clad in strange hues. Man was conscious of himself only as a member of a race, people, party, family or corporation—only through some general category. In Italy this veil first melted into air; an *objective* treatment and consideration of the state and of all the things of this world became possible. The *subjective* side at the same time asserted itself with corresponding emphasis; man became a spiritual *individual*, and recognized himself as such. . . . In far earlier times we can here and there detect a development of free personality which in northern Europe either did not occur at all, or could not display itself in the same manner. . . . But at the close of the thirteenth century Italy began to swarm with individuality; the ban laid upon human personality was dissolved; and a thousand figures meet us each in its own special shape and dress.

. . . This period, as we have seen, first gave the highest development to individuality, and then led the individual to the most zealous and thorough study of himself in all forms and under all conditions. Indeed, the development of personality is essentially involved in the recognition of it in oneself and in others. Between these two great processes our narrative has placed the influence of ancient literature, because the mode of conceiving and representing both the individual and human nature in general was defined and coloured by that influence. But the power of conception and representation lay in the age and in the people.

. . . Every period of civilisation, which forms a complete and consistent whole, manifests itself not only in political life, in religion, art, and science, but also sets its characteristic stamp on social life. Thus the Middle Ages had their courtly and aristocratic manners and etiquette, differing but little in the various countries of Europe, as well as their peculiar forms of middle-class life.

Italian customs at the time of the Renaissance offer in these respects the sharpest contrast to medievalism. The foundation on which they rest is wholly different. Social intercourse in its highest and most perfect form now ignored all distinctions of caste, and was based simply on the existence of an educated class as we now understand the word. Birth and origins were without influence, unless combined with leisure and inherited wealth. Yet this assertion must not be taken in an absolute and unqualified sense, since medieval distinctions still sometimes made themselves felt to a greater or less degree, if only as a means of maintaining equality with the aristocratic pretensions of the less advanced countries of Europe. But the main current of the time went steadily towards the fusion of classes in the modern sense of the phrase.

. . . The Italians of that day lived in the belief that they were more cleanly than other nations. There are in fact general reasons which speak rather for than against this claim. Cleanliness is indispensable to our modern notion of social perfection, which was developed in Italy earlier than elsewhere.

. . . We note with admiration the thousand ways in which art ennobles luxury, not only adorning the massive sideboard or the light brackets with noble vases, clothing the walls with the moving splendour of tapestry, and covering the toilet-table with numberless graceful trifles, but absorbing whole branches of mechanical work—especially carpentering—into its province. All western Europe, as soon as its wealth enabled it to do so, set to work in the same way at the close of the Middle Ages. But its efforts produced either childish and fantastic toy-work, or were bound by the chains of a narrow and purely Gothic art, while the Renaissance moved freely, entering into the spirit of every task it undertook and working for a far larger circle of patrons and admirers the northern artists.

. . . The games and contests of the popular classes did not differ essentially from those which prevailed elsewhere in Europe. In the maritime cities boat-racing was among the number, and the Venetian regattas were famous at an early period. The classical game of Italy was and is the ball; and this was probably played at the time of the Renaissance with more zeal and brilliancy than elsewhere. But on this point no distinct evidence is forthcoming.

. . . To understand the higher forms of social intercourse at this period, we must keep before our minds the fact that women stood on a footing of perfect equality with men. . . . There was no question of "woman's rights" or female emancipation, simply because the thing itself was a matter of course. The educated woman, no less than the man, strove naturally after a characteristic and complete individuality. The same intellectual and emotional development which perfected the man was demanded for the perfection of the woman.

Jacob Burckhardt, excerpts from *The Civilisation of the Renaissance in Italy*, translated by S. G. C. Middlemore (London: S. Sonnenschein, 1904), 4, 129–30, 308, 359, 374, 377, 390, 395, and 397.

What Really Happened

Historians have fiercely debated the accuracy of identifying a "Renaissance" in culture and society starting in Italy during the 1300s. Some historians have claimed that, beyond the self-congratulatory claims of people like Petrarch or Leonardo Bruni, very little actually changed in Europe until the massive upheavals of the Reformations, the transatlantic voyages, the Scientific Revolution, and cheaper paper for the new printing presses during the sixteenth century. These writers argue that the 1100s brought about much greater changes to the economy, thought, politics, etc., than any so-called Renaissance during the 1300s or 1400s. Other historians claim that changes in the 1300s and 1400s altered society from previous centuries and set the foundation for later developments. Yet, despite such disagreements, historians are in wide agreement that breaking the past up into periods like "Renaissance" and "medieval" oversimplify very complicated things. Moreover, historians have long rejected the concept of a "Dark Age" and have devoted considerable time and effort to unpacking the complex and innovative centuries in Europe from the 400s to the 1500s.

Many historians have examined that medieval period. At the turn of the twentieth century, the "Revolt of the Medievalists" had already begun to challenge assumptions about any sort of "Dark Age" between Antiquity and the 1400s. Historians emphasized the renewed interest of people in ancient texts, especially the works of Aristotle, often through Islamic intermediaries. Later developments, then, were in many cases the continuation of earlier trends. Some historians have taken these sorts of arguments even further. They have shown that the medieval period brought forth technological changes, demographic increases, and economic changes that seemed to mirror modern ones. Some of them who looked at science in particular claimed that medieval thinkers were much more similar to us than so-called Renaissance thinkers: Whereas a "medieval" thinker like Roger Bacon embraced a form of empiricism, a Renaissance thinker like Petrarch rejected the natural sciences as pursuits with no practical relevance. These historians, thus, have claimed that the medieval period has more to offer the modern world than the Italian Renaissance.

Some historians have gone so far as to argue that life, for most people, seems to have either gotten worse after the early 1300s or changed so little that people should not really break up European history until the much later Industrial Revolution. This argument contends that for the vast majority of Europeans, life in the 1500s was basically the same as it had been for centuries. Largely illiterate men and women lived mostly outside the purview of central authorities and thus continued regional versions of Christianity with little outside intervention. They passed down the same oral stories that had been shared for generations. Disposable income was not an aspect of everyday life, and inexpensive goods for purchase were largely absent until the Industrial Revolution of the nineteenth century. Proponents of this view of a "premodern" or "traditional" Europe reject subperiods like "medieval," "Renaissance," and "early modern" as being focused unjustifiably on the lives and cultures of a handful of elites at the expense of understanding and/or emphasizing the lives of ordinary people.

Today, most historians argue that life had changed enough by the 1500s to warrant a different historical period. The Italian peninsula was a center—though not the only one—for changes like the printing press, cheaper paper, state consolidation, and transatlantic voyages, apart from changes in religion and philosophical and scientific thought, among many other things. Scholars of the Italian peninsula argue that developments continued and differed from those of the medieval period. The term "Renaissance" continues to be used by scholars studying Italy, especially around the period 1300–1600, but the term no longer carries its previous pejorative connotations and often is simply shorthand for those centuries. Some very recent scholars have attempted to once again imbue the term with period-changing connotations, but such efforts are controversial and still much debated among scholars.

Ultimately, most historians today are much less interested in comparing different periods of time to the present and much more interested in understanding the past on its own terms. It has become clear that the concept of a "Renaissance" itself is indebted to writers from the early modern and even modern periods who had far different agendas and views of the world than people possess today. Leaving behind stale questions about periodization, scholars have unpacked how people from all walks of life lived and interacted with others. The best studies are able to show convincing analyses of past artifacts and documents to interpret how and why the lives and views of past peoples and changed over time, regardless of how similar or different those cultures, changes, and people were to ourselves.

PRIMARY SOURCE DOCUMENTS

One of Peter Abelard's most famous works, The Story of My Misfortunes, *is a good example of a medieval autobiography, making any argument about "the birth of the individual" in the Italian Renaissance difficult to sustain. The most famous part of the work describes how Abelard fell in love with a student and the disastrous consequences that followed for both of them. In the excerpt below, Abelard summarizes the arguments that Héloïse, his student and lover, presented to him for why they should not marry, despite the recent birth of their son in secret at Abelard's country estate.*

Forthwith I [that is, Abelard] repaired to my own country, and brought back thence my mistress [that is, his former student Héloïse], that I might make her my wife. She, however, most violently disapproved of this, and for two chief reasons: the danger thereof, and the disgrace which it would bring upon me. She swore that her uncle [that is, Héloïse's guardian who had hired Abelard to teach her] would never be appeased by such satisfaction as this, as, indeed, afterwards proved only too true. She asked how she could ever glory in me if she should make me thus inglorious, and should shame herself along with me. What penalties, she said, would the world rightly demand of her if she should rob it of so shining a light! What curses would follow such a loss to the Church, what tears among the philosophers would result from such a marriage! How unfitting, how lamentable it would be for me, whom nature had made for the whole world, to devote myself to one woman solely, and to subject myself to such humiliation! She vehemently rejected this marriage, which she felt would be in every way ignominious and burdensome to me.

Besides dwelling thus on the disgrace to me, she reminded me of the hardships of married life, to the avoidance of which the Apostle exhorts us, saying: "Art thou loosed from a wife? seek not a wife. But and if thou marry, thou hast non sinned; and if a virgin marry, she hath not sinned. Nevertheless such shall have trouble in the flesh: but I spare you" (1 Cor. vii, 27). And again: "But I would have you to be free from cares" (1 Cor. vii, 32). But if I would heed neither the counsel of the Apostle nor the exhortations of the saints regarding this heavy yoke of matrimony, she bade me at least consider the advice of the philosophers, and weigh carefully what had been written on this subject either by them or concerning their lives. Even the saints themselves have often and earnestly spoken on this subject for the purpose of warning us. Thus St. Jerome, in his first book against Jovinianus, makes Theophrastus set forth in great detail the intolerable annoyances and the endless disturbance of married life, demonstrating with the most convincing arguments that no wise man should ever have a wife, and concluding his reasons for this philosophic exhortation with these words: "Who among Christians would not be overwhelmed by such arguments as these advanced by Theophrastus?"

Again, in the same work, St. Jerome tells how Cicero, asked by Hircius after his divorce of Terentia whether he would marry the sister of Hiricius, replied that he would do no such thing, saying that he could not devote himself to a wife and to philosophy at the same time. Cicero does not, indeed, precisely speak of "devoting himself," but he does add that he did not wish to undertake anything which might rival his study of philosophy in its demands upon him.

Then, turning from the consideration of such hindrances to the study of philosophy, Héloïse bade me observe what were the conditions of honourable wedlock. What possible concord could there be between scholars and domestics, between authors and cradles, between books or tablets and distaffs, between the stylus or the pen and the spindle? What man, intent on his religious or philosophical meditations, can possibly endure the whining of children, the lullabies of the nurse seeking to quiet them, or the noisy confusion of family life? Who can endure the continual untidiness of children? The rich, you may reply, can do this, because they have palaces or houses containing many rooms, and because their wealth takes no thought of expense and protects them from daily worries But to this the answer is that the condition of philosophers is by no means that of the wealthy, nor can those whose minds are occupied with riches and worldly cares find time for religious or philosophical study. For this reason the renowned philosophers of old utterly despised the world, fleeing from its perils rather than reluctantly giving them up, and denied themselves all its delights in order that they might repose in the embraces of philosophy alone. One of them, and the greatest of all, Seneca, in his advice to Lucilius, says: "Philosophy is not a thing to be studied only in hours of leisure; we must give up everything else to devote ourselves to it, for no amount of time is really sufficient thereto" (Epist. 73) . . .

Her final argument was that it would be dangerous for me to take her back to Paris, and that it would be far sweeter for her to be called my mistress than to be known as my wife; nay, too, that this would be more honourable for me as well. In such case, she said, love alone would hold me to her, and the strength of the marriage chain would not constrain us. Even if we should by chance be parted from time to time, the joy of our meetings would be all the sweeter by reason of its rarity. But when she found that she could not convince me or dissuade me from my folly by these and like arguments, and because she could not bear to offend me, with grievous sighs and tears she made an end of her resistance: "Then there is no more left but this, that in our doom the sorrow yet to come shall be no less than the love we two have already known." Nor in this, as now the whole world knows, did she lack the spirit of prophecy.

So, after our little son was born, we left him in my sister's care, and secretly returned to Paris. A few days later, in the early morning, having kept our nocturnal vigil of prayer unknown to all in a certain church, we were united there in the benediction of wedlock, her uncle and a few friends of his and mine being present. We departed forthwith stealthily and by separate ways, nor thereafter did we see each other save rarely and in private, thus striving our utmost to conceal what we had done. But her uncle and those of his household, seeking solace for their disgrace, began to divulge the story of our marriage, and thereby to violate the pledge they had given me on this point. Héloïse, on the contrary, denounced her own kin and swore that they were speaking the most absolute lies. Her uncle, aroused to fury thereby, visited her repeatedly with punishments. No sooner had I learned this than I sent her to a convent of nuns at Argenteuil, not far from Paris, where she herself had been brought up and educated as a young girl. I had them make ready for her all the garments of a nun, suitable for the life of a convent, excepting only the veil, and these I bade her put on.

When her uncle and kinsmen heard of this, they were convinced that now I had completely played them false and had rid myself forever of Héloïse by forcing her to become a nun. Violently incensed, they laid a plot against me, and one night, while I, all unsuspecting, was asleep in a secret room in my lodgings, they broke in with the help of one of my servants, whom they had bribed. There they had vengeance on me with a most cruel and most shameful punishment, such as astounded the whole world, for they cut off those parts of my body with which I had done that which was the cause of their sorrow. This done, straightway they fled, but two of them were captured, and suffered the loss of their eyes and their genital organs. One of these two was the aforesaid servant, who, even while he was still in my service, had been led by his avarice to betray me.

Peter Abelard, excerpt from *Historia Calamitatum: The Story of My Misfortunes* (Saint Paul, MN: Thomas A. Boyd, 1922), 23–30.

Often pointed to as one of the best exponents of medieval science, Roger Bacon was a Franciscan friar who lived during the 1200s. In some writings, he advocated for studying nature by observing it, even as he did not propose, like modern scientists, the testing of variables in controlled environments. Bacon's "medieval" ideas about the study of nature are much closer to our own ideas about science than common prescriptions by Renaissance thinkers, who were usually content to follow information found in classical and medieval texts on topics like this.

Excerpt from "On Experimental Science."

Having laid down the main points of the wisdom of the Latins as regards language, mathematics and optics, I wish now to review the principles of wisdom from the point of view of experimental science, because without experiment it is impossible to know anything thoroughly.

There are two ways of acquiring knowledge, one through reason, the other through experiment. Argument reaches a conclusion and compels us to admit it, but it neither makes us certain nor so annihilates doubt that the mind rests calm in the intuition of truth, unless it finds this certitude by way of experience. . . . Experience is of two kinds. One is through the external senses: such are the experiments that are made upon the heaven through instruments in regard to facts there, and the facts on earth that we prove in various ways to be certain in our own sight . . . but such experience is not enough for man, because it does not give full certainty as regards corporeal things because of their complexity and touches the spiritual not at all. Hence man's intellect must be aided in another way, and thus the patriarchs and prophets who first gave science to the world secured inner light and did not rest entirely on the senses. . . . In accordance with which Ptolemy says in the Centilogium that there is a double way of coming to the knowledge of things, one through the experiments of science, the other through divine inspiration, which latter is far the better as he says.

And because this experimental science is a study entirely unknown by the common people, I cannot convince them of its utility, unless its virtue and characteristics are shown. This alone enables us to find out surely what can be done through nature, what through the application of art, what through fraud, what is the purport and what is mere dream in chance, conjuration, invocations, imprecations, magical sacrifices and what there is in them; so that all falsity may be lifted and the truth alone of the art retained. This alone teaches us to examine all the insane ideas of the magicians in order not to confirm but to avoid them, just as logic criticizes the art of sophistry. This science has three great purposes in regard to the other sciences: the first is that one may criticize by experiment the noble conclusions of all the other sciences, for the other sciences know that their principles come from experiment, but the conclusions through arguments drawn from the principles discovered, if they care to have the result of their conclusions precise and complete. It is necessary that they have this through the aid of this noble science. It is true that mathematics reaches conclusions in accordance with universal experience about figures and numbers, which indeed apply to all sciences and to this experience, because no science can be known without mathematics. If we would attain to experiments precise, complete and made certain in accordance with the proper method, it is necessary to undertake an examination of the science itself, which is called experimental on our authority. I find an example in the rainbow and in like phenomena, of which nature are the circles about the sun and stars, also the halo beginning from the side of the sun or of a star which seems to be visible in straight lines and is called by Aristotle in the third book of the Meteorology a perpendicular, but by Seneca a halo, and is also called a circular corona, which have many of the colors of the rainbow. Now the natural philosopher discusses these things, and in regard to perspective has many facts to add which are concerned with the operation of seeing which is pertinent in this place. But neither Aristotle or Avicenna have given us knowledge of these things in their books upon Nature, nor Seneca, who wrote a special book concerning them. But experimental science analyzes such things.

The experimenter considers whether among visible things, he can find colors formed and arranged as given in the rainbow. He finds that there are hexagonal crystals from Ireland or India which are called rainbow hued in Solinus Concerning the Wonders of the World and he holds these in a ray of sunlight falling through the window, and finds all the colors of the rainbow, arranged as in it in the shaded part next the ray.

Moreover, the same experimenter places himself in a somewhat shady place and puts the stone up to his eye when it is almost closed, and beholds the colors of the rainbow clearly arranged, as in the bow. And because many persons making use of these stones think that it is on account of some special property of the stones and because of their hexagonal shape the investigator proceeds further and finds this in a crystal, properly shaped, and in other transparent stones. And not only are these Irish crystals in white, but also black, so that the phenomenon occurs in smoky crystal and also in all stones of similar transparency. Moreover, in stones not shaped hexagonally, provided the surfaces are rough, the same as those of the Irish crystals, not entirely smooth and yet not rougher than those, the surfaces have the same quality as nature has given the Irish crystals, for the difference of roughness makes the difference of color. He watches, also, rowers and in the drops falling from the raised oars he finds the same colors, whenever the rays of the sun penetrate the drops. The case is the same with water falling from the paddles of a water-wheel. And when the investigator looks in a summer morning at the drops of dew clinging to the grass in the field or plane, he sees the same colors. And, likewise, when it rains, if he stands in a shady place and the sun's rays beyond him shine through the falling drops, then in some rather dark place the same colors appear, and they can often be seen at night about a candle. In the summer time, as soon as he rises from sleep while his eyes are not yet fully opened, if he suddenly looks at a window through which the light of the sun is streaming, he will see the colors. Again, sitting outside of the sunlight, if he holds his head covering beyond his eyes, or, likewise, if he closes his eyes, the same thing happens in the shade at the edges, and it also takes place through a glass vase filled with water, sitting in the sunlight. Similarly, if any one holding water in his mouth suddenly sprinkles the water in jets and stands at the side of them; or if through a lamp of oil hanging in the air the rays shine in the proper way, or the light shines upon the surface of the oil, the colors again appear. Thus, in an infinite number of ways, natural as well as artificial, colors of this kind are to be seen, if only the diligent investigator knows how to find them . . .

Experimental science is also that which alone, as the mistress of the speculative sciences, can discover magnificent truths in the fields of the other sciences, to which these other sciences can in no way attain . . .

The third value of this science is this—it is on account of the prerogatives through which it looks, not only to the other sciences, but by its own power investigates the secrets of nature . . .

Roger Bacon, excerpts from "On Experimental Science," in Oliver J. Thatcher, ed., *The Library of Original Sources* (Milwaukee, WI: University Research Extension, 1901), vol. 4, pp. 369–75.

Excerpt from "On the Hidden Workings of Nature and Art and the Emptyness of Magic."

I will now enumerate the marvelous results of art and nature which will make all kinds of magic appear trivial and unworthy. Instruments for navigation can be made which will do away with the necessity of rowers, so that great vessels, both in rivers and on the sea, shall be borne about with only a single man to guide them and with greater speed than if they were full of men. And carriages can be constructed to move without animals to draw them, and with incredible velocity. Machines for lying can be made in which a man sits and turns an ingenious device by which skillfully contrived wings are made to strike the air in the manner of a flying bird. Then arrangements can be devised, compact in themselves, for raising and lowering weights indefinitely great. . . . Bridges can be constructed ingeniously so as to span rivers without any supports.

Roger Bacon, excerpts from "On the Hidden Workings of Nature and Art and the Emptyness of Magic," in James Harvey Robinson, *Readings in European History* (Boston: Athenaeum Press, 1904), vol. 1, p. 461.

A prolific writer, Thomas Aquinas is best known for his systematic attempts to reconcile the philosophical ideas found in the newly translated works of Aristotle with medieval understandings of Christianity. Although today Aquinas has become synonymous with medieval philosophy—especially scholasticism—and the Catholic Church, in medieval times Aquinas's ideas were often controversial. In the years after his death, Aquinas began to enjoy an elevated status. The following excerpt provides a sample of the style and type of argument on which Aquinas and other medieval scholastics focused their intellectual efforts.

Article III. Whether God exists.

Let us proceed to the third article. It is objected (1) that God does not exist, because if one of two contradictory things is infinite, the other will be totally destroyed; that it is implied in the name God that there is a certain infinite goodness: if then God existed, no evil would be found. But evil is found in the world; therefore it is objected that God does not exist.

Again, that what can be accomplished through a less number of principles will not be accomplished through more. It is objected that all things that appear on the earth can be accounted for through other principles, without supposing that God exists, since what is natural can be traced to a natural principle, and what proceeds from a proposition can be traced to the human reason or will. Therefore that there is no necessity to suppose that God exists.

But as against this note what is said of the person of God (Exod. III., 14) *I am that I am.*

Conclusion. There must be found in the nature of things one first immovable Being, a primary cause, necessarily existing, not created; existing the most widely, good, even the best possible; the first ruler through the intellect, and the ultimate end of all things, which is God.

I answer that it can be proved in five ways that God exists. The first and plainest is the method that proceeds from the point of view of motion. It is certain and in accord with experience, that things on earth undergo change. Now everything that is moved is moved by something; nothing, indeed, is changed, except it is changed to something which is in potentiality. Moreover, anything moves in accordance with something actually existing; change itself, is nothing else than to bring forth something from potentiality into actuality. Now nothing can be brought from potentiality to actual existence except through something actually existing: thus heat in action, as fire, makes fire-wood, which is hot in potentiality, to be hot actually, and through this process, changes itself. The same thing cannot at the same time be actually and potentially the same thing, but only in regard to different things. What is actually hot cannot be at the same time potentially hot, but it is possible for it at the same time to be potentially cold. It is impossible, then, that anything should be mover and the thing moved, in regard to the same thing and in the same way, or that it should move itself. Everything, therefore, is moved by something else. If, then, that by which it is moved, is also moved, this must be moved by something still different, and this, again, by something else. But this process cannot go on to infinity (1) because there would not be any first mover, nor, because of this fact, anything else in motion, as the succeeding things would not move except because of what is moved by the first mover, just as a stick is not moved except through what is moved from the hand. Therefore it is necessary to go back to some first mover, which is itself moved by nothing, and this all men know as God.

The second proof is from the nature of the efficient cause. We find in our experience that there is a chain of causes: nor is it found possible for anything to be the efficient cause of itself, since it would have to exist before itself, which is impossible. Nor in the case of efficient causes can the chain go back indefinitely, because in all chains of efficient causes, the first is the cause of the middle, and these of the last, whether they be one or many. If the cause is removed, the effect is removed. Hence if there is not a first cause, there will not be a last, nor a middle. But if the chain were to go back infinitely, there would be no first cause, and thus no ultimate effect, nor middle causes, which is admittedly false. Hence we must presuppose some first efficient cause, which all call God.

The third proof is taken from the natures of the merely possible and necessary. We find that certain things either may or may not exist, since they are found to come into being and be destroyed, and in consequence potentially, either existent or non-existent. But it is impossible for all things that are of this character to exist eternally, because what *may* not exist, at length *will* not. If, then, all things were merely possible (mere accidents), eventually nothing among things would exist. If this is true, even now there would be nothing, because what does not exist, does not take its beginning except through something that does exist. If then nothing existed, it would be impossible for anything to begin, and there would now be nothing existing, which is admittedly false. Hence not all things are mere accidents, but there must be one necessarily existing being. Now every necessary thing either has a cause of its necessary existence, or has not. In the case of necessary things that have a cause for their necessary existence, the chain of causes cannot go back infinitely, just as not in the case of efficient causes, as proved. Hence there must be presupposed something necessarily existing through its own nature, not having a cause elsewhere but being itself the cause of the necessary existence of other things—which all call God.

The fourth proof arises from the degrees that are found in things. For there is found a greater and a less degree of goodness, truth, nobility, and the like. But more or less are terms spoken of various things as they approach in diverse ways toward something that is the greatest, just as in the case of hotter (more hot) which approaches nearer the greatest heat. There exists therefore something that is the truest, and best, and most noble, and in consequence, the greatest being. For what are the greatest truths are the greatest beings, as is said in the Metaphysics Bk. II. 2. What moreover is the greatest in its way, in another way is the cause of all things of its own kind (or genus); thus fire, which is the greatest heat, is the cause of all heat, as is said in the same book (cf. Plato and Aristotle). Therefore there exists something that is the cause of the existence of all things and of the goodness and of every perfection whatsoever—and this we call God.

The fifth proof arises from the ordering of things for we see that some things which lack reason such as natural bodies are operated in accordance with a plan. It appears from this that they are operated always or the most frequently in this same way the closer they follow what is the

Highest; whence it is clear that they do not arrive at the result by chance but because of a purpose. The things, moreover, that do not have intelligence do not tend toward a result unless directed by some one knowing and intelligent; just as an arrow is sent by an archer. Therefore there is something intelligent by which all natural things are arranged in accordance with a plan—and this we call God.

In response to the first objection, then, I reply what Augustine says; that since God is entirely good, He would permit evil to exist in His works only if He were so good and omnipotent that He might bring forth good even from the evil. It therefore pertains to the infinite goodness of God that he permits evil to exist and from this bring forth good.

My reply to the second objection is that since nature is ordered in accordance with some defined purpose by the direction of some superior agent, those things that spring from nature must be dependent upon God, just as upon a first cause. Likewise what springs from a proposition must be traceable to some higher cause which is not the human reason or will, because this is changeable and defective and everything changeable and liable to non-existence is dependent upon some unchangeable first principle that is necessarily self-existent as has been shown . . .

> Thomas Aquinas, excerpts from the *Summa Theologica* ("On the Existence of God"), in *The Library of Original Sources*, edited by Oliver Thatcher (Milwaukee, WI: University Research Extension, 1901), vol. 4, pp. 360–63.

Many writers and thinkers during the Renaissance valued what we would consider as the humanities as the most important focus for study and learning. Humanists like Petrarch, Leonardo Bruni, Biondo Flavio, and others argued that the natural scientists and theologians studied topics of far less practical relevance than the life lessons and skills gained from studying the humanities. Humanist studies came to dominate both learned circles and schools during the Renaissance and for most of the early modern period. In the following excerpt, the Italian humanist Pier Paolo Vergerio advises a ruler on how to educate his son in the early 1400s.

. . . We call those studies *liberal* which are worthy of a free man; those studies by which we attain and practise virtue and wisdom; that education which calls forth, trains and develops those highest gifts of body and of mind which ennoble men, and which are rightly judged to rank next to dignity to virtue only. For to a vulgar temper gain and pleasure are the one aim of existence, to a lofty nature, moral worth and fame. It is, then, of the highest importance that even from infancy this aim, this effort, should constantly be kept alive in growing minds. For I may affirm with fullest conviction that we shall not have attained wisdom in our later years unless in our earliest we have sincerely entered on its search . . .

. . . We cannot deny that there is still a horde—as I must call them—of people who, like Licinius the Emperor, denounce learning and the Arts as a danger to the State and hateful in themselves. In reality the very opposite is the truth. . . . Consider the necessity of the literary art to one immersed in reading and speculation: and its importance to one absorbed in affairs. To be able to speak and write with elegance is no slight advantage in negotiation, whether in public or private concerns. Especially in administration of the State, when intervals of rest and privacy are accorded to a prince, how must he value those means of occupying them wisely which the knowledge of literature affords to him! . . .

. . . Literature indeed exhibits not facts alone, but thoughts, and their expression. Provided such thoughts be worthy, and worthily expressed, we feel assured that they will not die: although I do not think that thoughts without style will be likely to attract much notice or secure a sure survival. What greater charm can life offer than this power of making the past, the present, and even the future, our own by means of literature? How bright a household is the family of books! We may cry, with Cicero. In their company is no noise, no greed, no self-will: at a word they speak to you, at a word they are still: to all our requests their response is ever ready and to the point. Books indeed are a higher—a wider, more tenacious—memory, a storehouse which is the common property of all.

I attach great weight to the duty of handing down this priceless treasure to our sons unimpaired by any carelessness on our part. How many are the gaps which the ignorance of past ages has willfully caused in the long and noble roll of writers! Books—in part or in their entirety—have been allowed to perish. What remains of others is often sorely corrupt, mutilated, or imperfect. It is hard that no slight portion of the history of Rome is only to be known through the labours of one writing in the Greek language: it is still worse that this same noble tongue, once well nigh the daily speech of our race, as familiar as the Latin language itself, is on the point of perishing even amongst its own sons, and to us Italians is already utterly lost, unless we except one or two who in our time are tardily endeavouring to rescue something—if it be only a mere echo of it—from oblivion.

We come now to the consideration of the various subjects which may rightly be included under the name of "Liberal Studies." Amongst these

I accord the first place to History, on grounds both of its attractiveness and of its utility, qualities which appeal equally to the scholar and to the statesman. Next in importance ranks Moral Philosophy, which indeed is, in a peculiar sense, a "Liberal Art," in that its purpose is to teach men the secret of true freedom. History, then, gives us the concrete examples of the precepts inculcated by philosophy. The one shews what men should do, the other what men have said and done in the past, and what practical lessons we may draw therefrom for the present day. I would indicate as the third main branch of study, Eloquence, which indeed holds a place of distinction amongst the refined Arts. By philosophy we learn the essential truth of things, which by eloquence we so exhibit in orderly adornment as to bring conviction to differing minds. And history provides the light of experience—a cumulative wisdom fit to supplement the force of reason and the persuasion of eloquence. For we allow that soundness of judgment, wisdom of speech, integrity of conduct are the marks of a truly liberal temper . . .

Pier Paolo Vergerio, excerpts from "De ingenuis moribus," in *Vittorino Da Feltre and Other Humanist Educators*, edited by William Harrison Woodward (Cambridge: Cambridge University Press, 1921), 102–7.

Further Reading

Belozerskaya, Marina. *Rethinking the Renaissance: Burgundian Arts Across Europe*. Cambridge: Cambridge University Press, 2002.

Braudel, Ferdinand. *The Mediterranean and the Mediterranean World in the Age of Philip II*. 2 vols. New York: Harper & Row, 1972–3.

Burckhardt, Jacob. *The Civilization of the Renaissance in Italy*. London: Penguin, 1990.

Caferro, William. *Contesting the Renaissance*. Malden, MA: Wiley-Blackwell, 2011.

Celenza, Christopher S. *The Intellectual World of the Italian Renaissance*. Cambridge: Cambridge University Press, 2018.

Celenza, Christopher S. *The Lost Italian Renaissance: Humanists, Historians, and Latin's Legacy*. Baltimore: Johns Hopkins University Press, 2004.

Ferguson, Wallace K. *The Renaissance in Historical Thought: Five Centuries of Interpretation*. Cambridge, MA: Houghton Mifflin, 1948.

Haskins, Charles H. *The Renaissance of the Twelfth Century*. Rev. ed. Cambridge, MA: Harvard University Press, 1971.

Herlihy, David, and Christiane Klapisch-Zuber. *Tuscans and their Families: A Study of the Florentine Catasto of 1427*. New Haven, CT: Yale University Press, 1985.

King, Margaret L. *Women of the Renaissance*. Chicago: University of Chicago Press, 1991.

Kristeller, Paul Oskar. *Renaissance Thought and Its Sources*. Edited by Michael Mooney. New York: Columbia University Press, 1979.

Mazzocco, Angelo. "Decline and Rebirth in Bruni and Biondo." In *Umanesimo a Roma nel Quattrocento*, edited by Paolo Brezzi and Maristella De Panizza Lorch, 249–66. Rome: Istituto dei Studi Romani, 1984.

Molho, Anthony. "The Italian Renaissance, Made in the USA." In *Imagined Histories: American Historians Interpret the Past*, edited by Gordon S. Wood, 263–94. Princeton, NJ: Princeton University Press, 1998.

Muir, Edward. "The Italian Renaissance in America." *American Historical Review* 100, no. 4 (October 1995): 1095–118.

Panofsky, Ewin. *Renaissance and Renascences in Western Art*. Stockholm: Almquist & Wiksell, 1960.

Ruggiero, Guido. *The Renaissance in Italy: A Social and Cultural History of the Rinascimento*. Cambridge: Cambridge University Press, 2015.

Thorndike, Lynn. *A History of Magic and Experimental Science*. 8 vols. New York: Columbia University Press, 1923–58.

Trexler, Richard. *Public Ritual in Renaissance Florence*. Ithaca, NY: Cornell University Press, 1980.

Vasari, Giorgio. *The Lives of the Artists*. Translated by George Bull. 2 vols. London: Penguin, 1988.

Woodward, William Harrison. *Vittorino da Feltre and other Humanist Educations*. Cambridge: Cambridge University Press, 1921.

Wyatt, Michael, ed. *The Cambridge Companion to the Italian Renaissance*. Cambridge: Cambridge University Press, 2014.

2

Christopher Columbus Proved that the Earth Was Round

What People Think Happened

The story goes that people in the medieval period believed that the world was a flat disk. On this disk were Europe, lands to the east in Asia (about which they knew very little), and lands to the south called Africa (about which they knew even less). Conventional and expert wisdom accepted that anyone who sailed too far to the west of Europe would simply fall off the edge of the planet or perhaps run into an invisible wall. The senses clearly showed that the earth was a flat plane. The vast ocean to the west had to end somewhere. Woe to the traveler who embarked on such a voyage—to sail to the edge was to never return! In this context, in 1492, the fearless Italian sailor Christopher Columbus sailed the ocean blue.

Columbus had become absolutely convinced that the accepted "wisdom" was wrong. After years of experience and study, Columbus began presenting to the rulers of Europe the idea that the world was, in fact, round. Because it was round, Columbus argued, he could take ships westward and reach the "Spice Islands." He presented his sophisticated, radical arguments to ruler after ruler. But ruler after ruler, expert after expert laughed at him and mocked his preposterous claims. They refused to waste money on an enterprise destined to fall quite literally off the face of the earth. Beaten but not defeated, Columbus arrived at the court of Spain. There he met the young Queen Isabella who secretly admired, perhaps loved, the daring, bold explorer. She defied her advisors and funded

Columbus's voyage. Columbus in turn set sail with three magnificent ships—the *Nina*, the *Pinta*, and the *Santa Maria*. After a long journey, he arrived in what is now called North America. The lands were sparsely populated by friendly but primitive peoples who thought Columbus was a God. Columbus returned triumphantly to Spain and proved that he had been right all along. His detractors were silenced and the various peoples of Europe quickly began their own voyages to explore and claim these new pristine lands.

How the Story Became Popular

During the nineteenth century, historians were increasingly interested in telling stories about the triumphs of rationalism and science over superstition and religion. The story of how the belief in a spherical world triumphed over the belief in a flat one seemed to them to be a perfect example. It is true that some early Christian writers argued that the world was flat. And it is also true that some late medieval and early modern people may have believed that the earth ended somewhere with a bottomless cliff or some kind of wall. Perhaps the cliff ended in Hell or the wall held up the Heavens. During the 1800s, some authors built upon those foundations and added in their own assumptions. They ignored issues while putting forth their arguments. For example, few people in late medieval or early modern Europe actually read the classical authors who argued for flat-earth ideas. Moreover, it is extremely difficult to piece together what ordinary people thought in the premodern past. These nineteenth-century authors combined fact with a generous helping of fiction to turn Columbus into a sort of scientific protagonist facing off against people beholden to superstitious nonsense.

The myth took off in the first half of the nineteenth century. In particular, Washington Irving wrote a book called *A History of the Life and Voyages of Christopher Columbus* in which he created a fictional account of Columbus's dispute with intellectuals of the time about the shape of the earth. Irving was a skilled writer, but he also had a tendency to mix fantasy with fact. Nevertheless, the story took off. First in France, and then in other places, various works presented the idea that Columbus had turned conventional wisdom on its head by proving the earth was round.

By the early twentieth century, the myth that Columbus had fought for his round-earth ideas against the intellectual oppressors of his age was commonplace in school textbooks and popular culture. In some accounts, the emphasis was on Columbus himself. He became a heroic navigator who refused to accept conventional wisdom and proved his detractors wrong. In other accounts, the emphasis was on a barbaric medieval period. Medieval people, the narrative went, were so gullible and beholden to church power that they believed even the silliest things. The prime example, of course, was the idea of the flat earth. Columbus represented the shining Renaissance that was reviving classical ideas from rediscovered classical texts. One idea from Antiquity, long forgotten, was that the earth was round.

Most historical textbooks and all serious historical scholarship have long since discarded this myth. Nevertheless, it remains pervasive in our society. People still describe a wildly dated argument as being like a "flat earth." When people refer to Columbus, the initial thought for many remains that he heroically

Popular myth holds that Christopher Columbus proved to his contemporaries that the world was round, not flat, and discovered the American continents. In this image the artist has highlighted those accomplishments: Columbus points to a round globe and particularly the North American continent. The truth is that Columbus' contemporaries believed the world was round while people have debated the morality and significance of Columbus and his voyages since the 1490s themselves. (Playing Card, Christopher Columbus, Playing Card from Set of "Cartes héroïques" or "Des grands hommes"; stencil-colored lithograph on paper; Gift of Marquis Val Verde de la Sierra; 1923-51-10-22. Cooper Hewitt, Smithsonian Design Museum.)

set the world on a path to rejecting superstition and proving the earth was round. Television programs, YouTube videos, books, and all other media often treat the myth as fact. Such is the nature of a myth as pervasive as this one; it is so engrained in our society that people assume that because they have heard it so many times, it must be true. But it is not. The myth records, at best, an exaggeration passed down for almost two centuries. No scholar of early modern Europe would claim that Columbus proved to his disbelieving contemporaries that the earth was round.

PRIMARY SOURCE DOCUMENTS

Nineteenth-century thinkers wanted to prove the superiority and progress of scientific thought over religion. Thus, the poorly documented suggestion that some early modern people were confused about the earth's shape turned into the claim that all people before Columbus knew with certainty that the earth was flat. Nineteenth-century writers focused on two early Christian authors, Lactantius and Cosmas, as typical representatives of pre-Columbian thought. In fact, these two men were outliers with little influence on medieval or early modern geographical thought and conceptions. The following excerpt offers one example of the flat-earth myth in the early twentieth century.

. . . From this old conception of the universe as a sort of house, with heaven as its upper story and the earth as its ground floor, flowed important theological ideas into heathen, Jewish, and Christian mythologies. . . . Myths having this geographical idea as their germ developed in luxuriance through thousands of years. . . . Naturally, in this view of things, if heaven was a loft, hell was a cellar; and if there were ascensions into one, there were descents into the other. Hell being so near, interferences by its occupants with the dwellers of the earth just above were constant, and form a vast chapter in mediaeval literature. Dante made this conception of the location of hell still more vivid, and we find some forms of it serious barriers to geographical investigations. Many a bold navigator, who was quite ready to brave pirates and tempests, trembled at the thought of tumbling with his ship into one of the openings into hell which a widespread belief placed in the Atlantic at some unknown distance from Europe. This terror among sailors was one of the main obstacles in the great voyage of Columbus. In a mediaeval text-book, giving science the form of a dialogue, occur the following question and answer: "Why is the sun so red in the evening?" "Because he looketh down upon hell."

But the ancient germ of scientific truth in geography—the idea of the earth's sphericity—still lived. Although the great majority of the early fathers of the Church and especially Lactantius, had sought to crush it beneath the utterances attributed to Isaiah, David, and St. Paul, the better opinion of Eudoxus and Aristotle could not be forgotten. . . . The warfare of Columbus the world knows well: how the Bishop of Ceuta worsted him in Portugal; how sundry wise men of Spain confronted him with the usual quotations . . . how, even after he was triumphant, and after his voyage had greatly strengthened the theory of the earth's sphericity . . . the Church by its highest authority solemnly stumbled and persisted in going astray. . . .

Yet the theological barriers to this geographical truth yielded but slowly. Plain as it had become to scholars, they hesitated to declare it to the world at large. . . . But in 1519 science gains a crushing victory. Magellan makes his famous voyage. He proves the earth to be round, for his expedition circumnavigates it. . . . Yet even this does not end the war. Many conscientious men oppose the doctrine for two hundred years longer. . . .

In summing up the action of the Church upon geography, we must say, then, that the dogmas developed in strict adherence to Scripture and the conceptions held in the Church during many centuries "always, everywhere, and by all," were, on the whole, steadily hostile to truth; but it is only just to make a distinction here between the religious and the theological spirit. To the religious spirit are largely due several of the noblest among the great voyages of discovery. . . . Thus, in this field, from the supremacy accorded to theology, we find resulting the tendency to dogmatism which has shown itself in all ages the deadly foe not only of scientific inquiry but of the higher religious spirit itself, while from the love of truth for truth's sake, which has been the inspiration of all fruitful work in science, nothing but advantage has ever resulted to religion.

Andrew Dickson White, excerpts from *A History of the Warfare of Science with Theology in Christendom*, 2 vols. (New York: D. Appleton, 1922), vol. 1, pp. 96–113.

In the following excerpt, the author repeats the idea that medieval people thought the world was flat. As you read this, remember that the idea of a flat earth was not believed by literate members of society in the 1400s. Nevertheless, note how the author creates fictional dialogue, romance, a series of obstacles over which Columbus finally prevailed, and other literary devices to make the work more appealing. Note also the author's frequent use of sarcasm. Almost all of this account is false and inaccurate and speaks much more to nineteenth-century Romanticism than fifteenth-century history.

Columbus lived in a stirring age. Everywhere light was breaking in after centuries of darkness, and all Europe was restless with suggestions and beginnings of new life. Great men were plenty; rulers, like the Medici of Florence; artists, like Raphael and Angelo; preachers, like Savonarola, whose fiery prophecies brought him to fiery death; reformers, chief among them Luther, just beginning to think the thoughts that later set the world agog. Great inventions were spreading; gunpowder, invented before, now becoming terribly effective through the improvement in guns; printing, suddenly opening knowledge to every class; the little compass, with which mariners were just beginning to trust themselves boldly on the seas, in spite of the popular impression that it was a sort of infernal machine presided over by the devil himself.

. . .

The Idea

As to the date of Columbus's birth, historians cannot agree within some ten years. It was doubtless somewhere between 1435 and 1446. They also give different accounts as to his birthplace; but it seems most probable that he was born in Genoa, on the Mediterranean, the son of a woolcarder, and that he went to school in Pavia. At fourteen he became a sailor.

Up and down the seas, first in the sunny Mediterranean, later along the stormy Atlantic coast, sailed the lad, the young man, in the small sailing vessels of the time, and learned well the ocean which he afterward so boldly trusted.

He was a daring, quick-witted, handsome, bronzed young man when he went to Lisbon, where his brother Bartholomew was established as a cosmographer, making charts for seamen; and with all his enthusiasm for his sea-faring life, he had enough interest in ordinary pursuits to fall in love most romantically. It happened on account of his being so regular at church. Every day he must attend service, and every day to church came Donna Philippa Palestrello, who lived in a convent near by. Across the seats flitted involuntary glances between the cloistered maiden and the handsome brown sailor—with a dimple in his chin, some pictures have him; something besides prayers were read between the lines of the prayer-book, and the marriage which closed this churchly wooing proved the wisdom of both parties.

Philippa's father had been one of Prince Henry's famous seamen and the governor of Porto Santo, one of the new-found islands; and after his marriage, Columbus lived sometimes at Porto Santo, sometimes at Lisbon, and much of the time on the sea. He sailed south along the African coast to Guinea; north he sailed to England, and farther on to Iceland. Wherever ships could go, there went he, intent on learning all there was to know of the world he lived in. He read eagerly all that was written about the earth's shape and size. The modern science of his time he well understood. He pored over the maps of the ancient geographer Ptolemy, over the maps of Cosmas, a later geographer, over Palestrello's charts, given him by Philippa's mother.

Ptolemy said the world is round, but Cosmas, whom good Christians were bound to believe, since he founded his science on the Bible, said it is flat, with a wall around it to hold up the sky—very probable, certainly. But that notion of the ancients that the world is "round like a ball" had been caught up and believed by a handful of men scattered sparsely down through the centuries, and of late had gained, among advanced scientists, more of a following than ever. And Columbus, who, with all his enthusiasm for adventure and reverence for religion and the church, had a clear, unbiased, scientific head, mentally turned his back upon Cosmas, and clasped hands with the ancients and the wisest scientists of his own day.

The north was known, the south was fast becoming so, the east had been penetrated, but the west was unexplored. Stretching along from Thule, the distant Iceland, to the southern part of the great African continent, thousands of miles, lay the "Sea of Darkness," as the people called it. What lay beyond? The question had been asked before, times enough; times enough answered for any reasonable man. "Hell was there," said one superstition, "Haven't you seen the flames at sunset-time?" "A sea thick like paste, in which no ships can sail," said another. "Darkness," said another, "thick darkness, the blackness of nothing, and the end of all created things!"

There *was* a legend that over there beyond was Paradise, and St. Brendan, wandering about the seas, had reached it. The ancients told of an island Atlantis over there somewhere in the West, and one of them had said: "In the last days an age will come when ocean shall loose the chains of things; a wonderful country will be discovered, and Tiphis shall make known new worlds, nor shall Thule be the end of the earth."

Ah, to be the discoverer of Atlantis or Paradise! "but, if the world is round," said Columbus, "it is not hell that lies beyond that stormy sea. Over there *must* lie the eastern strand of Asia, the Cathay of Marco Polo, the land of the Kubla Khan, and Cipango, the great island beyond it." "Nonsense!" said the neighbors; "the world isn't round—can't you *see* it is flat? And Cosmas Indicopleustes, who lived hundreds of years before you were born, says it is flat; and he got it from the Bible. You're no good Christian to be taking up with such heathenish notions!" Thought Columbus, "I will write to Paolo Toscanelli, at Florence, and see what he will say."

So Columbus wrote, and Toscanelli, the wise scientist, answered that the idea of sailing west was good and feasible; and with the letter came a map, on which Asia and the great island Cipango were laid down opposite Europe, with the Atlantic between, exactly as Columbus imagined it. Toscanelli said it was easy enough: "You may be certain of meeting with extensive kingdoms, populous cities, and rich provinces, abounding in all sorts of precious stones; and your visit will cause great rejoicing to the king and princes of those distant lands, besides opening a way for communication between them and the Christians, and the instruction of them in the Catholic religion and the arts we possess." It was 1474 when this encouragement came, and from this time all the sailor's thoughts and plans turn toward the west.

The life at home between his voyages, whether spent with his brother, the cosmographer, at Lisbon, or with his wife and sailor brother-in-law, on the Porto Santo island, was hardly less nautical than the voyages themselves. Porto Santo was in line with the ship-routes to and from Spain and all the new-found African coast and islands; and the family there, with the men sailors and geographers, and the women, wives and daughters of sailors and geographers, lived in the bracing salt sea-air, full of the tingle of adventure.

Wild stories tell the sailors, coming and going, whom one can scarce contradict for lack of certain knowledge; and it is not an age of wonders in real life? And the round earth—*is* it round? And the empire of the Grand Khan just over the western water there—not far! The sailors said that on the shores of one of the islands two dead men of strange appearance had been washed in from the west. The sailors said they had picked up curiously-carved sticks drifting from the west. Pedro Correa himself, Columbus's brother-in-law, and a man to be trusted, had found one floating from the west. And there was a legend of the sight of land lying like a faint cloud along that western horizon.

"The world *is* round," said Columbus. "It is not very large" (he thought it much smaller than it is), "and opposite us across that sea lies Asia; and to Asia by way of that sea I will go. There, in the west, lies my duty to God and man; I will carry salvation to the heathen, and bring back gold for the Christians. From the 'Occident to the Orient' a path I will find through the waters."

The Waiting

Such a venture as Columbus proposed could scarcely be carried out at that time except by the help of kings, so to the kings went Columbus.

Naturally, Portugal, with her proved interest in discovery, came first in his thought; and before Portugal's king he laid his project. The king should fit him out with vessels and men, and with them Columbus would sail to the Indies, not by the route around Africa, which the Portuguese had so long been seeking, but by a nearer way—straight across the Atlantic. Think of the untold wealth from the empire of the khan rolling in to Portugal if this connection could be established! And think of converting those heathen to our blessed mother church! It was worth thinking about, and the king called a council of his wise men to consider the startling idea. Not long were the wise men in wisely deciding that the plan was the wild scheme of an adventurer, likely to come to no good, whatever; and when the king, hardly satisfied, laid it before another council, they, too, wisely declared it ridiculous.

O ye owlish dignitaries! Still, the king was not convinced. "We have discovered much by daring adventure, why not more?" "Stick to the coast, and don't go sailing straight away from all known land into waters unknown and mysterious," said the wise men. "But if the unknown waters bring us to the riches of Cathay?" said the king. "That's the extravagant dream of a visionary; it contains no truth and much danger," said the wise men. "Try it yourself, and see. Unbeknown to this Columbus, just send out a ship of your own to the west, and let them come back and tell us what they find."

It was a most underhand piece of business all around; but the king yielded and sent out a ship, which presently came back again with the report that there was no Cathay there, and they hadn't found any Cipango; it was all nonsense! And what they had met with was a big storm that scared them terribly. So Columbus retired, and left the king of Portugal to his brave sailors and wise councilors.

Next will come Spain, and meantime he will send his brother Bartholomew to present the plan at the English court.

The Spanish sovereigns, Ferdinand and Isabella, were down in Andalusia, that beautiful southern province of Spain, in the midst of a war with the Moors, who occupied certain portions of the land, and whom the Spaniards were trying to drive out. So, his wife being now dead, Columbus took his little boy Diego, and to Andalusia they went. They stopped at Palos by the sea, and from there set out on foot. The way was long, and Diego could not go far without getting very thirsty; and his father stopping at a great, dark, stone convent, called Maria de la Rabida, to get him a drink, the prior asked them in to rest a bit. As they talked,

Columbus soon told of his great project, to sail to the Indies by way of the western sea.

The prior, in his long dark robe and shaved head, opened his eyes at this and wanted to hear more. "Novel project this," thought he; "very novel—most astonishing! I must have my friend, Dr. Fernandez, hear it." So a messenger was sent to Palos to fetch the doctor, and Columbus went over again the wonderful plan—just to sail west, not so very far, over the round earth, and reach the stately cities of Cathay, and convert the Grand Khan to the faith, and gather of the plentiful gold and jewels of that land. Little Diego stood by and listened with wide-open eyes, and the doctor pondered, while the prior gazed out from the western window upon the Atlantic, and Columbus bent eager eyes and flushed face over his chart.

"Why, it may be possible! Send for Martin Alonzo Pinzon. He is a seaman; let us see what he thinks!"

To Palos again goes the messenger, to the rich and influential citizen, Alonzo Pinzon, and tells him he is wanted at La Rabida. "Ah, Alonzo Pinzon!" greets him the prior, "come and hear what a man proposes to do; and a wise and courageous sailor he seems, though poor enough!" And a third time they bend over the charts there in the dark stone convent, and Alonzo Pinzon hears of the western route to India; and Diego gazes from one to the other, and hopes in his heart that his father will take him along—he wants to see the unicorns. Pinzon catches the idea with enthusiasm, promising to help Columbus with money and influence, and to go with him if he goes. The doctor, cogitating upon the statements and arguments, concludes that they make quite a reasonable showing, and advises Columbus to go on.

The prior says: "Go at once to the court. Talavera, the queen's confessor, is a good friend of mine, and a letter of introduction to him will gain you access to the king and queen. They will surely help you." Diego clasps his hands. "Will you stay with me, Diego?" says the long-robed prior. "I'd rather go to court," says Diego. "Nay, my son," says Columbus, "if the good prior will keep you, I will leave you here while I go on my uncertain errand." So the little boy stands in the great stone doorway and watches his father out of sight toward Cordova.

At Cordova is nothing but excitement and confusion. The army is just starting upon a campaign against the Moors. Talavera is preoccupied, has his hands full of business, and can scarcely give Columbus time enough to state his errand. "Dear me, a new route to the Indies! But don't you see how busy we are with this war? It is probably all nonsense—sounds like it. The court in wartime can not waste precious hours over the consideration of such wild visions as this." So Columbus takes lodgings in Cordova, supports himself by chart-making, talks to everybody about the new route to Asia, and waits. Such a man with such a story is likely to gain some attention, and by and by he begins to have friends. Several of the important politicians come to know him, some are converts to his theory, and finally the grand cardinal himself procures him an audience with the king and queen. Enthusiastically the "one-idea'd man" unfolds his theories to royalty. The land of the Grand Khan, with its untold treasure, the salvation of millions of souls in the Indies, are the vivid points. The earth is a sphere, and a ship may sail straight from Spain to Cipango, urges this man of imagination and faith. The king was not slow to perceive the great advantages which success in such an enterprise would bring to the government that undertook it; but he must consult the wise men. Talavera should head a commission composed of the great men in the church, great men of science, and professors in the universities. Surely no man could ask for more. So to Salamanca, seat of the greatest Spanish university, Columbus went to convince the commission.

In the hall of the convent there was assembled the imposing company— shaved monks in gowns of black and gray, fashionably dressed men from the court in jaunty hats, cardinals in scarlet robes—all the dignity and learning of Spain, gathered and waiting for the man and his idea.

He stands before them with his charts, and explains his belief that the world is round, and that Asia stretches from the eastern boundary of Europe to a point something like four thousand miles from Spain. Hence Asia could be reached by sailing due west across the Atlantic. They had heard something of this before at Cordova, and here at Salamanca, before the commission was formally assembled, and they had their arguments ready.

You think the earth is round, and inhabited on the other side? Are you not aware that the holy fathers of the church have condemned this belief? Say the fathers, the Scriptures tell us all men are descended from Adam; but certainly no men descended from Adam live in such a region as this you speak of—the antipodes. Will you contradict the fathers? The Holy Scriptures, too, tell us expressly that the heavens are spread out like a tent, and how can that be true if the earth is not flat like the ground the tent stands on? This theory of yours looks heretical.

Columbus might well quake in his boots at the mention of heresy; for there was that new Inquisition just in fine running order, with its elaborate bone-breaking, flesh-pinching, thumb-screwing, hanging, burning, mangling system for heretics. What would become of the Idea if he should get passed over to that energetic institution?

"I am a true and loyal Catholic," he cries; "I wish to convert the Grand Khan's people to our blessed faith. I believe the Bible, and God himself sends me on this mission. But these words of the Scriptures are to be taken as a figure, not as literal facts of science." "Will this sailor teach us how to read the Scriptures!" growl the monks.

"Well, for argument, suppose this world is round, and you could sail west to the Indies. The voyages would take years, and you could not carry food enough to keep you from starving."

"But I believe it is only a voyage of four thousand miles, and can, with favoring winds, be accomplished in a short time," says Columbus, stating his scientific reasons for this belief. "Will this sailor teach us science!" growl the professors. "Well, all this *may* be true; but really, can you expect us to believe that there is a land beneath us where people walk with their feet *up*, and trees grow *down*?" Oh, foolish Columbus! What an absurd idea! "And, besides, if the signor should succeed in sailing down around the earth to this peculiar region, how does he propose to get back again? Will his ship sail up-hill?"

Oh, the nudging and winks among the monks at this poser! And the professors smile triumphantly. "And anyway who are you Signor Columbo, to set yourself up to know more than all the world beside? Haven't men been sailing in all the seas ever since the time of Noah, and, if such a thing as this were possible, would not somebody have found it out long ago?" With sound science, reverent religion, enthusiastic imagination and faith, he answered them, this unknown sailor, and left them bewildered by his views and impressed by his personality. "Perhaps there is truth in the matter," said the monks of St. Stephen. They said they would think about it, and they did think about it, and it took them four years to think about it. Meantime they adjourned and went about their own affairs, and Columbus went back to court.

The campaign against the Moors began, and from that time to the end of those weary years Columbus followed the court from place to place, over the hills and valleys of beautiful Andalusia. Sometimes he made charts for his support, sometimes he fought in the battles, sometimes he talked with the courtiers, or begged audience with the king to urge him to a decision; but always was with him that one dream on which he was staking all his time and strength—the best years and the fullest power of his manhood—hope of his heart, purpose of his will, that one Idea possessing him in vivid, unwavering faith.

The queen was kind. His enthusiasm and sound judgment, his persistent faith in his idea, his dignity and strong determination, tempered by the most manly religion, made him friends even among his examiners at Salamanca; and so he hoped and waited. Think of it—four years of suspense on top of thirteen years of thought and study and investigation toward on end! And when at last Talavera assembled the wise men of the commission to announce the result of their long deliberation, they had come to this wise conclusion: that the whole thing was foolish and impossible, unworthy of a great king's attention.

Better give it up, Cristoforo Colombo, and make charts for a living the rest of your days. No, says Colombo, that western ocean must be crossed. He turns to the powerful Spanish nobles. They are friendly, but hardly dare take up the project. He will go to France and present his case. But first to La Rabida to see Diego, a tall lad now. "What!" says the prior, "no success? Too bad, too bad! But Spain must not give the glory of this great undertaking to France. I know the queen, and I will write to her; I was her confessor once."

He wrote with such force that he was summoned to the queen at once, and his earnest pleading determined Isabella to send again for Columbus. But again disappointment came, for they took offense at Columbus's high demands and would not grant them. The Spanish sovereigns were to furnish the largest share of the equipment; he should be admiral of the seas, and he and his sons after him were to rule, under the king, the countries discovered, and share in all the profits of the enterprise. Bold demands from an adventurer! Seventeen years of waiting might have taught him common sense; but with his absurd faith and uncommon sense he would accept no other terms, and turned away again with his Idea and his determination.

"Too bad, too bad!" said St. Angel, the tax-collector; "*I* will plead with the queen. She must not let slip this chance of enriching the king—*and* converting the khan. I will myself lend the money necessary, if the king can't afford it." Said Isabella to St. Angel: "I think as you do. This is a wonderful plan. Let them say what they will, by my own right I am queen of Castile, as well as queen of Spain, and I pledge the crown of Castile to raise for Cristoforo Columbo a suitable equipment to sail to the Indies by the west. Let him make his own terms."

At last the fretting applications, the repeated explanations, the harrowing suspense, the long restriction are over, and the strong wings of the sea-bird are free to bear away over the Atlantic.

James Johonnot, excerpt from *Ten Great Events in History* (New York, D. Appleton & Company, 1887), 117–33.

What Really Happened

Christopher Columbus's requests for funding fit into a broader context of sea voyages and theoreticians during the 1400s. Throughout much of the fifteenth century, the Portuguese had been commissioning sailors to move down the coast of West Africa in search of the fabled gold mines of Mali; the lost Christian society overseen by Prester John; and a means to procure spices from far-off places at a cheaper price. What we now consider Spain was then broken up into different lands. One of these, Castile, had begun contesting Portuguese expansion into some islands in the Atlantic Ocean. Another part of what eventually became Spain, the Kingdom of Aragon, had a long history of holding maritime territories across the Mediterranean Sea. In 1469, the marriage between the rulers of Castile and Aragon united their Mediterranean and Atlantic ambitions. Additionally, in 1492, the combined forces of Castile and Aragon conquered yet another area of present-day Spain, Granada, which was the last stronghold of an earlier Islamic empire. The rulers of Castile and Aragon viewed the conquests through the prism of the Crusades of old. They believed that their conquests fit into a narrative about the last days and the return of Christ. When Columbus arrived at court, he presented his arguments to two rulers who were interested in overseas expansion and exploration and who were also looking for possible new fronts to fight against Islam.

Columbus initially struggled to find support, not because his radical ideas were dismissed by ignorant academics, but because Columbus's calculations were viewed as—and in fact were—wrong. Already, in ancient Greece, mathematicians had determined that the earth was a sphere and had even roughly calculated its circumference. In Columbus's day all educated people knew that the earth was round. Some, certainly, questioned whether or not a person could sail too far south or too far north. Others accepted that sailing west would eventually lead to China, Japan, and the Spice Islands, but they wondered if such a venture was possible. Europeans had absolutely no knowledge that the American continents obstructed them from sailing west to Asia. Of course, centuries earlier the Vikings had traveled to what is now Newfoundland in Canada, and possibly even farther south, but few outside of the far north had even heard a legend of such voyages. Thus, when Europeans thought about sailing west, they assumed the trip would be impossible because it would take too many weeks across undrinkable water, under an unbearable sun, and with unforgiving winds.

To get around this problem, Columbus argued that the experts of his own day were wrong: the earth, Columbus claimed, was much smaller than anyone realized and the transatlantic voyage was not only plausible but could also be accomplished without much difficulty. After years of rejections at several European courts—rejections made in no small part because people correctly thought that Columbus had miscalculated and underestimated the size of the earth—the unified kingdoms of Castile and Aragon determined to invest some money into the expedition.

After several weeks at sea, Columbus arrived in the Caribbean. He believed that he had arrived on the eastern coast of Asia and immediately began searching for gold and the fabled kingdom of Japan. Through gestures, he established trade with local Amerindians, who at first seemed puzzled by Columbus's arrival. Confusion between the two peoples quickly deteriorated into violence and disaster. Columbus enslaved people to return them to Spain. He incessantly demanded that people tell him where to find precious metals, and soon, people began giving him answers to get rid of him or to avoid him. Soon after, Columbus began to arrive in empty villages. Columbus's firsthand accounts of his voyages reveal a man who was obsessed with his role in a divine plan. He was also driven by economic motives. He repeatedly noted that the peoples he found would be easy for his sovereigns to conquer. Far from being sparsely populated, the Caribbean encountered by Columbus was full of people with different cultures and different languages. Columbus returned to Spain and was granted titles and honors for his successes. He died believing that he had found a passage to Asia.

Columbus left behind a legacy that was controversial in his own day and that remains so. Columbus himself and then many individuals after him established systems of exploitation and enslavement that decimated Amerindian populations. In the early sixteenth century, people already questioned the morality of what was happening. Some argued that the conquests were legitimate and a necessary expansion of Christianity to new peoples. Others, however, condemned the despicable treatment of Amerindians and worried that it would bring down the wrath of God and then the end of the Spanish empire. Forced Amerindian labor, gold, and silver helped finance wars in Europe over the Italian peninsula and religion during the sixteenth, seventeenth, and later centuries. Disease—both intentionally and unintentionally spread—ravaged Amerindian populations. New diseases also entered Europe. Millions of Amerindians were enslaved or slaughtered. Certainly, the battles between Amerindians and Europeans were rarely one-sided. Early conquerors found successes largely through the assistance of Amerindian allies. But the ultimate result was the conquest of two continents and then a myth about a protagonist who fought the ignorance of his own day and discovered largely uninhabited lands.

PRIMARY SOURCE DOCUMENTS

Paolo Toscanelli was a learned man based in Florence, Italy. He was interested in the ongoing explorations of the Atlantic Ocean during the 1400s. He wrote a letter to Portugal in which he advised that the king consider sailing to the west in order to reach the riches of the Spice Islands. Toscanelli incorrectly argued that the world was much smaller than most previous thinkers had thought. Columbus ran with Toscanelli's miscalculation. In the following excerpt, Toscanelli sends a copy of a document to Columbus. Note what Toscanelli views as important about sailing west, what sorts of things he sees as novel, and what sorts of things he takes for granted.

Paul, the Physician, to Cristobal Colombo greeting. I perceive your magnificent and great desire to find a way to where the spices grow, and in reply to your letter I send you the copy of another letter which I wrote, some days ago, to a friend and favourite of the most serene King of Portugal before the wars of Castile, in reply to another which, by direction of his Highness, he wrote to me on the said subject, and I send you another sea chart like the one I sent him, by which you will be satisfied respecting your enquiries; which copy is as follows:

A Copy of the letter to Martins.
Paul, the Physician, to Fernan Martins, Canon at Lisbon, greeting. It was pleasant to me to understand that your health was good, and that you are in the favour and intimacy with the most generous and most magnificent Prince, your King. I have already spoken with you respecting a shorter way to the places of spices than that which you take by Guinea, by means of maritime navigation. The most serene King now seeks from me some statement, or rather a demonstration to the eye, by which the slightly learned may take in and understand the way. I know this can be shown from the spherical shape of the earth, yet, to make the comprehension of it easier, and to facilitate the work, I have determined to show that way by means of a sailing chart. I, therefore, send to his Majesty a chart made by my own hands, on which are delineated your coasts and islands, whence you must begin to make your journey always westward, and the

places at which you should arrive, and how far from the pole or the equi-noctial line you ought to keep, and through how much space or over how many miles you should arrive at those most fertile places full of all sorts of spices and jewels. You must not be surprised if I call the parts where the spices are west, when they usually call them east, because to those always sailing west, those parts are found by navigation on the under side of the earth. But if by land and by the upper side, they will always be found to the east. The straight lines shown lengthways on the map indicate the dis-tance from east to west, and those that are drawn across show the spaces from south to north. I have also noted on the map several places at which you may arrive for the better information of navigators, if they should reach a place different from what was expected, by reason of the wind or any other cause; and also that they may show some acquaintance with the country to the natives, which ought to be sufficiently agreeable to them. It is asserted that none but merchants live on the island. For there the number of navigators with merchandize is so great that in all the rest of the world there are not so many as in one most noble port called Zaitun. For they affirm that a hundred ships laden with pepper discharge their cargoes in that port in a single year, besides other ships bringing other spices. That country is very populous and very rich, with a multitude of provinces and kingdoms, and with cities without number, under one prince who is called Great Kan, which name signifies *Rex Regum* in Latin, whose seat and residence is generally in the province Katay. His ancestors desired intercourse with Christians now 200 years ago. They sent to the Pope and asked for several persons learned in the faith, that they might be enlightened, but those who were sent, being impeded in their journey, went back. Also in the time of Eugenius one of them came to Eugenius, who affirmed their great kindness towards Christians, and I had a long conversation with him on many subjects, about the magnitude of their rivers in length and breadth, and on the multitude of cities on the banks of the rivers. He said that on one river there were near 200 cities with marble bridges great in length and breadth, and everywhere adorned with columns. This country is worth seeking by the Latins, not only because great wealth may be obtained from it, gold and silver, all sorts of gems, and spices, which never reach us; but also on account of its learned men, philosophers, and expert astrologers, and by what skill and art so powerful and magnificent a province is governed, as well as how their wars are con-ducted. This is for some satisfaction to his request, so far as the shortness of time and my occupations admitted. Being ready in future more fully to satisfy his royal Majesty as far as he may wish.

Given at Florence, June 24th, 1474.

Excerpts of letters from Paolo Toscanelli to Christopher Columbus, published in Christopher Columbus, *The Journal*, translated by Clements R. Markham (London: Hakluyt Society, 1893), 3–7.

Christopher Columbus wrote a diary to chronicle his first voyage across the Atlantic Ocean. The original has been lost and all that remains is a copy that is somewhat removed from the original text. Nevertheless, the work reveals a great deal about Columbus's thoughts and views about himself, his voyages, and the people whom he encountered. The following excerpts suggest moments of anxiety in the ocean crossing but say nothing about a belief that the earth was flat.

. . .

Friday, 3d of August.

We departed on Friday, the 3d of August, in the year 1492, from the bar of Saltes, at 8 o'clock, and proceeded with a strong sea breeze until sunset, towards the south, for 60 miles, equal to 15 leagues; afterwards S.W. and W.S.W., which was the course for the Canaries.

. . .

Thursday, 9th of August.

The Admiral was not able to reach Gomera until the night of Sunday, while Martin Alonso remained on that coast of Gran Canaria by order of the Admiral, because his vessel could not be navigated. Afterwards the Admiral took her to Canaria, and they repaired the *Pinta* very thoroughly through the pains and labour of the Admiral, of Martin Alonso, and the rest . . .

. . .

Thursday, 6th of September.

He departed on that day from the port of Gomera in the morning, and shaped a course to go on his voyage; having received tidings from a caravel that came from the island of Hierro that three Portuguese caravels were off that island with the object of taking him. (This must have been the result of the King's annoyance that Colon should have gone to Castille.) There was a clam all that day and night, and in the morning he found himself between Gomera and Tenerife.

. . .

Monday, 10th of September.

In this day and night he made 60 leagues, at the rate of 10 miles an hour, which are 2½ leagues; but he only counted 48 leagues, that the people might not be alarmed if the voyage should be long.

. . .

Friday, 14th of September.

That day they navigated, on the westerly course, day and night, 20 leagues, counting a little less. Here those of the caravel *Niña* reported that they had seen a tern and a boatswain bird, and these birds never go more than 25 leagues from the land.

. . .

Saturday, 22nd of September.

They shaped a course W.N.W. more or less, her head turning from one to the other point, and made 30 leagues. Scarcely any weed was seen. They saw some sandpipers and another bird. Here the Admiral says: "This contrary wind was very necessary for me, because my people were much excited at the thought that in these seas no wind ever blew in the direction of Spain." Part of the day there was no weed, and later it was very thick.

. . .

Monday, 1st of October

Course west, and 25 leagues made good, counted for the crew as 20 leagues. There was a heavy shower of rain. At dawn the Admiral's pilot made the distance from Hierro 578 leagues to the west. The reduced reckoning which the Admiral showed to the crew made it 584 leagues; but the truth which the Admiral observed and kept secret was 707.

. . .

Wednesday 10th of October.

The course was W.S.W., and they went at the rate of 10 miles an hour, occasionally 12 miles, and sometimes 7. During the day and night they made 59 leagues, counted as no more than 44. Here the people could endure no longer. They complained of the length of the voyage. But the Admiral cheered them up in the best way he could, giving them good hopes of the advantages they might gain from it. He added that, however much they might complain, he had to go to the Indies, and that he would go on until he found them, with the help of our Lord.

Thursday, 11th of October.

The course was W.S.W., and there was more sea than there had been during the whole of the voyage. They saw sandpipers, and a green reed near the ship. Those of the caravel *Pinta* saw a cane and a pole, and they took up another small pole which appeared to have been worked with iron; also another bit of cane, a land-plant, and a small board. The crew of the caravel *Niña* also saw signs of land, and a small branch covered with berries. Everyone breathed afresh and rejoiced at these signs. The run until sunset was 26 leagues.

After sunset the Admiral returned to his original west course, and they went along at the rate of 12 miles an hour. Up to two hours after midnight they had gone 90 miles, equal to 22½ leagues. As the caravel *Pinta* was a better sailer, and went ahead of the Admiral, she found the land, and made the signals ordered by the Admiral. The land was first seen by a sailor named Rodrigo de Triana. But the Admiral, at ten in the previous night, being on the castle of the poop, saw a light, though it was so uncertain that he could not affirm it was land. He called Pero Gutierrez, a gentleman of the King's bedchamber, and said that there seemed to be a light, and that he should look at it. He did so, and saw it . . .

Christopher Columbus, excerpts from *The Journal,* translated by Clements R. Markham (London: Hakluyt Society, 1893), 15–35.

Columbus increased the Spanish presence in the growing world of Atlantic trade and exploration. Previously, the Portuguese had dominated that area. Thus, conflicts broke out between the two powers. The two rival states turned to the pope to mediate their disagreements. In 1494, Pope Alexander VI issued the Treaty of Tordesillas, which ordered western lands to the Spanish while eastern lands went to the Portuguese. Experts were then asked to interpret what the treaty might mean in practice. One opinion is excerpted below. Note that the expert never questions the circularity of the earth. Instead, he is concerned about figuring out how information from classical sources, especially Ptolemy, fit into the new geographical knowledge.

1. The manner of determining the terminus or end of the three hundred and seventy leagues, starting from the Islands of Cape Verde on a westerly line is as follows:

2. First, it must be noted that the said Cape Verde and its islands lie fifteen degrees from the equator, and it is likewise to be noted that the said 370 leagues, starting from the said islands, comprise to the west eighteen degrees, and each degree on that parallel contains twenty leagues and five-eights. Moreover, it is necessary to make a straight line, in latitude [*sic*] from pole to pole only in this our hemisphere, intersecting the said parallel exactly at the end of the said eighteen degrees; and everything lying within this line on the left hand, turning towards the side of Guinea, will be belong to the King of Portugal, and the other part by the West as far as it turns by the East towards the Arabian Gulf will belong to the Kings our Lords, if their ships first sail thither. And this is

what I understand by the treaty made by your Highnesses with the King of Portugal.

. . .

5. And because the sailing chart is not wholly useful and does not suffice for the mathematical demonstration of the above rule, a world map in spherical form is necessary, divided into two hemispheres by its lines and degrees, and the situation of the land, islands and sea, each in its own place—which world map I put down together with these expressions of my meaning and opinion, the more clearly to demonstrate the truth.

. . .

9. And if in this my decision and opinion any error appear, I will always defer to the correction of those who know and understand more than I, especially to the Admiral of the Indies, who at the present time knows more than any other person in this subject, for he is greatly learned in the theory and admirably practical, as his famous achievements demonstrate; and I believe that Divine Providence holds him as elect to carry out its great mystery and service in this undertaking, which I believe is the disposition and preparation of that (result) which, hereafter, the same Divine Providence will manifest to its great glory—the salvation and good of the world.

10. Here is shown the navigation of the Admiral of the Main-land. Ptolemy in the eighth book *de situ orbis* says at chapter five:

That the true circumference of the earth at the equator is 180,000 stades, at the rate of five hundred stades of a degree according to his calculation, and counting eight stades per mile, are 22,500 miles, which are 5,625 leagues at the rate of four miles per league in Castillian reckoning. . . . Moreover, according to Strabo, Alfragano, Ambrosi, Macrobi, Teodosi and Euristhenes, the said circumference of the earth is 252,000 stades, the which 252,000 stades, at the rate of eight stades per mile, are . . .

The said circle of the tropics is shorter than the equinoctial circle by 670 ½ leagues, which is, at four miles per league, 2,682 miles, according to the above calculation summed up and proved throughout . . .

. . .

15. And the Admiral says in his letter that Cape Verde is nine and a quarter degrees distant from the equator. According to Ptolemy, I see him allowing fifteen and two-thirds leagues to a degree; nevertheless, I decide with the other learned men as to the distance of the said islands from the equator. The division into stades, although the number given by Ptolemy is different from that given by the above cited learned men, Strabo, Alfragano, Macrobi, Teodosi, and Euristhenes, they are all essentially in

agrement, because Ptolemy makes use of longer stades; so that his 180,000 stades are equal to the 252,000 stades of the above mentioned learned men for the equinoctial line as above said.

Samuel Edward Dawson, excerpt from *The Lines of Demarcation of Pope Alexander VI* (Toronto: J. Hope & Sons, 1899), 542–45.

In the following excerpt, the Florentine historian Francesco Guicciardini describes Columbus's voyages from his viewpoint during the mid-1500s. Guicciardini relates that Europeans before 1492 believed southern lands were too hot for habitation and that the ocean was impossible to transverse. However, he never claimed that medieval or early modern people believed the world was flat.

Those who were of a speculative Genius, and had considered the admirable Structure and Motions of the Heavens, have taught Posterity to imagine, from their globular Form, a Line drawn from East to West, equidistant in all Points from the Northern and Southern Poles; and called it the Equinoctial, because when the Sun is under it the Days and Nights are equal. The Length of this Line they divided, in their Imagination into 360 Parts, which they called Degrees; and in like manner is a Circle that passes through the Poles divided into 360 Degrees. According to this Rule of theirs, our Cosmographers have measured and divided the Earth, and imagined an Equinoctial Line on the Earth, which falls perpendicularly under the celestial Line figured by Astronomers, and have divided it in like manner, together with the Circuit of the Earth, measured by a Line falling perpendicularly under the Poles, into 360 Degrees of Latitude; so that from our Pole to the southern Pole they estimate 180 Degrees, and from either of the Poles to the Equinoctial Line is a Distance of 90 Degrees. These are the general Principles established by Cosmographers; but as to Particulars relating to the habitable Parts of the Earth, after delivering down to us their Notions of that Part which lies under our Hemisphere, they had persuaded themselves, that that Part of the Earth which lies under the torrid Zone represented in the Heavens by Astronomers, and containing within it the Equinoctial, as being nearest the Sun, is, by reason of its Heat, uninhabitable; and that from our Hemisphere it was impossible to proceed to the Countries under the torrid Zone, or to those which lie beyond it towards the Southern Pole, which *Ptolemy*, who is universally acknowledged to be the Prince of Cosmographers, called Lands and Seas unknown. Hence that Author and others presupposed, that if a Person had a Mind to pass from our Hemisphere to the *Arabian* and *Persian* Gulphs, or to that Part of *India* which the victories of *Alexander* first discovered to the *Europeans*, he must be obliged to go thither by Land, or after approaching thither as far as possible, by sailing up the *Mediterranean* Sea, to perform the rest of the Journey by Land.

The Falsity of these Opinions and Suppositions has been demonstrated in our Times by the Navigation of the *Portuguese*, who had begun, many Years ago, under the Kings of *Portugal*, from a Desire of mercantile Gain, to coast it along the Shores of *Africa*, till by little and little they proceeded as far as the Isles of *Cape Verde*, called by the Antients, as many are of opinion, the *Hesperides*, distant 14 Degrees from the Equinoctial Line towards the North Pole. Their Boldness still increasing, they ventured farther and farther, till after fetching a long Compass, they arrived at length at the *Cape of Good Hope* in South Latitude. This Promontory is the most distant of any Part of *Africa* from the Equinoctial Line, being removed from it 38 Degrees. From this Cape they stretched away to the East as far as the *Arabian* and *Persian* Gulfs, in which Places the Merchants of *Alexandria* used to purchase their Spices, which were partly of the Growth of the Country, but the greater Part of them was brought from the *Molucca* Islands and some from *India*, and afterwards conveyed by Land through a long and very inconvenient Road, at a great Expence, to *Alexandria*. There they were brought up by the *Venetian* Merchants, who exported them to *Venice*, from whence they supplied all Christendom with Spices, to their immense Profit. For having monopolized that Commodity, they set what Price they pleased on it; and in the same Ships that exported it from *Alexandria* they carried thither great Quantities of mercantile Goods; and their Vessels which carried these Spices into *France, Flanders, England,* and other Places, returned with Ladings of other Merchandise to *Venice*; which Way of trafficking at the same time greatly increased the Revenues of the Republic, by the Duties and Customs.

But the *Portuguese* sailing from *Lisbon*, the Seat of the King of *Portugal*, into these remote Parts, contracted Acquaintance and Friendship with the Kings of *Calicut*, and other neighbouring Towns in the *Indian* Sea; and afterwards, by degrees, penetrating into the most remote Places, in process of Time erected Fortresses in convenient Situations, and entering into Alliances with some Cities of the Country, subjected others by Force of Arms. By virtue of these Discoveries and Settlements, they transferred the Spice Trade, which used to be managed in *Alexandria*, into their own Hands, first conveying the Spices by Sea to *Portugal*, and afterwards exporting that rich Commodity to the same Countries, which had before been supplied with it by the *Venetians*. A Navigation truly wonderful for the Space of Sixteen Thousand Miles, through Seas wholly unknown, under other Stars, and other Heavens, and with other Instruments; for after passing the Equinoctial Line they are no longer guided by the Pole Star, and remain deprived of the Use of the Magnet; and they have no Place to put in for Shelter or Refreshments in so long a Voyage, but on the unknown Coasts of Lands inhabited by hostile Barbarians of strange Language, Religion, and Manners. But yet, in spite of all these Difficulties, this Navigation is by length of Time become so familiar, that the same Voyage which formerly required Ten Months, is now performed with less Danger in Six.

But yet more astonishing was the Navigation of the *Spaniards*, which commenced in the Year 1490, for the Discoveries of *Christopher Columbus* a *Genoese*. That Gentleman had made several Voyages on the Ocean, and conjecturing, from his observations on certain Winds, what afterwards appeared to be Truth, he obtained of the *Spanish* Monarchs some Ships, with which he sailed Westwards, and at the End of 33 Days discovered in the utmost Extremity of our Hemisphere certain Islands, of which none had the least Notice before; they were situated in a happy Climate, were of a fertile Soil; and the Inhabitants, except some Tribes of Savages, who fed on human Flesh, were in general of great Simplicity of Manners, and contended with what the Bounty of Nature afforded them; were never tormented with Ambition or Avarice, but deserved Compassion in that they had no established Religion, no Notion of Learning, or Skill in mechanic Arts, were unpractised in Arms and the Art of War, and knew nothing by Speculation or Experience; in short, they were a kind of tame Animals, and ready to fall a very easy Prey to any Invader. The *Spaniards*, afterwards allured by the Facility of seizing the Country, and the Richness of it, for there had been discovered very rich Veins of Gold, soon transported themselves thither in great Numbers, and settled as in their own proper Habitations.

Columbus pushed his Discoveries much farther, as did after him *Americus Vespucius*, a *Florentine*; and many others successively discovered other Islands, and very large Tracts of Land on the Continent, and in some few Parts of them the Marks of an established System of Customs and civil Polity; for the Inhabitants had public and private Edifices, were well cloathed, and affable in their Conversation; but all of them, in general, knew not the Use of Arms, and were easy to become a Prey. But this vast Extent of Land, which, without comparison, exceeds all that was known to be inhabited, the *Spaniards* have peopled with a new Race of People, transported thither by their frequent Navigations; and sometimes by digging Gold and Silver from Veins, which are to be found in many Places, or clearing them from the Sands of Rivers, or procuring them of the Inhabitants in Exchange for Toys of very small Value, and sometimes by robbing the Places where they are reposited, an infinite Quantity of those precious Metals has been imported into *Spain* by private Adventurers, tho' with the King's Licence, at their own Charges, every one paying his Majesty a fifth Part of what he got possessed of, by digging in the Mines, or by any other Means. Nay, the Boldness of the *Spaniards* has carried them yet much farther, for some Ships of theirs having stretched along the Coast of the Continent towards the Southern Pole, to the Latitude of 53 Degrees South, afterwards entered into a narrow Sea, which opened them a Passage into a vast Ocean, through which they sailed to the East Indies, and thence returned home by the same Course which the *Portuguese* take in their Eastern Voyage, having, as it appears with the Highest Degree of Certainty, fetched a Compass round the Globe of the Earth, Worthy, indeed, are those *Portuguese* and *Spaniards*, and particularly *Columbus*, the first Undertaker of this wonderful and most dangerous Navigation, to be celebrated with eternal Praises, Vigilance, and Hardiness, which have enlightened our Age with the Knowledge of such great and marvellous Things, that were hitherto buried in Obscurity. But yet more worthy would they be to be celebrated for their Undertaking, had they not been induced to undergo such great Perils and Fatigues by an immoderate Thirst after Gold and Riches, but by a Desire to improve themselves or others in Knowledge, or to propagate the Christian Faith, tho' these Ends were in some measure answered by their Discoveries, the Natives in many Places being converted to our Religion. By these Navigations it is manifest, that the Antients were mistaken in many Things relating to the Knowledge of the Earth. For the Equinoctial Line has been passed, the torrid Zone found habitable, as well as the Zones next the Poles, contrary to their Opinion, who held that these Polar Zones were not habitable because of their immoderate Cold, on account of their Situation, with respect to the Heavens, so remote from the Course of the Sun. These Navigators have made plain what some of the Antients believed, others rejected, that there are Inhabitants on our Globe who had their Feet opposite to ours, and are called *Antipodes*.

Francesco Guicciardini, excerpt from *The History of Italy*, translated by Austin Parke Goddard (London: John Towers, 1753), vol. 3, pp. 300–312.

Further Reading

Abulafia, David. *The Discovery of Mankind: Atlantic Encounters in the Age of Columbus*. New Haven, CT: Yale University Press, 2008.

Bedini, Silvio A. *The Christopher Columbus Encyclopedia*. 2 vols. New York: Simon & Schuster, 1991.

Columbus, Christopher. *The Four Voyages*. Edited and translated by J. M. Cohen. New York: Penguin, 1969.

Connell, William J. "Italians in the Early Atlantic World." In *The Routledge History of Italian Americans*, edited by William J. Connell and Stanslao G. Pugliese, 17–41. London: Routledge, 2018.

Crosby, Alfred. *The Columbian Exchange: Biological and Cultural Consequences of 1492*. Westport, CT: Greenwood, 1972.

Garwood, Christine. *Flat Earth. The History of an Infamous Idea*. New York: St. Martin's, 2008.

Greenblatt, Stephen. *Marvelous Possessions. The Wonder of the New World*. Chicago: University of Chicago Press, 1991.

Heike, Paul. *The Myths that Made America: An Introduction to American Studies*. Bielefeld: Transcript Verlag, 2014.

Phillips, William D. "Christopher Columbus." In *Oxford Bibliographies*. Found online at https://www.oxfordbibliographies.com/view/document/obo-9780195399301/obo-9780195399301-0029.xml (accessed August 19, 2020).

Phillips, William D., and Carla Rahn. *The Worlds of Christopher Columbus*. Cambridge: Cambridge University Press, 1992.

Russell, Jeffrey Burton. *Inventing the Flat Earth: Columbus and Modern Historians*. Westport, CT: Praeger, 1991.

3

Early Modern Women Were Uneducated and Uninfluential

What People Think Happened

The story goes that all early modern women lived lives of total subservience to men. Fathers, and then husbands, expected absolute obedience from women. Women were to be silent until and unless they were spoken to. All women suffered the same dreary existence: The birth of a girl was seen as a tragedy. Disappointed parents forced little girls to learn housework by the side of their miserable mothers. Eventually, the men in the family arranged a marriage for the girl. The girl had no input in the marriage plans. She did not know her soon-to-be spouse. A loveless marriage and more obedient servitude ensued. As a wife, a woman did what she was told to do and asked no questions. The husband ruled the household. As a mother, she taught her unfortunate daughters to be subservient themselves. Eventually, death put her out of her misery. It is not fair for modern people to ask if early modern women enjoyed their existence because they simply did not know better. It was only in the 1800s that women began to break free from near-total oppression and only in the 1970s that they enjoyed any real success. Today's arguments for equality between the sexes stand against traditions as old as history itself.

A part of the problem for early modern women was that education was out of their reach. A few very elite women might have received enough of an education to be able to provide entertainment for their husbands. Perhaps a handful could understand a few words in a prayer book, especially if the text had pictures. But most women never saw a book, let alone read or write one. One or two women, through a bizarre series of chance accidents, became queens. In those cases, the women rulers were obviously puppets. Behind the scenes, male advisors dictated their actions and made decisions for them. If queens were so controlled, what hope did other women have? Early modern women enjoyed no economic or political freedom. Their husbands controlled all their money, and the very idea that a woman could hold political power was seen as so ludicrous that it was never even considered. For all of these reasons, women, the myth goes, are not really important to understand the early modern period. Their lives were insignificant and unchanging, while men wrote the literature that we know, painted the pictures we recognize, were responsible for the innovations that we still prize, and held the political, social, and military positions where they could actually do important things.

How the Story Became Popular

The history of women was not a recognized area of study prior to the mid-twentieth century. Before that time, historians focused on the sorts of things that continue to be popularly associated with historical scholarship: wars, battles, diplomacy, and political leaders. Women were not a part of most historical treatments, and certainly not the focus. People in the 1800s and the first half of the 1900s rarely challenged their assumptions about the lives of women who lived centuries ago. These assumptions affected the focus of their studies and how they treated the few women in power whom they deemed worthy of mention; at times, they led to comical misunderstandings of the roles that women fulfilled in early modern societies. The early modern world was unquestionably full of misogynism, and therefore earlier historians were able to find plenty of examples of early modern writers who seemed to confirm a subordinate and unimportant role for women during the early modern period.

In terms of focus, the assumption that women were incapable of holding positions of power or creating noteworthy literary or artistic pieces led earlier historians to simply pass them over in their studies. An artist like Artemisia Gentileschi, for example, was enormously popular and influential in the late 1500s and found employment in both Italy and England. But historians, working under nineteenth-century assumptions that historical women simply were not artists, excluded her from the canon of great sixteenth-century artists. The work of female writers fared no better. No matter the popularity of women writers and their works, earlier

Esther before Ahasuerus, painting by Artemisia Gentileschi. Popular myth holds that early-modern women lived uniform, mostly insignificant lives of minor impact. However, early-modern women held all different kinds of roles—some powerful, some less so—even as they lived in a society very different than our own. Artemisia Gentileschi was an influential and sought-after painter during her lifetime. (The Metropolitan Museum of Art, Gift of Elinor Dorrance Ingersoll, 1969)

historians simply glossed over their contributions. The same story holds when it comes to the history of other areas such as science and politics. Such is the power of "paradigms." A paradigm is an assumption that we hold to be true about our world: we don't think about these assumptions, and we don't question them, we just know that they are the way things are and, for many, the way that they have always been. Working within late-nineteenth-century paradigms, historians saw the past as exactly what they expected to see: men made significant contributions and women did not.

Paradigms also helped shape the ways in which earlier historians treated the history and lives of women whom they *did* deem worthy of comment. For example, historians have studied figures like Queen Elizabeth I of England for a long time. Yet, older scholarship tended to highlight how exceptional and unusual it was that a woman could assume power over a rising state. Scholarship emphasized that Elizabeth ruled and acted like a man would have, a conclusion that reinforced their assumption that women in power were an oddity. Important women writers, when discussed, were usually viewed through the same lens. A woman writing something down was viewed as strange. A woman publishing something was unusual. Comments by women about matters outside the household, or even comments about expressing power within the household, were glossed over in favor of an emphasis upon areas where women accepted or admitted to subservience. If a woman seemed to have agency in early modern Europe, the consensus was that that agency was a facade masking the true male power behind the scenes.

Working within dated, older paradigms led some earlier historians to make wild claims about women in early modern Europe, claims that have been overwhelmingly rejected by historical work over the past sixty years. The most famous example of this was found in the writings of Jacob Burckhardt. Burckhardt wrote a book where he argued that things like individualism and secularism originated in Italy during the 1400s. Burckhardt also argued that Italy in those years began to prize social equality and to reject older ideas about inherited nobility. The vast majority of Burckhardt's arguments pertained to the experiences of elite men, but he also included a short section on women where he claimed that women and men were completely equal during the Italian Renaissance. Certainly, women were not as powerless as popular imagination often assumes, but Burckhardt's claim went too far in the other direction. Historians have, especially over the past sixty years, developed a much more sophisticated and nuanced understanding of women in early modern Europe. However, the ill-informed statements of nineteenth-century and early-twentieth-century scholars, based more upon their assumptions than actual historical evidence, continue to shape popular conceptions of the period. Certainly, women were not viewed by most people in early modern Europe as equal and there is no doubt that early modern Europe was a patriarchy. However, women did contribute a significant voice to many important stories about early modern Europe. Their prolific cultural productions were second to none. They directly or indirectly held influence over the most powerful political offices of their day. They possessed daily agency in a world very different from our own.

PRIMARY SOURCE DOCUMENTS

Aristotle viewed women as physically inferior to men and consequently argued for their just subordination to men. Aristotle's ideas were not universally shared in Antiquity (Plato, for example, had different ideas) but his views became extremely influential in medieval and early modern Europe. In the following excerpt, Aristotle discusses the role of women in a marriage and the importance of obedience. For further context, Aristotle argued, in other works, that women should ideally marry in their late teens to men in their late thirties.

A Good and perfect wife ought to be mistress of every thing within the house, and to have the care of every thing within the house, and to have the care of everything according to fixed laws; allowing no one to come in unbidden by her husband, and especially keeping on her guard against everything which can be noised abroad relating to a woman's dishonour. So that if any mischance has happened within doors, she alone ought to know about it; but when those who have come in have done any thing wrong, the husband should bear the blame. And she should manage the expenses laid out upon such festivals as her husband has agreed with her in keeping, and make an outlay of clothes and other ornaments on a somewhat lesser scale than is encouraged by the laws of the state; considering that neither splendour of vestments, nor pre-eminence of beauty, nor the amount of gold, contributes so much to the commendation of a woman, as good management in domestic affairs, and a noble and comely manner of life; since all such array of the soul is far more lovely, and has greater force (than any thing besides), to provide herself and her children true ornament till old age. A wife therefore ought to inspire herself with confidence, and perpetually to be at the head of domestic affairs. For it is unseemly for a man to know all that goes on in the house; in all respects indeed she ought to be obedient to her husband, and not to busy herself about public affairs, nor to take part in matrimonial concerns. And when it is time to give his daughters in marriage, or to get wives for his sons, by all means in these respects she should obey her husband. And she ought to show herself a fellow-counsellor to her husband, so as to assent to what pleases him, remembering that it is less unseemly for a husband to take in hand domestic matters, than for a wife to busy herself in affairs out of doors. But the well-ordered wife will justly consider the behaviour of her husband as a model of her own life, and a law to herself, invested with a divine sanction by means of the marriage tie and the community of life. For if she can persuade herself to bear her husband's ways patiently, she will most easily manage matters in the house; but if she cannot, she will have greater difficulty. So that it will be seemly for her to show herself of one mind with her husband, and tractable, not only when her husband is in good luck and prosperity, but also when he is in misfortune; and when good fortune has failed him, or sickness has laid hold of his bodily frame, or when he has been deprived of his sense, she ought gently and sympathetically to yield in any matter which is not base and unworthy; but if her husband has been ailing and made a mistake, she ought not to keep it on her mind, but to lay the blame on the disease or ignorance. For in proportion as she is now more careful to give way, so much the more gratitude will her husband feel towards her, when his ailment has passed by; and if she fails to obey him when he commands something which is unseemly, he will be able to pardon her with a better grace when he recovers. Observing such rules as these, the wife ought to show herself even more obedient to the rein than if she had entered the house as a purchased slave. For she has been bought at a high price, for the sake of sharing life and bearing children; than which no higher or holier tie can possibly exist.

Aristotle, excerpt from "Economics," in *The Politics and Economics of Aristotle*, translated by Edward Walford (London: Henry G. Bohn, 1853), 296–98.

In the following excerpt, Burckhardt seeks to fit women into his view that social hierarchies dissolved in fifteenth-century Italy. Historians have universally rejected these claims by Burkchardt and have shown convincingly the complex interplay of agency and oppression for women in medieval, Renaissance, and early modern Europe. But Burckhardt's claims reveal just how little serious attention was being paid to the history of women in the mid-nineteenth century.

To understand the higher forms of social intercourse at this period, we must keep before our minds the fact that women stood on a footing of perfect equality with men. We must not suffer ourselves to be misled by the sophistical and often malicious talk about the assumed inferiority of the female sex, which we meet with now and then in the dialogues of this time, nor by such satires as the third of Ariosto, who treats woman as a dangerous grown-up child, whom a man must learn how to manage, in spite of the great gulf between them. There is, indeed, a certain amount of truth in what he says. Just because the educated woman was on a level with the man, that communion of mind and heart which comes from the sense of mutual dependence and completion, could not be developed in marriage at this time, as it has been developed later in the cultivated society of the North.

The education given to women in the upper classes was essentially the same as that given to men. The Italian, at the time of the Renaissance, felt no scruple in putting sons and daughters alike under the same course of literary and even philological instruction. . . . Indeed, looking at this ancient culture as the chief treasure of life, he was glad that his girls should have a share in it. We have seen what perfection was attained by the daughters of princely houses in writing and speaking Latin. Many others must at least have been able to read it, in order to follow the conversation of the day, which turned largely on classical subjects. An active interest was taken by many in Italian poetry, in which, whether prepared or improvised, a large number of Italian women . . . made themselves famous. One, indeed, Vittoria Colonna, may be called immortal. If any proof were needed of the assertion made above, it would be found in the manly tone of this poetry. Even the love-sonnets and religious poems are so precise and definite in their character, and so far removed from the tender twilight of sentiment, and from all the dilettantism which we commonly find in the poetry of women, that we should not hesitate to attribute them to male authors, if we had not clear external evidence to prove the contrary.

For, with education, the individuality of women in the upper classes was developed in the same way as that of men. Till the time of the Reformation, the personality of women out of Italy, even of the highest rank, comes forward but little . . . throughout the whole of the fifteenth century, the wives of the rulers, and still more those of the Condottieri, have nearly all a distinct, recognizable personality, and take their share of notoriety and glory. To these came gradually to be added a crowd of famous women of the most varied kind . . . among them those whose distinction consisted in the fact that their beauty, disposition, education, virtue, and piety, combined to render them harmonious human beings. There was no question of "woman's rights" or female emancipation, simply because the thing itself was a matter of course. The educated woman, no less than the man, strove naturally after characteristic and complete individuality. The same intellectual and emotional development which perfected the man, was demanded for the perfection of the woman. Active literary work, nevertheless, was not expected from her, and if she were a poet, some powerful utterance of feeling, rather than the confidences of the novel or the diary, was looked for. These women had no thought of the public; their function was to influence distinguished men, and to moderate male impulse and caprice.

The highest praise which could then be given to the great Italian women was that they had the mind and the courage of men. We have only to observe the thoroughly manly bearing of most of the women in the heroic poems. . . . Women of this stamp could listen to novels . . . without social intercourse suffering from it. The ruling genius of society was not, as now, womanhood, or the respect for certain presuppositions, mysteries, and susceptibilities, but the consciousness of energy, of beauty, and of a social state full of danger and opportunity. And for this reason, we find, side by side with the most measured and polished social forms, something our age would call immodesty, forgetting that by which it was corrected and counterbalanced—the powerful characters of the women who were exposed to it.

That in all the dialogues and treatises together we can find no absolute evidence on these points is only natural, however freely the nature of love and the position and capacities of women were discussed.

What seems to have been wanting in this society were the young girls, who, even when not brought up in the monasteries, were still carefully kept away from it. It is not easy to say whether their absence was the cause of the greater freedom of conversation, or whether they were removed on account of it.

Even the intercourse with courtesans seems to have assumed a more elevated character. . . . It is clear from all we read on the subject that the famous courtesans were treated with no slight respect and consideration. Even when relations with them were broken off, their good opinion was still desired, which shows that departed passion had left permanent traces behind. But on the whole this intellectual intercourse is not worth mentioning by the side of that sanctioned by the recognised forms of social life, and the traces which it has left in poetry and literature are for the most part of a scandalous nature.

Jacob Burckhardt, excerpt from *The Civilisation of the Renaissance in Italy*, translated by S. G. C. Middlemore (London: S. Sonnenschein, 1904), 395–401.

The following excerpt is from a story within Giovanni Boccaccio's The Decameron, *a collection of stories written during the mid-1300s. In the story, two men, Buffalmacco and Bruno, play a trick on their friend Calandrino. The two men convince Calandrino that a nearby river possesses a magical stone that makes the person holding it turn invisible. The three men travel to the river and, after a time, Buffalmacco and Bruno pretend that they are unable to see Calandrino. Calandrino, thinking he has found the magical stone and is invisible, returns to Florence. The end of the story, included here, contains passages that seem to confirm popular myths about the subordination of women in early modern society.*

. . . The officers, forewarned by them, feigned not to see Calandrino and let him pass, laughing heartily at the jest, whilst he, without stopping, made straight for his house, which was near the Canto alla Macina, and fortune so far favored the cheat that none accosted him, as he came up the stream and after through the city, as, indeed, he met with few, for that well nigh every one was at dinner. Accordingly, he reached his house, thus laden, and as chance would have it, his wife, a fair and virtuous lady, by name Mistress Tessa, was at the stairhead. Seeing him come and somewhat provoked at his long tarriance, she began to rail at him saying, "Devil take the man! Wilt thou never think to come home betimes? All the folk have already dined whenas thou comest back to dinner." Calandrino, hearing this and finding that he was seen, was overwhelmed with chagrin and vexation and cried out, "Alack, wicked woman that thou art, wast thou there? Thou hast undone me: but, by God His faith, I will pay thee therefor!" Therewithal he ran up to a little saloon he had and there disburthened himself of the mass of stones he had brought home; then, running in a fury at his wife, he laid hold of her by the hair and throwing her down at his feet, cuffed and kicked her in every part as long as he could wag his arms and legs, without leaving her a hair on her head or a bone in her body that was not beaten to a mash, nor did it avail her aught to cry him mercy with clasped hands.

Meanwhile Bruno and Buffalmacco, after laughing awhile with the keepers of the gate, proceeded with slow step to follow Calandrino afar off and presently coming to the door of his house, heard the cruel beating he was in act to give his wife; whereupon, making a show of having but then come back, they called Calandrino, who came to the window, all asweat and red with anger and vexation, and prayed them come up to him. Accordingly, they went up, making believe to be somewhat vexed and seeing the room full of stones and the lady, all torn and disheveled and black and blue in the face for bruises, weeping piteously in one corner of the room, whilst Calandrino sat in another, untrussed and panting like one forspent, eyed them awhile, then said, "What is this, Calandrino? Art thou for building, that we see all these stones here? And Mistress Tessa, what aileth her? It seemeth thou hast beaten her. What is all this ado?" Calandrino, outwearied with the weight of the stones and the fury with which he had beaten his wife, no less than with chagrin for the luck which him seemed he had lost, could not muster breath to give them aught but broken words in reply; wherefore, as he delayed to answer, Buffalmacco went on, "Harkye, Calandrino, whatever other cause for anger thou mightest have had, thou shouldst not have fooled us as thou hast done, in that, after thou hadst carried us off to seek with thee for the wonder-working stone, thou leftist us in the Mugnone, like a couple of gulls, and madest off home, without saying so much as God be with you or Devil; the which we take exceeding ill; but assuredly this shall be the last trick thou shalt ever play us."

Therewithal, Calandrino, enforcing himself, answered, "Comrades, be not angered; the case standeth otherwise than as you deem. I (unlucky wretch that I am!) had found the stone in question, and you shall hear it I tell the truth. When first you questioned one another of me, I was less than half a score yards distant from you; but; seeing that you made off and saw me not, I went on before you and came back hither, still keeping a little in front of you." Then, beginning from the beginning, he recounted to them all that they had said and done, first and last, and showed them how the stones had served his back and shins; after which, "And I may tell you," continued he, "that, whenas I entered in at the gate, with all these stones about me which you see here, there was nothing said to me, albeit you know how vexatious and tiresome these gatekeepers use to be in wanting to see everything; more by token that I met by the way several of my friends and gossips, who are still wont to accost me and invite me to drink; but none of them said a word to me, no, nor half a word, as those who saw me not. At last, being come home hither, this accursed devil of a woman presented herself before me, for that, as you know, women cause everything to lose its virtue, wherefore I, who might else have called myself the luckiest man in Florence, am become the most unlucky. For this I have beaten her as long as I could wag my fists and I know not what hindereth me from slitting her weasand, accursed be the hour when first I saw her and when she came to me in this house." Then, flaming out into fresh anger, he offered to rise and beat her anew.

Bruno and Buffalmacco, hearing all this, made believe to marvel exceedingly and often confirmed that which Calandrino said, albeit they had the while so great a mind to laugh that they were like to burst: but, seeing him start up in a rage to beat his wife again, they rose upon him and withheld him, avouching that the lady was nowise at fault, but that he had only himself to blame for that which had happened, since he knew that women caused things to lose their virtue and had not bidden her beware of appearing before him that day, and that God had bereft him of foresight to provide against this, either for that the adventure was not to be his or because he had had it in mind to cozen his comrades, to whom he should have discovered the matter, as soon as he perceived that he had found the stone. Brief, after many words, they made peace, not without much ado, between him and the woebegone lady and went their ways, leaving him disconsolate, with the house full of stones.

Giovanni Boccaccio, excerpt from *The Decameron*, translated by John Payne (London: n.p., 1895), vol. 3, pp. 57–61.

What Really Happened

The history of women in the early modern world is a complicated story of how half of the European population lived their lives. Scholarly understanding of it changes all the time. It is true that misogyny existed in the early modern period and that, in many ways, women were—explicitly and implicitly—treated and considered as inferior. Men did hold most positions of political power. Men did monopolize most routes to formal education. Men did hold advantages in the law. It is indisputable that early modern Europe, in most of its facets, was a patriarchy and that even some of the most abhorrent misogynistic ideas could be presented and defended with impunity. However, these generalities overshadow the complexity of historical specifics. Too often, the most extreme examples are taken as typical of the experiences or opinions of most early modern men and women. In other cases, these generalities pretend that the experiences of women were simply static during the centuries of the early modern period. That was not the case, and the lives of women were dramatically different in 1450 compared to what they were in 1650, and very different in northern France or England, for example, compared to what they were in northern Italy.

Since the 1970s, historians have repeatedly illustrated how the practical experiences of women reveal a much more complicated reality than that suggested by popular myths. At times, laws banned married or young women from speaking for themselves in court, but such bans were not always followed. Additionally, many different routes existed for women to formally or informally advocate on their own behalf. Unmarried women and nuns could be their own advocates in different proceedings and could hold property in their own names. Widows controlled their own finances. They frequently served as literary or artistic patrons. Even married women, in practice, exercised a surprising amount of agency. When husbands were out of town, their wives became trusted substitutes to oversee local business interests. Women exercised informal political power, oversaw the organization of the household, and possessed varying degrees of influence over the family's daily affairs. In the event of troubles like political exile, the role of women in navigating family affairs took center stage. Women held power in states, as regents, with surprising regularity. All aspects of the lives of women varied by person, by place, and by time. Women held important roles as well as mundane roles. Negative, atemporal generalizations are not only false but also force people to miss the complexity of life and experience in the past.

Moreover, especially from the year 1500 onward, many women received some form of education. For example, in a city like Florence in Italy, probably a little over a third of women were literate to some degree at the very beginning of the early modern period. Many women received their education at home from their fathers. These women could in turn use that education to fulfill all of the responsibilities they would shoulder later in life. The numbers of educated women only increased as the decades and centuries passed. Many women from the sixteenth and seventeenth centuries were famous and best-selling writers. Countless publications penned by them during those centuries have survived. Additionally, a seemingly infinite number of unpublished records written by them—with their own hands and expressing their own voices—survive to document their lives. Women wrote works that were emulated and admired. Indeed, the popularity and sheer quantity of their works illustrates that early modern people were also willing to entertain new ideas and enjoy as well as emulate the style of women writers and thinkers.

PRIMARY SOURCE DOCUMENTS

Early modern women had many different experiences and lived many different lives. One of the best sources for information on them are letters. In the mid-1400s, Alessandra Macinghi Strozzi wrote many letters to her sons who had been exiled from Florence and thus had to live in other cities. In those letters, Alessandra described her challenges and successes in Florence, including her efforts to secure pardons for her sons and her family affairs. Through these letters she also relayed the latest social and political news and discussed many other topics. In the following letter, Alessandra relates her indecision about whether she should send her youngest son, Matteo, to live with her elder brothers abroad or if he should stay with her a bit longer in Florence. Alessandra's wealth and unusual political circumstances made her, in some ways, an unusual case but in many other ways her letters reveal the common experiences of early modern women.

To Filippo degli Strozzi in Naples
In the name of God, the 8th day of November 1448. Upon the 6th day of this month I did receive from thee a letter written upon the 16th of last month, whereunto I will herewith reply.

Thou dost tell me of Matteo's doing, how that he hath written thee a letter concerning our condition. And it is true; it is even worse than he did say. God be praised for all things. Thou didst well to show the letter unto Niccolò. Seeing that our condition is known unto strangers, it should be known likewise unto those who are our kinsmen, and do continually assist us. Neither hath Niccolò waited until now to show his goodwill towards us, but hath been ever ready to do good unto us; this do I well know by experience, and thou shouldst know it even better than I. Thou dost tell me that Matteo being still here, Niccolò is desirous that I should make him ready and send him unto thee, partly because of the pestilence which doth render it dangerous to abide here, and partly because he hath no occupation and wasteth his days. It is true that the pestilence hath commenced here, and that all who could go unto their villas have departed thither; some have already died in the country, and in almost every place in the neighbourhood one or another is dying of it. The family is still at the villa, but if there be no further peril, I do think they will presently return to Florence. It is believed that for this winter the pestilence will do no more hurt, but that in the springtime it will cause great destruction. May God help us! Matteo hath heard me say that now the pestilence is come I have no money to give away, and it is true. I know not how I can send him away from me, for he is little and hath need of my care, nor know I how that I may live without him. Of my five children how shall I abide with one only, and she Alessandra whom I do expect to marry at any time? The utmost that I can keep her with me is less than two years, and at thought thereof must great grief fall upon me so to remain alone. A while ago Matteo went unto Marco's villa, and there sojourned six days; methought I should not live until his return. I had none to do me a service, and I was greatly hindered without him, for he writeth all my letters. Moreover, he had a grievous sickness this summer, and I did think he would die; but good nursing saved him. And when I took counsel with the physician concerning the sending of him away, he said, "An ye hold him dear, send not him away, for he is of a delicate nature, and should he fall sick without your care, then surely were he like to die. Wherefore, if ye hold him dear, send him not away from you so young." For this reason, and because I have need of him, I may think no more of it. True it is that about a year ago I was desirous of sending him; but then was Caterina at home, so that I felt not so lonely. But when I heard of the ill-health of Lorenzo, I grieved so deeply for them both that if they had been dead, I could not more have grieved. And, between one thing and another, I did determine not to send him away saving there were great need of it. I have taken counsel with Marco and with Antonio degli Strozzi. They did both advise me not to send him away for the present, but that if there should be a great pestilence in the spring, as they do expect, and if the pestilence have abated at Siena, and upon all that road even unto Rome, then might I send him. Truly it were madness in me to send him away now, wherefore, though I do determine to send him, it will not be yet awhile. Therefore think ye no more upon it at this present. I am acquainted with your needs better than anyone, and if ye are not able to earn money for yourself ye must not be put to the charge of other persons. For my part, I will use all mine endeavour—and if the Commune take it not from me, for I am no longer able to defend myself—by good management and every other means to preserve for you the little that I have. God will be mine aid, and unto you may He give virtue and health according to my desires.

Concerning the flax, I will trust in thy judgment. If thou sendest it, set within it 10 lbs of almonds against Lent; they will travel well within the bale of flax. I ask them of thee because I hear that in Naples they cost but little, and here are they dear. See that thou send them, for so shall the expense be small.

Concerning Marco Parenti, I can inform thee that he is a good youth, and doth treat Caterina exceeding well; also dealeth he fairly with all men, which doth much content me. He is of good character, but the contributions he is forced to pay are too heavy, for he hath been taxed at eleven florins. Hitherto he hath paid everything, and so be he doeth no worse, I am content with him. May God bestow His grace upon him. Caterina is not yet with child, at which, considering these times of pestilence, I do rejoice. She is lean in her body, and herein resembles she her father. May God give her strength.

I did write unto thee upon the fourth of this month, and did enclose my letter in one from Marco, and since the messenger departed more soon than I did expect, I think that thou wilt receive it at the same time as this. Therein write I unto thee concerning the little house of Niccolò Popoleschi, which hath been sold unto Donato Rucellai; it standeth close by ours, adjoining our court, so that on no account will we lose it out of our hands. Filippo, answer me quickly, for I must write unto Jacopo in Bruges.

No more at present. God guard thee from evil. Thine Alessandra, widow of Matteo degli Strozzi in Florence.

See that thou art obedient unto Niccolò, and do thy duty towards him, showing thyself grateful for the good he doeth thee. For if thus thou do, I shall likewise be satisfied. May God in His mercy grant thee grace. A few days since hath Matteo written a letter unto Lorenzo in Avignon.

Isidoro del Lungo, excerpt from *Women of Florence*, translated by Mary C. Steegmann (London: Chatto and Windus, 1907), 290–94.

The education of early modern women varied greatly from place to place and across different times. In some places, even by the early 1400s there was the basic expectation that women, or at least elite women, should receive some schooling. In the excerpt that follows, the learned humanist Leonardo Bruni offers his ideas about what sorts of things should be the educational focus for elite women. Bruni thought that certain subjects and foci were more appropriate for men vis-à-vis women, and vice versa, but he also recommended a degree of overlap that defies many myths about the lives and learning of early modern women.

I am led to address this Tractate to you, Illustrious Lady, by the high repute which attaches to your name in the field of learning; and I offer it, partly as an expression of my homage to distinction already attained, partly as an encouragement to further effort. Were it necessary I might urge you by brilliant instances from antiquity: Cornelia, the daughter of Scipio, whose Epistles survived for centuries as models of style; Sappho, the poetess, held in so great honour for the exuberance of her poetic art; Aspasia, whose learning and eloquence made her not unworthy of the intimacy of Socrates. Upon these, the most distinguished of a long range of great names, I would have you fix your mind; for an intelligence such as your own can be satisfied with nothing less than the best. You yourself, indeed, may hope to win a fame higher even than theirs. For they lived in days when learning was no rare attainment, and therefore they enjoyed no unique renown. Whilst, alas, upon such times are we fallen that a learned man seems well-nigh a portent, and erudition in a woman is a thing utterly unknown. For true learning has almost died away amongst us. True learning, I say: not a mere acquaintance with that vulgar, thread-bare jargon which satisfied those who devote themselves to Theology, but sound learning in its proper and legitimate sense, viz., the knowledge of realities—Facts and Principles—united to a perfect familiarity with Letters and the art of expression. Now this combination we find in Lactantius, in Augustine, or in Jerome; each of them at once a great theologian and profoundly versed in literature. But turn from them to their successors of to-day: how must we blush for their ignorance of the whole field of Letters!

This leads me to press home this truth—though in your case it is unnecessary—that the foundations of all true learning must be laid in the sound and thorough knowledge of Latin: which implies study marked by a broad spirit, accurate scholarship, and careful attention to details. Unless this solid basis be secured it is useless to attempt to rear an enduring edifice. Without it the great monuments of literature are unintelligible, and the art of composition impossible. To attain this essential knowledge we must never relax our careful attention to the grammar of the language, but perpetually confirm and extend our acquaintance with it until it is thoroughly our own. We may gain much from Servius, Donatus and Priscian, but more by careful observation in our own reading, in which we must note attentively vocabulary and inflexions, figures of speech and metaphors, and all the devices of style, such as rhythm, or antithesis, by which fine taste is exhibited. To this end we must be supremely careful in our choice of authors, lest an inartistic and debased style infect our own writing and degrade our taste; which danger is best avoided by bringing a keen, critical sense to bear upon select works, observing the sense of each passage, the structure of the sentence, the force of every word down to the least important particle. In this way our reading reacts directly upon our style.

You may naturally turn first to Christian writers . . .

. . . But the wider question now confronts us, that of the subject matter of our studies, that which I have already called the realities of fact and principle, as distinct from literary form. Here, as before, I am contemplating a student of keen and lofty aspiration to whom nothing that is worthy in any learned discipline is without its interest. But it is necessary to exercise discrimination. In some branches of knowledge I would rather restrain the ardour of the learning, in others, again, encourage it to the uttermost. Thus there are certain subjects in which, whilst a modest proficiency is on all accounts to be desired, a minute knowledge and excessive devotion seem to be a vain display. For instance, subtleties of Arithmetic and Geometry are not worthy to absorb a cultivated mind, and the same must be said of Astrology. You will be surprised to find me suggesting (though with much more hesitation) that the great and complex art of Rhetoric should be placed in the same category. My chief reason is the obvious one, that I have in view the cultivation most fitting of a woman. To her neither the intricacies of debate nor the oratorical artifices of action and delivery are of the least practical use, if indeed they are not positively unbecoming. Rhetoric in all its forms—public discussion, forensic argument, logical fence, and the like—lies absolutely outside the province of woman.

What Disciplines then are properly open to her? In the first place she has before her, as a subject peculiarly her own, the whole field of religion and morals. The literature of the Church will thus claim her earnest study. Such a writer, for instance, as St. Augustine affords her the fullest scope for reverent yet learned inquiry. Her devotional instinct may lead her to value the help and consolation of holy men now living; but in this case let her not for an instant yield to the impulse to look into their writings, which, compared with those of Augustine, are utterly destitute of sound and melodious style, and seem to me to have no attraction whatever.

Moreover, the cultivated Christian lady has no need in the study of this weighty subject to confine herself to ecclesiastical writers. Morals, indeed, have been treated of by the noblest intellects of Greece and Rome. What they have left to us upon Continence, Temperance, Modesty, Justice, Courage, Greatness of Soul, demands your sincere respect. You must enter into such questions as the sufficiency of Virtue to Happiness; or whether, if Happiness consist in Virtue, it can be destroyed by torture, imprisonment or exile; whether, admitting that these may prevent a man from being happy, they can be further said to make him miserable. Again, does Happiness consist (with Epicurus) in the presence of pleasure and the absence of pain: or (with Xenophon) in the consciousness of uprightness: or (with Aristotle) in the practice of Virtue? These inquiries are, of all others, most worthy to be pursued by men and women alike; they are fit material for formal discussion and for literary exercise. Let religion and morals, therefore, hold the first place in the education of a Christian lady.

But we must not forget that true distinction is to be gained by a wide and varied range of such studies as conduce to the profitable enjoyment of life, in which, however, we must observe due proportion in the attention and time we devote to them.

First amongst such studies I place History: a subject which must not on any account be neglected by one who aspires to true cultivation. For it is our duty to understand the origins of our own history and its development; and the achievements of Peoples and of Kings.

For the careful study of the past enlarges our foresight in contemporary affairs and affords to citizens and to monarchs lessons of incitement or warning in the ordering of public policy. From History, also, we draw our store of examples of moral precepts.

In the monuments of ancient literature which have come down to us History holds a position of great distinction. We specially prize such authors as Livy, Sallust and Curtius; and, perhaps even above these, Julius Caesar; the style of whose Commentaries, so elegant and so limpid, entitles them to our warm admiration. Such writers are fully within the comprehension of a studious lady. For, after all, History is an easy subject: there is nothing in its study subtle or complex. It consists in the narration of the simple matters of fact which, once grasped, are readily retained in the memory.

The great Orators of antiquity must by all means be included. Nowhere do we find the virtues more warmly extolled, the vices so fiercely decried. From them we may learn, also, how to express consolation, encouragement, dissuasion or advice. If the principles which orators set forth are portrayed for us by philosophers, it is from the former that we learn how to employ the emotions—such as indignation, or pity—in driving home their application in individual cases. Further, from oratory we derive our store of those elegant or striking turns of expression which are used with so much effect in literary compositions. Lastly, in oratory we find that wealth of vocabulary, that clear easy flowing style, that verve and force, which are invaluable to us both in writing and in conversation.

I come now to Poetry and the Poets—a subject with which every educated lady must shew herself thoroughly familiar. For we cannot point to any great mind of the past for whom the Poets had not a powerful attraction. Aristotle, in constantly quoting Homer, Hesiod, Pindar, Euripides and other poets proves that he knew their works hardly less intimately than those of the philosophers. Plato, also frequently appeals to them, and in this way covers them with his approval . . .

. . . We know, however, that in certain quarter—where all knowledge and appreciation of Letters is wanting—this whole branch of Literature, marked as it is by something of the Divine, and fit, therefore, for the highest place, is decried as unworthy of study. But when we remember the value of the best poetry, its charm of form and the variety and interest of its subject-matter, when we consider the ease with which from our childhood up it can be committed to memory, when we recall the peculiar affinity of rhythm and metre to our emotions and our intelligence, we must conclude that Nature herself is against such headlong critics . . .

. . . To sum up what I have endeavoured to set forth. That high standard of education to which I referred at the outset is only to be reached by one who has seen many things and read much. Poet, Orator, Historian, and the rest, all must be studied, each must contribute a share. Our learning thus becomes full, ready, varied and elegant, available for action or for discourse in all subjects. But to enable us to make effectual use of what we know we must add to our knowledge the power of expression. These two sides of learning, indeed should not be separate: they afford mutual aid and distinction. Proficiency in literary form, not accompanied by broad acquaintance with facts and truths, is a barren attainment; whilst information, however vast, which lacks all grace of expression, would seem to be put under a bushel or partly thrown away. Indeed, one may fairly ask what advantage it is to possess profound and varied learning if one cannot convey it in language worthy of the subject. Where, however, this double capacity exists—breadth of learning and grace of style—we allow the highest title to distinction and to abiding fame. If we review the great names of ancient literature, Plato, Democritus, Aristotle, Theophrastus, Varro, Cicero, Seneca, Augustine, Jerome, Lactantius, we shall find it hard to say whether we admire more their attainments or their literary power.

But my last word must be this. The intelligence that aspires to the best must aim at both. In doing so, all sources of profitable learning will in due proportion claim your study. None have more urgent claim than the subjects and authors which treat of Religion and of our duties in the world; and it is because they assist and illustrate these supreme studies that I press upon your attention the works of the most approved poets, historians and orators of the past.

Leonardo Bruni, excerpt from "Concerning the Study of Literature—A Letter Addressed to the Illustrious Lady, Baptista Malatesta," in *Vittorino da Feltre and Other Humanist Educators*, edited by William Harrison Woodward (Cambridge: Cambridge University Press, 1921), 123–33.

In The Book of the Courtier, *Baldassare Castiglione offers advice on how people could act and appear in early modern courts in order to earn rewards. This book presents a "dialogue" where different characters bearing real historical names debate different topics. The dialogue in the Book of the Courtier is presided over by a female ruler and included long sections devoted to topics related to women and their experiences. In the following excerpt, the characters Gaspar and the Magnifico argue about women's equality. These passages suggest that Castiglione agreed with the Magnifico's arguments that women and men could be equals in many areas.*

. . . Moreover, many women have been the cause of countless benefits to their men-folk, and sometimes have corrected many a one of his errors. Wherefore, women being (as we have shown) naturally capable of the same virtues as men, and the effects thereof being often seen, I do not perceive why—in giving them what it is possible for them to have, what they more than once have had and still have—I should be regarded as relating miracles, whereof my lord Gaspar has accused me; seeing that there have always been on earth, and now still are, women as like the Court Lady I have fashioned, as men like the man these gentlemen have fashioned.

Then my lord Gaspar said:

Those arguments that have experience against them do not seem to me good; and certainly if I were to ask you who these great women were that have been as worthy of praise as the great men whose wives or sisters or daughters they were, or that have been the cause of any benefit, and who those were that have corrected the errors of their men folk—I think you would be embarrassed.

Verily, replied the Magnifico Giuliano, no other thing could make me embarrassed save their multitude; and had I time enough I should tell you here the story of Octavia, wife of Mark Antony and sister of Augustus; that of Porcia, Cato's daughter and wife of Brutus; that of Caia Caecilia, wife of Tarquinius Priscus; that of . . .

Here the Magnifico made a little pause; then he added:

Do you not know that the wife and daughters of Mithridates showed much less fear of death than Mithridates? And Hasdrubal's wife than Hasdrubal? Do you know that Harmonia, daughter of Hiero the Syracusan, chose to perish in the burning of her native city?

Then Frisio said:

Where obstinacy is concerned, it is certain that some women are occasionally to be found who never change their purpose . . .

The Magnifico Giuliano laughed, and said:

Obstinacy that tends to a worthy end ought to be called steadfastness; as was the case of the famous Epicharis, a Roman freedwoman . . .

Then madonna Margarita Gonzaga said:

Methinks you narrate too briefly these virtuous deeds done by women; for these enemies of ours, although having heard and read them, yet pretend not to know them and fain would have the memory of them lost: but if you will let us women hear them, we at least shall deem ourselves honoured by them.

Then the Magnifico Giuliano replied:

So be it. I wish to tell you now of one who did what I think my lord Gaspar himself will admit very few men do; and he began: In Massilia there was once a custom that is believed to have been brought from Greece, which was that they publicly kept a poison compounded of hemlock, and allowed anyone to take it who proved to the Senate that he ought to lay down his life because of any trouble that he found therein, or for other just cause, to the end that whoever had suffered a too hostile fortune or had enjoyed a too prosperous fortune, should not drag on the one or change the other. Now Sextus Pompey, finding himself . . .

Here Frisio, not waiting for the Magnifico Giuliano to go on, said:

Methinks this is the beginning of a long story.

Then the Magnifico Giuliano turned to madonna Margarita laughing, and said:

You see that Frisio will not let me speak. I wished to tell you now about a woman who, having shown to the Senate that she had good reason to die, cheerfully and fearless took the poison in Sextus Pompey's presence, with such steadfastness of spirit and with such affectionate and thoughtful reembraces to her family, that Pompey and all the others who saw such wisdom and confidence on a woman's part in the dread hour of death, were lost in wonderment and tears.

Then my lord Gaspar said, laughing:

I too remember having read a speech in which an unhappy husband asks leave of the Senate to die, and proves that he has just cause for it in that he cannot endure the continual annoyance of his wife's chatter, and prefers to drink the poison, which you say was publicly kept for such purposes, than his wife's words.

The Magnifico Giuliano replied:

How many poor women would have just cause for asking leave to die because they cannot endure, I will not say the evil words, but the very evil deeds of their husbands! I know several such, who suffer in this world the pains that are said to be in hell.

Do you not believe, replied my lord Gaspar, that there are also many husbands who have such torment of their wives that they hourly wish for death?

And what pain, said the Magnifico, can wives give their husbands that is as incurable as are those that husbands give their wives? Who if not for love, at least for fear, are submissive to their husbands.

Certain it is, said my lord Gaspar, that the little good they sometimes do proceeds from fear, since there are few in the world who in their secret hearts do not hate their husbands.

Nay, quite the contrary, replied the Magnifico; and if you recall aright what you have read, we see in all the histories that wives nearly always love their husbands more than husbands love their wives . . .

Frisio replied: . . . But even supposing this were true, I tell you that such women are no longer to be found in the world.

Indeed they are to be found, said the Magnifico; and that this is true, listen:

In my time there was a . . . [here is a list of examples]

My lord Gaspar said:

It may be that this lady was too loving, for women always run to extremes in everything, which is bad; and you see that by being too loving she wrought evil to herself, and to her husband and children, for whom she turned to bitterness the joy of his perilous and longed-for deliverance. So you ought by no means to cite her as one of those women who have been the cause of such great benefits.

The Magnifico replied:

I cite her as one of those who bear witness that there are wives who love their husbands; for of those who have been the cause of great benefits to the world, I could tell you of an endless number, and discourse to you of some so ancient that they almost seem fabulous, and of those who among men have been the inventors of such things, that they deserved to be esteemed as goddesses . . .

Here having paused a little, and seeing that my lord Gaspar did not speak, the Magnifico Giuliano said:

Do you not think that these women were the cause of good to their men-folk and contributed to the greatness of Rome?

My lord Gaspar replied:

No doubt they were worthy of much praise; but had you been as willing to tell the sins of women as their good works, you would not have omitted to say that in this war of Titus Tatius a woman betrayed Rome and showed the enemy the way to seize the Capital, whereby the Romans came near being all destroyed.

The Magnifico Giuliano replied:

You tell me of a single bad woman, while I tell you of countless good ones; and besides those already mentioned, I could show you a thousand other instances on my side, of benefits done to Rome by women. . . . And had I time enough, I should further show you that women have often corrected many of men's errors; but I fear that this discourse of mine is already too long and wearisome . . .

Then my lady Emilia said:

Do not deprive women of those true praises that are their due; and remember that if my lord Gaspar, and perhaps my lord Ottaviano as well, listen to you with weariness, we and all these other gentlemen listen to you with pleasure.

The Magnifico still wished to stop, but all the ladies began begging him to speak: whereupon he said, laughing:

In order not to make my lord Gaspar more my enemy than he is, I will tell briefly of a few women who occur to my mind, omitting many that I might mention . . . [here is a list of examples]

. . . Then my lord Gaspar said:

Ah, my lord Magnifico, but God knows how those things happened; for that age is so remote from us that many lies can be told and there is none to refute them.

The Magnifico said:

If in every age you will compare women's worth with that of men, you will find that they have never been and are not now at all inferior to men in worth . . . [another list of examples]

But laying all others aside, tell me, my lord Gaspar, what king or what prince has there been in our days, or even for many years past in Christendom, who deserves to be compared with Queen Isabella of Spain?

My lord Gaspar replied:

King Ferdinand, her husband.

The Magnifico continued:

That I shall not deny; for since the queen judged him worthy to be her husband, and so loved and honoured him, we cannot say that he did not deserve to be compared with her: yet I believe that the fame he had by her was a dowry not inferior to the kingdom of Castile . . .

Baldassare Castiglione, excerpt from *The Book of the Courtier*, translated by Leonardo Eckstein Opdycke (New York: Charles Scribner's Sons, 1903), 190–242.

During the 1800s, movements for women's suffrage and equality meant that many writers revisited older works to support their arguments. In this context, the American writer Thomas Higginson weighed in to support women's rights. The following excerpt from Higginson provides examples from the early modern history of women. These examples are but a few in an essay designed to argue for the fundamental equality in both female and male potential. It is included here to provide a glimpse of the number of women writers in early modern Europe.

It is true that Eve ruined us all, according to theology, without knowing her letters. Still there is something to be said in defence of that venerable ancestress. The Veronese lady, Isotta Nogarola, five hundred and thirty-six of whose learned epistles were preserved by De Thou, composed a dialogue on the question, Whether Adam or Eve had committed the greater sin. But Ludovico Domenichi, in his "Dialogue on the Nobleness of Women," maintains that Eve did not sin at all, because she was not even created when Adam was told not to eat the apple. It was "in Adam all died," he shrewdly says; nobody died in Eve: which looks plausible . . .

It has been seriously asserted, that during the last half century more books have been written by women and about women than during all the previous uncounted ages. It may be true; although, when we think of the innumerable volumes of *Mémoires* by French women of the seventeenth and eighteenth centuries—each justifying the existence of her own ten volumes by the remark, that all her contemporaries were writing as many—we have our doubts. As to the increased multitude of general treatises on the female sex, however—its education, life, health, diseases, charms, dress, deeds, sphere, rights, wrongs, work, wages, encroachments, and idiosyncrasies generally—there can be no doubt whatever; and the poorest of these books recognizes a condition of public sentiment of which no other age ever dreamed.

Still, literary history preserves the names of some reformers before the Reformation, in this matter. There was Signora Moderata Fonte, the Venetian, who left a book to be published after her death, in 1592, "Dei Meriti delle Donne." There was her townswoman, Lucrezia Marinella, who followed, ten years after, with her essay, "La Nobilità e la Eccelenza delle Donne, con Difetti e Mancamenti degli Uomini,"—a comprehensive theme, truly! Then followed the all-accomplished Anna Maria Schurman, in 1645, with her "Dissertatio de Ingenii Muliebris ad Doctrinam et meliores Literas Aptitudine," with a few miscellaneous letters appended in Greek and Hebrew. At last came boldly Jacquette Guillaume, in 1665, and threw down the gauntlet in her title-page, "Les Dames Illustres; où par bonnes et fortes Raisons il se prouve que le Sexe Feminin surpasse en toute Sorte de Genre le Sexe Masculin"; and with her came Margaret Boufflet and a host of others; and finally, in England, Mary Wollstonecraft, whose famous book, formidable in its day, would seem rather conservative now; and in America, that pious and worthy dame, Mrs. H. Mather Crocker, Cotton Mather's grandchild, who, in 1848, published the first book on the "Rights of Woman" ever written on this side the Atlantic.

Meanwhile there have never been wanting men, and strong men, to echo these appeals . . .

Thomas Wentworth Higginson, excerpt from *The Writings* (Cambridge: Riverside Press, 1900), vol. 4, pp. 5–7.

Further Reading

Barker, Sheila, ed. *Artemisia Gentileschi in a Changing Light*. Turnhout: Brepols, 2018.

Bennett, Judith M. *A Medieval Life: Cecilia Penifader of Brigstock, c. 1295–1344*. 2nd ed. New York: McGraw-Hill, 2021.

Cox, Virginia. *The Prodigious Muse: Women's Writing in Counter-Reformation Italy*. Baltimore: Johns Hopkins University Press, 2011.

Dabbs, Julia K. *Life Stories of Women Artists, 1550–1800. An Anthology*. London: Routledge, 2009.

Davis, Natalie Zemon. *The Return of Martin Guerre*. Cambridge, MA: Harvard University Press, 1983.

Davis, Natalie Zemon. *Women on the Margins*. Cambridge, MA: Harvard University Press, 1995.

Garrard, Mary D. *Artemisia Gentileschi and Feminism in Early Modern Europe*. London: Reaktion, 2020.

Hopkins, Lisa, and Aidan Norrie, eds. *Women on the Edge in Early Modern Europe*. Amsterdam: Amsterdam University Press, 2019.

Kaborycha, Lisa. *A Corresponding Renaissance*. Oxford: Oxford University Press, 2015.

King, Margaret. *Women of the Renaissance*. Chicago: University of Chicago Press, 1991.

King, Margaret, and Albert Rabil, series eds. *The Other Voice in Early Modern Europe*. Chicago: University of Chicago Press, 1996–2010; Toronto: CRRS, 2010–2014; Toronto: Iter, 2015–present.

Monter, William. *The Rise of Female Kings in Europe, 1300–1800*. New Haven, CT: Yale University Press, 2012.

Morton, Peter A., ed. *The Trial of Tempel Anneke: Records of a Witchcraft Trial in Brunswick, Germany, 1663*. Translated by Barbara Dähms. 2nd ed. Toronto: University of Toronto Press, 2017.

Murphy, Caroline P. *The Pope's Daughter: The Extraordinary Life of Felice della Rovere*. Oxford: Oxford University Press, 2006.

Ray, Meredith K. *Daughters of Alchemy. Women and Scientific Culture in Early Modern Italy*. Cambridge, MA: Harvard University Press, 2015.

Robin, Diana, Anne R. Larsen, and Carole Levin, eds. *Encyclopedia of Women in the Renaissance. Italy, France, and England*. Santa Barbara, CA: ABC-CLIO, 2007.

Ross, Sarah Gwyneth. *The Birth of Feminism: Woman as Intellect in Renaissance Italy and England*. Cambridge, MA: Harvard University Press, 2009.

Scott, Joan W. "Gender: A Useful Category of Historical Analysis." *American Historical Review* 91, no. 5 (December, 1986): 1053–75.

Stjerna, Kiris. *Women and the Reformation*. Hoboken, NJ: Wiley-Blackwell, 2008.

Strocchia, Sharon T. *Forgotten Healers: Women and the Pursuit of Health in late Renaissance Italy*. Cambridge, MA: Harvard University Press, 2019.

Strocchia, Sharon T. *Nuns and Nunneries in Renaissance Florence*. Baltimore: Johns Hopkins University Press, 2009.

Wiesner-Hanks, Merry. *Women and Gender in Early Modern Europe*. 4th ed. Cambridge: Cambridge University Press, 2019.

4

Humanists Introduced Secularism to Early Modern Europe

What People Think Happened

The myth goes that even the most educated people in medieval Europe were slaves to superstition and ignorance. They held an unquestioning belief in even the strangest parts of their religion. Rewards on earth were earned by pleasing God, while those less fortunate had, obviously, done something to incur God's wrath. A handful of usually greedy churchmen forbade anyone from reading the Bible directly. Those foolhardy individuals who challenged the Church were tortured and killed. There were few original writers, and they all wrote about theology. These men argued abstract, irrelevant points: How many angels could dance upon the head of a pin? Their impenetrable answers mattered to no one. In medieval times, original thought was associated with heresy, while accepted thought was tightly controlled, always religious, and always irrelevant to ordinary people.

In the fourteenth and fifteenth centuries, people known as humanists began to free themselves from this intellectual darkness and challenge the oppression of religious tyranny. In some ways, their rebellion offered changes that people today find pleasing. For example, when writing about history, medieval writers had always ascribed historical change to the direct hand of God. Humanists, by contrast, began to argue that cause and effect or things like chance drove historical narratives. Medieval thinkers had shunned the classical past as a den of pagan vipers. Humanists, by contrast, drank in the lost teachings of ancient Greece and ancient Rome. Consequently, their writings began to approach questions with more sophistication and without the blinders of religious superstition.

Under the influence of the humanists, people finally began to break free from the mental shackles of the medieval church. Humanists pursued science for the first time and thus initiated a new age of technology and progress. They challenged assumptions that people had accepted from the Church for centuries. The humanists, according to the myth, brought forth new secular ways of understanding the world that did not need demons and superstition. Sometimes, in fact, their challenges went too far and strayed into immoral areas. A man like Poggio Bracciolini, for example, spun risqué tales. Niccolò Machiavelli spurned all morality to argue that power, and only power, mattered in politics. The moral man, for Machiavelli, was a dead man. Although most humanists were less extreme, all humanists contributed to a progression of knowledge that ushered in the Scientific Revolution. Their works met with resistance. The ancient and powerful Catholic Church tried to track down and control these heretics and their heretical writings. They censored, tortured, and killed those authors and thinkers whom they could find. Despite its best efforts, the Church could not put pandora back in her box. From the humanists came the secularism and progress synonymous with the Enlightenment, and on the shoulders of humanists was built the modern world.

How the Story Became Popular

In the nineteenth century, scholars turned to investigations of the literary and intellectual revival of Antiquity that seemed to characterize fourteenth-century Italy and then the rest of Europe in the early modern period. Early modern thinkers who prized Antiquity were called "humanists." Nineteenth-century writers credited these humanists with all sorts of accomplishments. According to some writers, the humanists turned the subject of philosophy away from stale, esoteric theological questions and toward the nature of human beings. These nineteenth-century writers argued that the central tenet of humanist thought was the positive potential of people. The humanists, they claimed, turned European culture away from religion and toward concerns about this world. Their secularism helped usher in modern science. Historians argued that humanists removed God as a causal agent, both in historical narratives and in natural developments. The removal of God opened the way toward deeper analyses of human actions and much more sophisticated understandings of how the natural world works.

But there was a price. Historians argued that some humanist writers turned their backs upon Christianity and revived pagan cults. Some even became atheists. Scholars pointed to lewd humanist texts to prove their arguments. They quoted merciless condemnations of actions by churchmen as proof that the humanists had left the faith. The very term "humanist" invited most people to associate them with human rather than religious affairs; it brought about conflations between early modern scholars and modern "secular humanists." Today, secular humanists try to follow moral codes created outside of religious structures. Although secular humanist groups may do many of the same sorts of things that churches do, secular humanists tend to be agnostics or atheists. The shared name between humanists and modern secular humanists, combined with the lingering effects of nineteenth-century writers, has created the popular conception that Renaissance and early modern intellectuals introduced a modern secular society that rejected medieval religious thought.

PRIMARY SOURCE DOCUMENTS

Lorenzo Valla was a brilliant—but polemical—writer and scholar during the fifteenth century. He is best known today for his works related to religion and clergymen. In one of his works, he studied the accuracy of the long-accepted Latin version of the Bible and made suggestions for corrections to it. In another, On the Donation of Constantine, *Valla attacked the legal and historical foundations of papal claims to be rulers over much of Europe. Because of these texts, later writers have often credited Valla with helping to free people's minds from the influence of the medieval church and with helping to set the stage for the Protestant Reformations in the next century. In truth, Valla's work on the Bible was little noticed in his own day, and his criticism of papal political claims was rooted in the political context of fifteenth-century Italy: Valla's patron, Alfonso of Aragon, was waging a war against the papacy and Valla's document was clearly designed to assist that cause. The following excerpt comes from Valla's* On the Donation of Constantine. *For centuries, the papacy had used the* Donation of Constantine *as the legal basis for their territorial holdings. Valla argued that the text was a forgery and disputed these papal claims.*

. . . O Roman pontiffs, the model of all crimes for other pontiffs! O wickedest of scribes and Pharisees, who sit in Moses' seat and do the deeds of Dathan and Abiram! Will the raiment, the habiliments, the pomp, the cavalry, indeed the whole manner of life of a Caesar thus befit the vicar of Christ? What fellowship has the priest with the Caesar? Did Sylvester put on this raiment; did he parade in this splendor; did he live and reign with such a throng of servants in his house? Depraved wretches! They did not know that Sylvester ought to have assumed the vestments of Aaron, who was the high priest of God, rather than those of a heathen ruler.

But this must be more strongly pressed elsewhere. For the present, however, let us talk to this sycophant about barbarisms of speech; for by the stupidity of his language his monstrous impudence is made clear, and his lie.

. . .

This terrible threat is the usual one, not of a secular ruler, but of the early priests and flamens, and nowadays, of ecclesiastics. And so this is not the utterance of Constantine, but of some fool of a priest who, stuffed and pudgy, knew neither what to say nor how to say it, and, gorged with eating and heated with wine, belched out these wordy sentences which convey nothing to another, but turn against the author himself. First he says, "shall be subject to damnation," then as though more could be added, he wishes to add something else, and to eternal penalties he joins penalties in the present life; and after he frightens us with God's condemnation, he frightens us with the hatred of Peter, as though it were something still greater . . .

. . .

Estopped from defending the Donation, since it never existed and, if it had existed, it would now have expired from lapse of time, our adversaries take refuge in another kind of defense; figuratively speaking, the city being given up for lost, they betake themselves to their citadel—which forthwith they are constrained by lack of provisions to surrender. "The Roman church," they say, "is entitled by prescription to what it possesses." Why then does it lay claim to that, the greater part, to which it has no title by prescription, and to which others are entitled by prescription; unless others cannot act toward it as it can act toward them?

The Roman church has title by prescription! Why then does it so often take care to have the Emperors confirm its right? Why does it vaunt the Donation, and its confirmation by the Caesars? If this alone is sufficient, you seriously weaken it by not at the same time keeping silent about the other title [by prescription]. Why don't you keep silent about that other? Obviously because this is not sufficient.

The Roman church has prescribed! And how can it have entered a prescription where no title is established by only possession through bad faith? Or if you deny that the possession was a case of bad faith, at least you cannot deny that the faith [in the Donation] was stupid. Or, in a matter of such importance and notoriety, ought ignorance of fact and of law to be excused? Of fact, because Constantine did not make a grant of Rome and the provinces; a fact of which a man of the common people might well be ignorant, but not the supreme pontiff. Of law, because they could not be granted; which any Christian ought to know. And so, will stupid credulity give you a right to that which, had you been more conscientious, would never have been yours? Well! Now, at least, after I have shown that you held possession through ignorance and stupidity, do you not lose that right, if it was such? and what ignorance unhappily brought you, does not knowledge happily take away again? and does not the property revert from the illegal to the legal master, perchance even with interest? But if you continue to keep possession in the future, your ignorance is henceforth changed into malice aforethought and into deceit, and you become a fraudulent holder.

The Roman church has entered a prescription! O simpletons, O ignoramuses in divine law! No length of years whatever can destroy a true title. Or indeed, if I were captured by barbarians and supposed to have perished, and should return again home after a hundred years of captivity, as a claimant of my paternal inheritance, should I be excluded? What could be more inhuman! And, to give another example, did Jephthah, the leader of Israel, when the Ammonites demanded back the land from "the borders of Arnon even unto Jabbok and unto Jordan," reply, "Israel has prescribed this now through three hundred years' occupation"? Or did he not show that the land which they demanded as theirs, had never been theirs, but had been the Amorites'? And the proof that it did not belong to the Ammonites was that they had never in the course of so many years claimed it.

The Roman church has prescribed! Keep still, impious tongue! You transfer "prescription," which is used of inanimate, senseless objects, to man; and holding man in servitude is the most detestable, the longer it lasts. Birds and wild animals do not let themselves be "prescribed," but however long the time of captivity, when they please and occasion is offered, they escape. And may not man, held captive by man, escape?

Let me tell why the Roman pontiffs show fraud and craft rather than ignorance in using war instead of law as their arbiter—and I believe that the first pontiffs to occupy the city [of Rome] and the other towns did about the same. Shortly before I was born, Rome was led by an incredible sort of fraud, I call those then present there to witness, to accept papal government or rather usurpation, after it had long been free. The Pope was Boniface IX, fellow of Boniface VIII in fraud as in name—if they are to be called Boniface (benefactor) at all, who are the worst malefactors. And when the Romans, after the treachery had been detected, stirred up trouble, the good Pope, after the manner of Tarquinius, struck off all the tallest poppies with his stick. When his successor, Innocent [VII], afterwards tried to imitate this procedure he was driven out of the city. I will not speak of other Popes; they have always held Rome down by force of arms. Suffice it to say that as often as it could it has rebelled; as for instance, six years ago, when it could not obtain peace from Eugenius, and it was not equal to the enemies which were besieging it, it besieged the Pope within his house, and would not permit him to go out before he either made peace with the enemy or turned over the administration of the city to the citizens. But he preferred to leave the city in disguise, with a single companion in flight, rather than to gratify the citizens in their just and fair demands. If you give them the choice, who does not know that they would choose liberty rather than slavery?

We may suspect the same of the other cities, which are kept in servitude by the supreme pontiff, though they ought rather to be liberated by him from servitude. It would take too long to enumerate how many cities taken from their enemies the Roman people once set free; it went so far that Titus Falminius [Flaminius] set free the whole of Greece, which had been under Antiochus, and directed that it enjoy its own laws. But the Pope, as may be seen, lies in wait assiduously against the liberty of countries; and therefore one after another, they daily, as opportunity affords, rebel. (Look at Bologna just now.) And if at any time they have voluntarily accepted papal rule, as may happen when another danger threatens them from elsewhere, it must not be supposed that they have accepted it in order to enslave themselves, so that they could never withdraw their necks from the yoke, so that neither themselves nor those born afterwards should have control of their own affairs; for this would be utterly iniquitous.

"Of our own will we came to you, supreme pontiff, that you might govern us; of our own will we now leave you again, that you may govern us no more. If you have any claim against us, let the balance of debit and credit be determined. But you want to govern us against our will, as though we were wards of yours, we who perhaps could govern you more wisely than you do yourself! Add to this the wrongs all the time being committed against this state either by you or by your magistrates. We call God to witness that our wrong drives us to revolt, as once Israel did from Rehoboam. And what great wrong did they have? What [a small] part of our calamity is the [mere] payment of heavier taxes! What then if you impoverish the Republic? You *have* impoverished it. What if you despoil our temples? You *have* despoiled them. What if you outrage maidens and matrons? You *have* outraged them. What if you drench the city with the blood of its citizens? You *have* drenched it. Must we endure all this? Nay, rather, since you have ceased to be a father to us, shall we not likewise forget to be sons? This people summoned you, supreme pontiff, to be a father, or if it pleases you, to be their lord, not to be an enemy and a hangman; you do not choose to act the father or the lord, but the enemy and the hangman. But, since we are Christians, we will not imitate your ferocity and your impiety, even though by the law of reprisal we might do so, nor will we bare the avenging sword above your head; but first your abdication and removal, and then we will adopt another father or lord. Sons may flee from vicious parents who brought them into the world; may we not flee from you, not our real father but an adopted one who treats us in the worst way possible? But do you attend to your priestly functions; and don't take your stand in the north, and thundering there hurl your lightning and thunderbolts against this people and others."

But why need I say more in this case, absolutely self-evident as it is? I contend that not only did Constantine not grant such great possessions, not only could the Roman pontiff not hold them by prescription, but that even if either were a fact, nevertheless either right would have been extinguished by the crimes of the possessors, for we know that the slaughter and devastation of all Italy and of many provinces has flowed from this single source. If the source is bitter, so is the stream; if the root is unclean, so are the branches; if the first fruit is unholy, so is the lump. And *vice versa*, if the stream is bitter, the source must be stopped up, if the branches are unclean, the fault comes from the root; if the lump is unholy, the first fruit must also be accursed. Can we justify the principle of papal power when we perceive it to be the cause of such great crimes and of such great and varied evils?

Wherefore I declare, and cry aloud, nor, trusting God, will I fear men, that in my time no one in the supreme pontificate has been either a faithful or a prudent steward, but they have gone so far from giving good to the household of God that they have devoured it as food and a mere morsel of bread! And the Pope himself makes war on peaceable people, and sows discord among states and princes. The Pope both thirsts for the goods of others and drinks up his own . . .

Lorenzo Valla, excerpt from *On the Donation of Constantine*, edited and translated by Christopher B. Coleman (New Haven, CT: Yale University Press, 1922), 105, 131, and 169–79.

Poggio Bracciolini was one of the most important Renaissance humanists of the early 1400s. He is credited with creating the sorts of fonts that we still use to make our letters and with reintroducing many works from Antiquity that had not been read in centuries. He was also a very successful secretary for multiple popes and a prominent author of original humanist texts. Poggio is often brought forward as a perfect example of an irreligious or secular humanist. Critics point to many different works, including his Facetiae, *excerpted below. The* Facetiae *is a collection of short anecdotes, many of which Poggio claimed to have heard or witnessed in his years working for the popes. The intention behind these anecdotes was to entertain readers and make them laugh, although Poggio's humor, which is from nearly 600 years ago, is often very different from our own. The following excerpts have been chosen from among the 283 such tales in Poggio's book.*

"A Jew who had been persuaded to become a Christian"

A Jew, who was much exhorted to embrace the Christian faith, could not make up his mind to part with his property. Many advised him to give it to the poor, since, according to the word of the Gospel, which is truth itself, it would be repaid him a hundredfold. Persuaded at last, he became a convert, and divided his goods and chattels among the poor, the needy and the beggars. In consequence, during nearly one month, many Christians vied in receiving him hospitably and honorably; complimentary praises of him were echoed on every side. But he, whose livelihood was precarious, kept expecting from day to day the hundredfold he had been promised: many people growing tired of having to feed him, and invitations being scarce, he became so destitute that he had to go to the hospital, where he was taken most grievously ill with dysentery. Despairing of ever recovering his health, and diffident as to the hundredfold, he, one day, impelled by some pain or other to seek the open air, got out of his bed, and repaired to a neighbouring little meadow for the relief of his belly. When the thing was over, as he was looking for a handful of grass to wipe his backside, he found a piece of linen rolled up and filled with precious stones. Thus grown rich, he took medical advice, got cured, bought a house and grounds, and lived thenceforward in the greatest affluence.

Every body saying to him: "Had we not told you that God would repay you a hundredfold?"—"Yes, indeed," he replied, "so He has; but not before my stools had nearly bled me to death." The saying applies to such as are slow at bestowing or acknowledging a kindness.

"A dolt who believed his wife had 'duos cunnos'"

A rustic of our parts, rather silly and assuredly a raw hand at love-deeds, took unto himself a wife. Now, it happened one night that she, *renes versus virum volvens*, had put *nates in ejus gremio*; the bow was bent, the shaft was shot, and perchance hit the mark. Amazed at that, our clodhopper enquires of his wife whether she had two, and being answered in the affirmative: "Ho, ho!," saith he, "one will do for me; the other is really a superfluity." The woman, a sly hussy, who was courted by the parish priest, rejoined, "The second one we can give as an alms: let us make a present of it to the Church and to our vicar; to him it will be most acceptable, and will not prejudice you in the least, since one is enough for you." The man assented, equally anxious to please the priest, and to rid himself of a superfluity. So, the vicar having been asked to supper and had matters explained to him, the meal over, all three got into the same bed, the woman in the middle, the husband in front, and the other behind, so as to avail himself of the gift made him. Famished, and greedy of the long coveted dainty, the priest was the first to open fire; the woman participating in the engagement, gave a few sighs. Fearing lest his allotment should be trespassed upon, "Observe our agreement, my friend," cried the husband, "use thy share, but leave mine untouched." To which the priest replied: "So help me God: I care little for what is thine provided I enjoy what belongs to the Church." Our blockhead acquiesced, and bade him use freely what he had conceded to the Church.

"Rustics commissioned to buy a crucifix, and asked whether they wanted a dead or a live one"

Some good folks were sent from the same place to Arezzo, in order to buy a wooden crucifix for the country-church. They went to a maker of such things, who perceiving, from the very first words spoken, that he had to do with regular dolts and blockheads, resolved upon having a laugh at their expense, and enquired whether they wanted a living or a dead Christ. They, having taken some time to consider, and stepped aside to consult together, answered at last they had rather have a living one, and that their people could easily put to death on the spot, if not satisfied with.

"A friend of mine who grieved at seeing preferred to himself many who were his inferiors in learning and honesty"

At the Roman Court good fortune generally prevails, and there is but seldom room for talent or honesty; every thing is obtained through intrigue or luck, not to mention money, which seems to hold supreme sway all over the world. A friend of mine, sore at the preference given over him to men very much his inferiors, both in learning and merit, complained to Angelotto, Cardinal of Saint-Mark, that no account was taken of his worth, that he was left aside for people who could not bear comparison with himself; and he spoke of the pains he had been at for his education and the acquisition of knowledge. The Cardinal was never slow at animadverting upon the pravity of Court: "Here," quoth he, "learning and merit stand for nothing; however, be not disheartened, but devote some of your time to unlearning the good you know and learning some of the bad you know not, if you wish to be acceptable to the Pope."

"Reply of the Roman priest Lorenzo"

The day when the Roman Angelotto was made a Cardinal by Pope Eugene, a jocular priest, named Lorenzo, went home cheering merrily, and overflowing with mirth and joy. His neighbours asked him what good fortune had befallen him, that he should be so cheerful and so jolly: "It is all right with me now," said he, "and I may indeed feel sanguine, when I see fools and lunatics made Cardinals of; Angelotto being still more crazed than I am, I also shall soon be a Cardinal."

"A parson who had buried a little dog"

There was in Tuscany a very rich country-parson, who, having lost a little dog he was very fond of, buried it in the church-yard. This came to the ears of the Bishop, who, covetous of the parson's money, summoned him for punishment, as if he had been guilty of the greatest crime. The parson, who had his Bishop at his fingers' ends, complied with the summons, and came provided with fifty golden ducats: the Prelate taunted him sharply for the burial of his dog and ordered him to prison: "Oh! my Father," then said the sly parson, "if you knew how great was that little dog's wisdom, you would not wonder at his having deserved to be buried amongst men; for his intelligence was more than human, in life and especially at the point of death." "What does that mean?" asked the Bishop. "At the end of his days," rejoined the parson, "he made his will, and knowing you are a poor man, bequeathed you fifty golden ducats, which I have brought with me." The Bishop hastened to approve of the will and of the burial, pocketed the money, and discharged the parson.

"A jocular reply"

A man, who plied his tongue rather too freely, was saying, in the very palace of the Pope, some inconsiderate things which he illustrated by funny but expressive gestures. "What are you up to?" exclaimed a friend; "people would take you for a fool." "That is the very best thing that could befall me," he replied; "for I have no other way of ingratiating myself with the powers that be, since now is the hey-day of fools, and everything is in their hands."

"A joke of Everardo, apostolic secretary, who let a fart at a cardinal"

Cardinal de' Conti, a stout and burly man, had been out hunting, and, towards noon, feeling hungry, came down to dinner; he took his seat at table, perspiring copiously (it was summer time) and requested that some-one should air him with a fan. The servants had left the room on various duties, and he asked a certain Everardo Lupi, Apostolic Secretary, to ventilate him. "But," said the latter, "I do not know how that is done with you." "Never mind," answered the Cardinal, "do it as you like, in your own way." "All right, by Jove," replied the Secretary, and raising his right leg he emitted from the very depths of his bowels the most sonorous fart, saying at the same time that that was how he was accustomed to make a breeze for himself. There was a numerous company, who could not help bursting out into a fit of laughter.

"Conclusion"

I think I should not omit to mention the place where most of the above tales were related, I might almost say, acted. That place is our *Bugiale*, a sort of laboratory for fibs, which the Pope's Secretaries had formerly instituted for their amusement. Until the reign of Pope Martin we were wont to select, within the precincts of the Court, a secluded room where we collected the news of the day, and conversed on various subjects, mostly with a view to relaxation, but sometimes also with serious intent. There nobody was spared, and whatever met with our disapprobation was freely censured; oftentimes the Pope himself was the first subject-matter of our criticism, so that many people attended our parties, lest they should themselves be the objects of our first chapter. Foremost among the relaters were Razello of Bologna, many of whose contributions are found in our tales; Antonio Lusco, a most witty man, whom we have frequently referred to; and the Roman Cincio, who was also very fond of a joke; I have also added some good things of my own. Now that those boon companions have departed this life, the *Bugiale* has come to an end: whether men or the times are to be held responsible, it is a fact that genial talk and merry confabulations have gone out of fashion.

Poggio Bracciolini, excerpts from *The Facetiae* (Paris: Isidore Liseux, 1879), vol. 1, pp. 16–21, 33, 49–50, 56, 65–66, 129; vol. 2, pp. 22–23 and 230–32.

In this excerpt from his highly influential work, The History of the Popes, *vol. 1, Ludwig von Pastor paints the still-common view that many Renaissance humanists were anti-religious or a-religious. Pastor's work claimed that the Renaissance began well with pious figures like Petrarch and Bocaccio but things took a turn for the worse during the fifteenth century. Pastor frequently criticizes fifteenth-century humanists as attacking Christianity, especially the papacy. The excerpt below is drawn from Pastor's general introduction.*

The contrasts here apparent became more and more marked as time went on. On the one side the banner of pure heathenism was raised by fanatics of the classical ideal. Its followers wished to bring about a radical return to paganism both in thought and manners. The other side strove to bring the new element of culture into harmony with the Christian ideal, and the political and social civilization of the day. These two parties represented the false and the true, the heathen and the Christian Renaissance.

The latter party, whose judgment was sufficiently free from fanatical bias to perceive that a reconciliation between existing tendencies would be more profitable than a breach with the approved principles of Christianity and the development of more than a thousand years, could alone produce real intellectual progress. To its adherents the world owes it, that the Renaissance was saved from bringing about its own destruction.

Not a few Humanists wavered between the two streams. Some sought to find a happy mean, while others were in youth carried away by one current, and in mature age by the other.

No one has better expressed the programme of the radical heathenizing party than Lorenzo Valla, in his book on Pleasure, published in 1431. . . .

Valla was not alarmed by the attacks of theologians on his daring opinions, for King Alfonso of Naples was his firm protector. On the contrary, he now betook himself to the realm of theology, and eagerly sought opportunities of encountering his ecclesiastical opponents. His dialogue on religious vows, the first of his works to become known in recent times, here comes under our notice. It is of special interest, as in its pages Valla goes far beyond the previous attacks of the Humanists on the monastic life . . .

With equal audacity and venom, Valla turned his arms against the temporal power of the Papacy, in his pamphlet, "On the falsely credited and invented Donation of Constantine." . . .

It will be seen that it is Valla, not Machiavelli, who started the often-repeated assertion that the Popes are to blame for all Italy's misfortunes . . .

Valla's audacious attack on Christian morals in his dialogue "On Pleasure" was far surpassed by Antonio Beccadelli Panormita (died 1471). Repulsive though the subject be, we must speak of his "Hermaphroditus" or collection of epigrams, because the spirit of the false Renaissance is here manifested in all its hideousness. "The book," says the Historian of Humanism, "opens a view into an abyss of iniquity, but wreathes it with the most beautiful flowers of poetry." The most horrible crime of heathen antiquity, crimes whose very name a Christian cannot utter without reluctance, were here openly glorified . . .

Beccadelli's disgraceful work did not, unfortunately, stand alone, for Poggio, Filelfo and Aeneas Sylvius Piccolomini have much to answer for in the way of highly seasoned anecdotes and adventures. No writing of the so-called Humanists, however, equals Beccadelli's collection of epigrams in impurity. The false heathen Renaissance culminates in this repulsive "Emancipation of the Flesh," sagaciously characterized by a modern historian as the forerunner of the great Revolution, which in the following centuries shook Europe to its centre . . .

The corrupting effects of the false, profligate Humanism represented by Valla and Beccadelli made themselves felt to an alarming extent in the province of religion, as well as in that of ethics. The enthusiasm for everything connected with the ancient world was carried to such an excess, that the forms of antiquity alone were held to be beautiful, and its ideas alone to be true. The Ancient literature came to be looked upon as capable of satisfying every spiritual need, and as sufficing for the perfection of humanity. Accordingly its admirers sought to resuscitate ancient life as a whole, and that, the life of the period of the decadence with which alone they were acquainted. Grave deviations from Christian mode of thought and conduct were the necessary consequences of such opinions.

In the beginning of the fifteenth century Cino da Rinuccini brought forward a list of serious charges against the adherents of the false Renaissance. . . . There may be, perhaps some exaggeration in these charges, but it cannot be denied, that enthusiastic admiration for the ancients exercised a most deleterious influence . . .

The adherents of the false Renaissance, with scarcely an exception, were, during life, indifferent to religion. They looked on their classical studies, their ancient philosophy, and the faith of the Church as two distinct worlds, which had no point of contact. From considerations of worldly prudence or convenience they still professed themselves Catholics, while in their hearts they were more or less alienated from the Church. In many cases, indeed, the very foundations of faith and morals were undermined by the triumph of false Humanism. The literary men and artists of this school lived in their ideal world of classic dreams; theirs was a proud and isolated existence. The real work of social and, yet, more, that of moral and religious life, with its needs, its struggles, and its sacrifices, was far too common and too burdensome for their notice; and they only condescended to take part in it, in so far as was necessary in order to bring themselves into view and to share in its advantages.

Overweening self-esteem was a characteristic of all these men; they never thought themselves sufficiently appreciated. Some of them, as for example, Filelfo, cherished a fixed idea that they were the geniuses of their age, and that the whole world must give way to them because they spoke Greek and wrote Latin with elegance. Notwithstanding all the Stoical phrases, which adorned their discourses and writings, the Humanists were fond of money and good cheer, desirous of honour and admiration, eager to find favour with the rich and noble, quarrelsome amongst themselves, ready for any intrigue, calumny, or baseness, that would serve to ruin a rival.

Poggio Bracciolini may be taken as a genuine representative of this false Humanism. This gifted writer, "the most fortunate discoverer the world has ever known in the field of literature," is, as a man, one of the most repulsive figures of the period. Almost all the vices of the profligate Renaissance are to be found combined in his person, and it would be hard to say whether his slanderous disposition or the gross immorality of his life is most worthy of condemnation.

Notwithstanding occasional expressions of another kind in his writings, there can be no doubt that Poggio's point of view was more heathen than Christian. Christianity and the Church were entirely outside his sphere. To quote the words of the biographer Aeneas Sylvius Piccolomini, "he was such a worshipper of heathen antiquity, that he would certainly have given away all the treasures of dogmatic theology for a new discourse of Cicero." A remarkable example of his heathen, or rather indifferent, state of mind is furnished by his well-known letter to the Council of Constance on the occasion of the burning of Jerome of Prague. Poggio speaks with the greatest enthusiasm of Jerome, from which, however, it is not to be inferred that he approved of his opinions. On the contrary, the conception of a martyr to any faith was as foreign to the mind of this follower of the false Renaissance as to that of a heretic. The thing which he admired in Jerome was of a very different kind. The courage with which this man met death reminded him of Cato, and of Mutius Scevola, and he considered the eloquence of his address to the Council as approaching that of the ancients. The decision of the ecclesiastical authority is scarcely noticed by Poggio; he only regrets that so noble an intellect should have turned to heresy; "If," he adds, "the accusations brought against him are true." This doubt is, however, disposed of by the cool observation, "it is not my business to judge of the matter: I contented myself with the opinion of those who are considered wiser than I am."

Almost all the writings of Poggio are offensively obscene and coarse. The worse in this respect, after his "Facetiae," are his shameless and immoral letter on the license which prevailed at the baths of Zurich, and his libels on Filelfo and Valla. "Like the lowest boy out of the streets," says the historian of Humanism, "Poggio assails his adversary with the coarsest abuse and the basest calumny." He accuses these two Humanists of every kind of turpitude, and the greater part of the work is unfit for translation.

The impression produced is a strange one, when a writer, whose own life was so far from respectable, sets himself up as a censor of the depraved morals of the monks and clergy. Poggio cannot find words sufficiently stinging with which to brand the hypocrisy, cupidity, ignorance, arrogance, and immorality of the clergy. The monks, however, are everywhere the especial object of his sarcasm, often, indeed, in discourses, letters, and treatises, where such sentiments might least have been looked for. Violent attacks upon them are to be found, as in his dialogues on Avarice and on Human misery, and in his book against hypocrites . . .

In order to understand how unjustifiable is this caricature of the monks, we must remember that the Religious Orders gave to Italy in the fifteenth century a line of preachers whose devotion to their calling and whose power and earnestness have, even after the lapse of ages, commanded the esteem of those who differ from them. The limits of his work do not permit us to enter into a detailed account of all the brilliant and truly popular orators who produced the remarkable and copious pulpit literature of the age of the Renaissance . . .

"An age," as a modern historian observes, "which thus perceives and acknowledges its faults, is certainly not among the worst of ages. If in the individual the recognition of a fault is the first step to amendment, it cannot be otherwise in regard to whole classes of men, to nations, and to the Church itself. No one who bestows even a superficial glance on the literature of the period, can deny that this recognition existed in the Church in the time of the Renaissance. The first and most essential step towards amendment had been taken, and there was well grounded hope that further energetic measure would follow."

From this point of view, the general unfavourable judgment of the religious and moral condition of the Renaissance period may be essentially modified. At all events, as the first German authority on Italian history has lately observed, it is a mistake to suppose from the numerous testimonies of Pagan tendencies furnished by the Italian Humanists, that these were absolutely general. This gifted nation—and this is especially true of Florence, the intellectual home of the Renaissance—still retained its warm religious feeling in the midst of all party struggles, excommunications, and external conflicts . . .

The magnificent gifts, by which the pomp and dignity of religious worship were maintained, the countless works of Christian art, and the innumerable and admirably organized charitable foundations, also bear testimony to the continuance of "heartfelt piety and ardent faith" in the Italy of the fifteenth century.

Side by side with these evidences of religious feeling in the Italian people, the age of the Renaissance certainly exhibits alarming tokens of moral decay; sensuality and license reigned, especially among the higher classes. Statistics on this subject, however, are so incomplete, that a certain estimate of the actual moral condition of the age or a trustworthy comparison with later times is impossible.

But if those days were full of failings and sins of every kind, the Church was not wanting in glorious manifestations, through which the source of her higher life revealed itself . . .

. . .

From the beginning, the true Christian Renaissance existed side by side with the false.

Its followers were equally enthusiastic in their admiration of the treasures of antiquity, and they recognized in the classics a most perfect means of intellectual culture, but they also clearly perceived the danger attendant on the revival of the old literature, especially under the circumstances of the time . . .

Ludwig von Pastor, excerpt from *The History of the Popes*, vol. 1, translated by Frederick Antrobus (London: Kegan Paul, 1891), 13–40.

In The following excerpt, from The Civilisation of the Renaissance in Italy, *Jacob Burckhardt concludes a discussion about Renaissance humanists. Like Pastor, Burckhardt viewed many humanists as irreligious. In general, Burckhardt had an ambivalent view of humanists, as he looked to attribute to them many of the accomplishments of the Italian Renaissance, even as he did not approve of their cultivation of the Latin language instead of Italian.*

After a brilliant succession of poet-scholars had, since the beginning of the fourteenth century, filled Italy and the world with the worship of antiquity, had determined the forms of education and culture, had often taken the lead in political affairs and had, to no small extent, reproduced ancient literature—at length in the sixteenth century, before their doctrines and scholarship had lost hold of the public mind, the whole class fell into deep and general disgrace. Though they still served as models to the poets, historians, and orators, personally no one would consent to be reckoned of their number. To the two chief accusations against them—that of malicious self-conceit, and that of abominable profligacy—a third charge of irreligion was now loudly added by the rising powers of the Counter-Reformation.

Why, it may be asked, were not these reproaches, whether true or false, heard sooner? As a matter of fact, they were heard at a very early period, but the effect they produced was insignificant, for the plain reason that men were far too dependent on the scholars for their knowledge of antiquity— that the scholars were personally the possessors and diffusers of ancient culture. But the spread of printed editions of the classics, and of large and well-arranged hand-books and dictionaries, went far to free the people from the necessity of personal intercourse with the humanists, and, as soon as they could be but partly dispensed with, the change in popular feeling became manifest. It was a change under which the good and bad suffered indiscriminately.

The first to make these charges were certainly the humanists themselves. Of all men who ever formed a class, they had the least sense of their common interests, and least respected what there was of this sense. All means were held lawful, if one of them saw a chance of supplanting another. From literary discussion they passed with astonishing suddenness to the fiercest and the most groundless vituperation. Not satisfied with refuting, they sought to annihilate an opponent. Something of this must be put to the account of their position and circumstances; we have seen how fiercely the age, whose loudest spokesmen they were, was borne to and fro by the passion for glory and the passion for satire. Their position, too, in practical life was one that they had continually to fight for. In such a temper they wrote and spoke and described one another. Poggio's works alone contain dirt enough to create a prejudice against the whole class—and these "Opera Poggii" were just those most often printed, on the north, as well as on the south, side of the Alps. We must take care not to rejoice too soon, when we meet among these men a figure which seems immaculate; on further inquiry there is always a danger of meeting with some foul charge, which, even when it is incredible, still discolours the picture. The mass of indecent Latin poems in circulation, and such things as the ribaldry on the subject of his own family, in Pontano's dialogue, "Antonius," did the rest to discredit the class. The sixteenth century was not only familiar with all these ugly symptoms, but had also grown tired of the type of the humanist. These men had to pay both for the misdeeds they had done, and for the excess of honour which had hitherto fallen to their lot. Their evil fate willed it that the greatest poet of the nation wrote of them in a tone of calm and sovereign contempt.

Of the reproaches which combined to excite so much hatred, many were only too well founded. Yet a clear and unmistakable tendency to strictness in matters of religion and morality was alive in many of the philologists, and it is a proof of small knowledge of the period, if the whole class is condemned. Yet many, and among them the loudest speakers, were guilty.

Three facts explain, and perhaps diminish their guilt: the overflowing excess of favour and fortune, when the luck was on their side: the uncertainty of the future, in which luxury or misery depended on the caprice of a patron or the malice of an enemy; and finally, the misleading influence of antiquity. This undermined their morality, without giving them its own instead; and in religious matters, since they could never think of accepting the positive belief in the old gods, it affected them only on the negative and sceptical side. Just because they conceived of antiquity dogmatically—that is, took it as the model for all thought and action—its influence was here pernicious. But that an age existed, which idolised the ancient world and its products with an exclusive devotion, was not the fault of individuals. It was the work of a historical providence, and all the culture of the ages which have followed, and of the ages to come, rests upon the fact that it was so, and that all the ends of life but this one were then deliberately put aside.

The career of the humanists was, as a rule, of such a kind that only the strongest characters could pass through it unscathed. The first danger came, in some cases, from the parents, who sought to turn a precocious child into a miracle of learning, with an eye to his future position in that class which then was supreme. Youthful prodigies, however, seldom rise above a certain level; or, if they do, are forced to achieve their further progress and development at the cost of the bitterest trials. For an ambitious youth, the fame and the brilliant position of the humanists were a perilous temptation; it seemed to him that he too "through inborn pride could no longer regard the low and common things of life." He was thus led to plunge into a life of excitement and vicissitude, in which exhausting studies, tutorships, secretaryships, professorships, offices in princely households, mortal enmities and perils, luxury and beggary, boundless admiration and boundless contempt, followed confusedly one upon the other, and in which the most solid worth and learning were often pushed aside by superficial impudence. But the worst of all was, that the position of the humanist was almost incompatible with a fixed home, since it either made frequent changes of dwelling necessary for a livelihood, or so affected the mind of the individual that he could never be happy for long in one place. He grew tired of the people, and had no peace among the enmities which he excited, while the people themselves in their turn demanded something new . . . the scholar of the Renaissance was forced to combine great learning with the power of resisting the influence of ever-changing pursuits and situations. Add to this the deadening effect of licentious excess, and—since do what he might, the worse was believed of him—a total indifference to the moral laws recognised by others. Such men can hardly be conceived to exist without an inordinate pride. They needed it, if only to keep their heads above water, and were confirmed in it by the admiration which alternated with hatred in the treatment they received from the world. They are the most striking examples and victims of an unbridled subjectivity.

The attacks and the satirical pictures began, as we have said, at an early period. For all strongly marked individuality, for every kind of distinction, a corrective was at hand in the national taste for ridicule. And in this case the men themselves offered abundant and terrible materials which satire had but to make use of . . .

Jacob Burckhardt, excerpt from *The Civilisation of the Renaissance in Italy*, translated by S. G. C. Middlemore (London: S. Sonnenschein, 1904), 271–75.

What Really Happened

The characteristics and contributions of humanists to history continue to be debated, but scholars agree that early modern humanists and

Popular myth holds that intellectuals during the Renaissance, called humanists, introduced secularism after the religious Middle Ages. The humanists, however, were in almost all cases just as religious as writers and thinkers before them had been. Erasmus, for example, depicted in this image, was a leading humanist, devoted Catholic, and wrote extensively on religious topics. (Erasmus of Rotterdam ca. 1532 Hans Holbein the Younger German. The Metropolitan Museum of Art, Robert Lehman Collection, 1975)

their broader society were deeply religious. Certainly, some humanists developed more secular outlooks during the sixteenth, seventeenth, and eighteenth centuries. But as many, or more, devoted their studies entirely to religious texts and religious reforms. Humanists, at times, contributed directly to stories that continue to unfold in our own day—our conception of the humanities, for example, comes from them. But most of the time, humanists directly impacted historical developments and events in their own day and the years after, which are now long past.

Renaissance and early modern humanists showed varied levels of religious devotions, just as all other people during that time. One of the earlier humanists, Francesco Petrarch, worked diligently to combine his deep Christian piety with his classical studies. Throughout his oeuvre, Petrarch revealed his love for classical texts, classical Latin, and the humanities. But even as he emulated pagan authors, he also shaped those emulations into mainstream Christian texts. Humanists after Petrarch sometimes professed similar piety and sometimes less in their original works, but research into their lives almost always reveals some level of commitment to Christianity. A man like Poggio Bracciolini, for example, published the risqué stories excerpted earlier in this chapter, but he also found solace in early Christian texts at different times of his career and spent most of his life working as a secretary for various popes and other religious figures. Fifteenth-century popes like Nicholas V and Pius II were renowned for their classical learning. Both men supported new humanist studies. But both men also made new crusades to spread and defend the Christian faith central aspects of their respective papacies.

The relationship between humanist studies and religion continued to be complicated, perhaps even more so, in later centuries. As humanism became increasingly popular in northern Europe, it took on distinctive characteristics. Many humanists aimed their writings and textual studies at religious texts, religious reform, and religious propagation. These humanists were so tied to religious matters that scholars have dubbed them "Christian humanists." Additionally, many humanists helped spread the Protestant Reformations by supporting Protestant authors and printing their books. Others rejected Protestant arguments and used their positions to defend and reform the Catholic faith.

Some of the best known early-modern humanists, consequently, focused their original texts on religious matters. For example, one of the most popular writers of the time, Desiderius Erasmus, urged contemporary churchmen to emulate what he viewed as the pristine practices of the early church. Erasmus also published commentaries on how the Latin Vulgate Bible could better reflect its original Greek text. Other humanists focused on similar topics. People turned to studying, and then even publishing, the Bible in each of its original languages. In schools, the studies of humanists dominated curricula. Indeed, the new Jesuit order began to play a dominant role in schools across Europe, and such schools focused on the disciplines deemed essential to humanist studies. It was not until much, much later that scholars began tying humanists to nationalist and secular narratives that reflected their own times much more than they reflected early modern Europe.

PRIMARY SOURCE DOCUMENTS

Petrarch was a pivotal figure in securing the success and popularity of humanism in the late medieval period. The son of an exile from Florence, Petrarch traveled widely in and beyond Italy. He maintained an extensive correspondence with people and tried to write Latin like a classical author. Petrarch was also a deeply pious man and his religion permeates his writings. In his "Ascent of Mont Ventoux," excerpted on the following page, Petrarch used the climbing of a mountain as a metaphor for the spiritual life and to show how people must focus on the next life rather than on worldly affairs.

To-day I made the ascent of the highest mountain in this region, which is not improperly called Ventosum. My only motive was the wish to see what so great an elevation had to offer . . .

But, as usually happens, fatigue quickly followed upon our excessive exertion, and we soon came to a halt at the top of a certain cliff. Upon starting on again we went more slowly, and I especially advanced along the rocky way with a more deliberate step. While my brother chose a direct path straight up the ridge, I weakly took an easier one which really descended. When I was called back, and the right road was shown me, I replied that I hoped to find a better way round on the other side, and that I did not mind going farther if the path were only less steep. This was just an excuse for my laziness; and when the others had already reached a considerable height I was still wandering in the valleys. I had failed to find an easier path, and had only increased the distance and difficulty of the ascent. At last I became disgusted with the intricate way I had chosen, and resolved to ascend with more ado. When I reached my brother, who, while waiting for me, had had ample opportunity for rest, I was tired and irritated. We walked along together for a time, but hardly had we passed the first spur when I forgot about the circuitous route which I had just tried, and took a lower one again. Once more I followed an easy, round-about path through winding valleys, only to find myself soon in my old difficulty. I was simply trying to avoid the exertion of the ascent; but no human ingenuity can alter the nature of things, or cause anything to reach a height by going down. Suffice it to say that, much to my vexation and my brother's amusement, I made this same mistake three times or more during a few hours.

After being frequently misled in this way, I finally sat down in a valley and transferred my winged thoughts from things corporeal to the imma-terial, addressing myself as follows—"What thou hast repeatedly experi-enced to-day in the ascent of this mountain, happens to thee, as to many, in the journey toward the blessed life. But this is not so readily perceived by men, since the motions of the body are obvious and external while those of the soul are invisible and hidden. Yes, the life which we call blessed is to be sought for on a high eminence, and strait is the way that leads to it. Many, also, are the hills that lie between, and we must ascend, by a glorious stairway, from strength to strength. At the top is at once the end of our struggles and the goal for which we are bound. All wish to reach this goal, but, as Ovid says, 'To wish is little; we must long with the utmost eagerness to gain our end.' Thou certainly dost ardently desire, as well as imply wish, unless thou deceives thyself in this matter, as in so many others. What, then, doth hold thee back? Nothing, assuredly, except that thou wouldst take a path which seems, at first thought, more easy, leading through low and worldly pleasures. But nevertheless in the end, after long wanderings, thou must perforce either climb the steeper path, under the burden of tasks foolishly deferred, to its blessed culmination, or lie down in the valley of thy sins, and (I shudder to think of it!), if the shadow of death overtake thee, spend an eternal night amid constant torments." . . .

One peak of the mountain, the highest of all, the country people call "Sonny," why, I do not know, unless by antiphrasis, as I have sometimes suspected in other instances; for the peak in question would seem to be the father of all the surrounding ones. On its top is a little level place, and here we could at last rest our tired bodies.

. . . At first, owing to the unaccustomed quality of the air and the effect of the great sweep of view spread out before me, I stood like one dazed. I beheld the clouds under our feet, and what I had read of Athos and Olympus seemed less incredible as I myself witnessed the same things from a mountain of less fame. I turned my eyes towards Italy, whither my heart most inclined. The Alps, rugged and snow-capped, seemed to rise close by, although they were really at a great distance; the very same Alps through which that fierce enemy of the Roman name once made his way, bursting the rocks, if we may believe the report, by the application of vinegar . . .

. . . The sinking sun and the lengthening shadows of the mountain were already warning us that the time was near at hand when we must go. As if suddenly wakened from sleep, I turned about and gazed toward the west. I was unable to discern the summits of the Pyrenees, which form the barrier between France and Spain; not because of any intervening obstacle that I know of but owing simply to the insufficiency of our mortal vision. But I could see with the utmost clearness, off to the right, the mountains of the region about Lyons, and to the left the bay of Marseilles and the waters that lash the shores of Aigues Mortes, altho' all these places were so distant that it would require a journey of several days to reach them. Under our very eyes flowed the Rhone.

While I was thus dividing my thoughts, now turning my attention to some terrestrial object that lay before me, now raising my soul, as I had done my body, to higher planes, it occurred to me to look into my copy of St. Augustine's *Confessions* . . . that I always have about me . . . I opened the compact little volume, small indeed in size, but of infinite charm, with the intention of reading whatever came to hand, for I could happen upon nothing that would be otherwise than edifying and devout.

Now it chanced that the tenth book presented itself. My brother, waiting to hear something of St. Augustine's from my lips, stood attentively by. I call him, and God too, to witness that where I first fixed my eyes it was written: "And men go about to wonder at the heights of the mountains, and the mighty circuit of the ocean, and the revolution of the stars, but themselves they consider not." I was abashed, and, asking my brother (who was anxious to hear more), not to annoy me, I closed the book, angry with myself that I should still be admiring earthly things who might long ago have learned from even the pagan philosophers that nothing is wonderful but the soul, which, when great itself, finds nothing great outside itself. Then, in truth, I was satisfied that I had seen enough of the mountain; I turned my inward eye upon myself, and from that time not a syllable fell from my lips until we reached the bottom again . . .

. . . I thought in silence of the lack of good counsel in us mortals, who neglect what is noblest in ourselves, scatter our energies in all directions, and waste ourselves in a vain show, because we look about us for what is to be found only within. I wondered at the natural nobility of our souls, save when it debases itself of its own free will, and deserts its original estate, turning what God has given it for its honour into dishonour. How many times, think you, did I turn back that day, to glance at the summit of the mountain, which seemed scarcely a cubit high compared with the range of human contemplation—when it is not immersed in the foul mire of earth? With every downward step I asked myself this: If we are ready to endure so much sweat and labour in order that we may bring our bodies a little nearer heaven, how can a soul struggling toward God, up the steeps of human pride and human destiny, fear any cross or prison or sting of fortune? How few, I thought, but are diverted from their path by the fear of difficulties or the love of ease! How happy the lot of those few, if any such there be! . . .

> Francesco Petrarch, excerpt from "The Ascent of Mont Ventoux," in *Petrarch, the First Modern Scholar and Man of Letters*, edited by James Harvey Robinson and Henry Winchester Rolfe (New York: G. P. Putnam's Sons, 1907), 307–19.

Erasmus was a leading humanist and popular author active in the first decades of the sixteenth century. He traveled throughout Europe and enjoyed the friendship and respect of many of the other literary figures of his day, in addition to the patronage of many powerful people. One of his most popular works was his frequently revised collection of famous adages. He also worked on annotations to the Latin Vulgate, a work in which he presented areas where the long-standard Latin translation of the Bible deviated from the original biblical languages. Erasmus spent much of his career traveling around Europe rather than settling down in one place. In one period, he befriended the English humanist Thomas More and wrote for him a short text, The Praise of Folly. *A word for "folly" in Greek is "moria," and thus the title and subject were intended as a pun on his friend's name. The text is both learned and funny, while also offering several critiques about religious practice and institutions. In the excerpt below, Erasmus takes aim at theologians.*

. . . And those too they pronounce like Oracles. This Proposition is scandalous; this Irreverent; this has a smatch of Heresie; this no very good sound: so that neither Baptisme, nor the Gospel, nor Paul, nor Peter, nor St. Jerome, nor St. Augustine, no nor most Aristotelian Thomas himself, can make a man a Christian, without these Batchelours too be pleas'd to give him his grace. And the like is their subtilty in judging; for who would think he were no Christian that should say these two Speeches "Matula Putes" and "matula Putet", or "Ollae fervere" and "ollam fervere" were not both good Latine, unless their wisdoms had taught us the contrary? Who had deliver'd the Church from such Mists of Errour, which yet no one e're met with, had they not come out with some University Seal for 't? And are they not most happy while they do these things?

Then for what concerns Hell, how exactly they describe every thing, as if they had been conversant in that Common-wealth most part of their time! Again, how do they frame in their fancy new Orbes, adding to those we have already an eighth! A goodly one, no doubt, and spatious enough, lest perhaps their happy Souls might lack room to walk in, entertain their friends, and now and then play at Foot-ball. And with these and a thousand the like fopperies their heads are so full stufft and stretcht, that I believe Jupiter's brain was not near so bigg when, being in labour with Pallas, he was beholding to the Midwifery of Vulcan's Axe. And therefore ye must not wonder if in their publique Disputes they are so bound about the head, lest otherwise perhaps their brains might leap out. Nay, I have sometimes laught my self, to see 'em so towre in their own opinion when they speak most barbarously; and when they Humh and Hawh so pitifully that none but one of their own Tribe can understand 'em, they call it heights which the Vulgar can't reach; for they say 'tis beneath the dignity of Divine Mysteries to be crampt and ty'd up to the narrow Rules of Grammarians: from whence we may conjecture the great Prerogative of Divines, if they onely have the priviledge of speaking corruptly, in which yet every Cobler thinks himself concern'd for his share. Lastly, they look upon themselves as somewhat more than Men, as often as they are devoutly saluted by the name of "Our Masters", in which they fancy there lyes as much as in the Jews' "Jehovah"; and therefore they reckon it a crime if "Magister noster" be written other than in Capital Letters; and if any one should preposterously say "Noster masters", he has at once overturn'd the whole body of divinity.

And next these come those that commonly call themselves the Religious and Monks; most false in both Titles, when both a great part of 'em are farthest from Religion, and no men swarm thicker in all places than themselves. Nor can I think of any thing that could be more miserable, did not I support 'em so many several wayes. For whereas all men detest 'em to that height, that they take it for ill luck to meet one of 'em by chance, yet such is their happiness that they flatter themselves. For first, they reckon it one of the main Points of Piety if they are so illiterate that they can't so much as read. And then when they run over their Offices, which they carry about 'em, rather by tale than understanding, they believe the Gods more than ordinarily pleas'd with their braying. And some there are among 'em that put off their trumperies at vast rates, yet roave up and down for the bread they eat; nay, there is scarce an Inne, Waggon, or Ship into which they intrude not, to the no small damage of the Common-wealth of Beggars. And yet, like pleasant fellows, with all this Vileness, Ignorance, Rudeness and Impudence, they represent to us, for so they call it, the lives of the Apostles. Yet what is more pleasant than that they do all things by Rule and, as it were, a kind of Mathematicks, the least swerving from which were a crime beyond forgiveness—as, how many knots their shoes must be ti'd with, of what colour every thing is, what distinction of habits, of what stuff made, how many straws broad their Girdles and of what fashion, how many bushels wide their Cowle, how many fingers long their Hair, and how many hours sleep; which exact equality, how disproportionable it is, among such variety of bodies and tempers, who is there that does not perceive it? And yet by reason of these fooleries they not onely set slight by others, but each different Order, men otherwise professing Apostolical Charity, despise one another, and for the different wearing of a habit, or that 'tis of darker colour, they put all things in combustion. And amongst these there are some so rigidly Religious that their upper Garment is hair-Cloth, their inner of the finest Linnen; and, on the contrary, others wear Linnen without, and hair next their skins. Others, agen, are as afraid to touch mony as poison, and yet neither forbear Wine nor dallying with Women. In a word, 'tis their onely care that none of 'em come near one another in their manner of living, nor do they endeavour how they may be like Christ, but how they may differ among themselves . . .

Erasmus, excerpt from *The Praise of Folly* (Oxford: Clarendon Press, 1913), 123–28.

Further Reading

Bentley, Jerry H. *Humanists and Holy Writ: New Testament Scholarship in the Renaissance.* Princeton, NJ: Princeton University Press, 1983.

Caferro, William. *Contesting the Renaissance.* Malden, MA: Wiley-Blackwell, 2011.

D'Amico, John. *Renaissance Humanism in Papal Rome.* Baltimore: Johns Hopkins University Press, 1983.

Dost, Timothy P. *Renaissance Humanism in Support of the Gospel in Luther's Early Correspondence.* New York: Routledge, 2001.

Erasmus, Desiderius. *Christian Humanism and the Reformation.* Edited by John C. Olin. New York: Fordham University Press, 1987.

King, Margaret, ed. and trans. *Renaissance Humanism. An Anthology of Sources.* Indianapolis: Hackett, 2014.

Kraye, Jill. *The Cambridge Companion to Renaissance Humanism.* Cambridge: Cambridge University Press, 1996.

Nauert, Charles. *Humanism and the Culture of Renaissance Europe.* 2nd ed. Cambridge: Cambridge University Press, 2006.

Palmer, Ada. "The Persecution of Renaissance Lucretius Readers Revisited." In *Lucretius Poet and Philosopher*, edited by Philip R. Hardie, Valentina Prosperi, and Diego Zucca, 167–98. Berlin: De Gruyter, 2020.

Peterson, David. "Out of the Margins: Religion and the Church in Renaissance Italy." *Renaissance Quarterly* 53 (2000): 835–79.

Price, David Hotchkiss. *Albrecht Dürer's Renaissance. Humanism, Reformation, and the Art of Faith.* Ann Arbor: University of Michigan Press, 2003.

Rummell, Erika, ed. *Biblical Humanism and Scholasticism in the Age of Erasmus.* Leiden: Brill, 2008.

Spitz, Lewis. *The Religious Renaissance of the German Humanists.* Cambridge, MA: Harvard University Press, 1963.

Stinger, Charles L. *Humanism and the Church Fathers: Ambrogio Traversari (1386–1439) and Christian Antiquity in the Italian Renaissance.* Albany: State University of New York Press, 1977.

Trinkaus, Charles. *In Our Image and Likeness: Humanity and Divinity in Italian Humanist Thought.* South Bend, IN: University of Notre Dame Press, 1970.
Trinkaus, Charles Edward, and Heiko Oberman. *The Pursuit of Holiness in Late Medieval and Renaissance Religion.* Leiden: Brill, 1972.

5

The Pope Was an All-Powerful Ruler in Early Modern Europe

What People Think Happened

The myth goes that from the fall of Rome until the eighteenth century, the pope was an all-powerful ruler pulling the strings and controlling the thoughts of all Europeans. It continues that during the chaos of the early medieval period, the pope took control of the crumbling Roman state. From that position the pope quickly seized European finances and political power. Then, for over 1,000 years all other rulers looked to the pope with anxiety, fearful of a man whose reach was far wider than theirs and whose resources were far more considerable. Rulers were picked, promoted, and discarded based on their obedience to the pope in Rome. These popes are usually imagined as older men, wise in the ways of coercion, corruption, and personal aggrandizement.

Papal control ushered in an historical stasis where the pope reigned supreme and nefariously controlled people's thoughts and beliefs. There was a single orthodoxy. Even those who believed the "right" things, in theory, were not safe because justice systems were so primitive that any sort of accusation, even the most ludicrous one, was believed to be true. Innocent people, consequently, were tortured, maimed, and executed simply because of their gullibility and the wickedness of papal representatives. People who believed the "wrong" things fared much worse. "Wrong" here meant anything contrary to or critical of the pope. Those who dared to challenge the Church with criticism or free thought were arrested. Their works were formally censored. Copies were rounded up and burned. Consequently, all texts revered the Church and its prelates.

After the Renaissance, according to the myth, the pope finally began to lose his stranglehold on belief, wealth, and political power. Free thinkers began to show the world as it was: the earth moved around the sun, it was round, blood circulated in the body, etc. Revolutionaries believed that people could make up their own minds about religion and thus the Bible was translated into languages people could read. Powerful kings in France, England, and Spain eclipsed the power and wealth of the pope. People were free to work to support their families and believe things as they saw fit. They could read things and make up their own minds. The theocratic tyranny of the papacy had finally ended.

How the Story Became Popular

The myth of papal power over the late medieval and early modern worlds derives from a combination of developments within the Catholic Church and writings by both Protestants and Catholics. Beginning in the sixteenth century, Christianity in Europe formally and permanently split into multiple competing versions of the faith. Each version sought to project a positive image of itself while vilifying its religious competitors. Some Protestant writers, for example, presented their founders as saint-like figures who fought against popes who were more than just wicked villains: the pope was the anti-Christ himself. Catholics in turn characterized the pope as the true descendant of the apostle Peter and thus the divinely chosen successor of Christ. As these battles—both in print and on the battlefield—continued in the sixteenth century, different faiths became increasingly rigid about their beliefs and the behaviors that they viewed as acceptable. Members of the Catholic and Protestant churches sought to better define their beliefs and their differences from other versions of Christianity. Toward that end, Catholics expanded the early modern papacy to have more power than before; created an index of forbidden books; and empowered an Inquisition to weed out and punish unacceptable practices and thoughts. Such practices were only applicable to Catholic states, and even in those states they worked only to varying degrees. The Pope never had the power to live up to his modern myth.

The myth of papal power is popular in the United States because the history of the United States has traditionally focused on the experiences of white, protestant settlers arriving from England, especially groups like the Pilgrims. The Pilgrims lived in an England that was still in the midst

Rome, Italy. Michelangelo's Moses on the tomb of Pope Julius II in Saint Peter in Chains San Pietro in Vincoli. Popular myth holds that the pope was an all-powerful ruler during medieval and early-modern periods. The pope often claimed to hold universal power, but all but a few popes struggled to turn those claims into reality. Pope Julius II, for example, was a powerful pope and key patron of the artist Michelangelo in the early 1500s. But Pope Julius also spent much of his papacy enmeshed in Italian politics while seeking to gain allies and oppose enemies among powerful northern European kingdoms. (ID 118049761 © Stefania Valvola | Dreamstime.com)

of struggles between Catholics and Protestants. Famously, King Henry VIII had, in 1534, split from Catholicism and established the Anglican faith. However, a royal proclamation was one thing and the beliefs of people quite another. For decades, England, like the rest of Europe, wrestled with religious turmoil and polemics. In the 1610s, 1620s, and 1630s, groups of English protestants began to urge religious reforms to better reflect their version of Christian piety. Some of these individuals, called puritans, believed that the best approach to reform was to work within the existing Anglican system. Other individuals, called separatists or pilgrims, believed that the Anglican Church was beyond reform and thus they had to break away from it. These Protestants took their beliefs to New England on the Mayflower in 1620. Their disdain for Catholics and even other Protestants came with them. The traditional narrative of American history then traced the experiences of these settlers within the thirteen English colonies. Such narratives stressed the righteousness of their Protestant beliefs and contended that the modern age, in fact, was born after the rejection of medieval, Catholic spirituality. The presentation of the historical Catholic Church contained a mixture of truth, fiction, and exaggeration. At its center stood an all-powerful pope and his tools of oppression. From the comedy troupe Monty Python's famous sketch on the omnipresent, always listening "Spanish Inquisition" to more recent blogs and YouTube videos professing the pope's ancient power, the incorrect idea that premodern popes somehow held unlimited power continues to creep into our popular imagination.

PRIMARY SOURCE DOCUMENTS

Starting in the mid-1000s, the popes and the kings of Europe began a series of conflicts, both in writing and by the sword, over who had more political power theoretically. Kings argued that they were the masters of all secular affairs and that the papacy was the master of all affairs of the church and faith. Popes argued that Christ had made them supreme masters over both religious and secular matters. The stakes were very high. Of prime importance was the right of the papacy to appoint and control the actions of secular rulers. Also of key importance was the fact that the Church possessed huge tracts of land throughout Europe. In recent years, popes had been so weak that kings had grown accustomed to personally appointing their allies and relatives to oversee those lands. Now the popes wanted that power back. One peak in the struggle between popes and secular rulers occurred in the early 1300s, when the king of France managed to temporarily defeat his papal opponent. The following excerpt is from a document from that struggle between Pope Boniface VIII and King Philip the Fair of France. In it, Pope Boniface makes a wide-ranging claim for papal power. King Philip, obviously, rejected these arguments and, soon after, defeated Boniface. The defeat strengthened France while weakening the pope.

We are compelled, our faith urging us, to believe and to hold—and we do firmly believe and simply confess—that there is one holy catholic and apostolic church, outside of which there is neither salvation nor remission of sins; her Spouse proclaiming it in the canticles: "My dove, my undefiled is but one, she is the choice one of her that bare her"; which represents one mystic body, of which body the head is Christ; but of Christ, God. In this church there is one Lord, one faith and one baptism. There was one ark of Noah, indeed, at the time of the flood, symbolizing one church; and this being finished in one cubit had, namely, one Noah as helmsman and commander. And, with the exception of his ark, all things existing upon the earth were, as we read, destroyed. This church, moreover, we venerate as the only one, the Lord saying through His prophet: "Deliver my soul from the sword, my darling from the power of the dog." He prayed at the same time for His soul—that is, for Himself the Head—and for His body—which body, namely, he called the one and only church on account of the unity of the faith promised, of the sacraments, and of the love of the church. She is that seamless garment of the Lord which was not cut but which fell by lot. Therefore of this one and only church there is one body and one head—not two heads as if it were a monster: Christ, namely, and the vicar of Christ, St. Peter, and the successor of Peter. For the Lord Himself said to Peter, Feed my sheep. My sheep, He said, using a general term, and not designating these or those particular sheep; from which it is plain that He committed to Him *all* His sheep. If, then, the Greeks or others say that they were not committed to the care of Peter and his successors, they necessarily confess that they are not of the sheep of Christ; for the Lord says, in John, there is one fold, one shepherd and one only. We are told by the word of the gospel that in this His fold there are two swords—a spiritual, namely, and a temporal. For when the apostles said "Behold here are two swords"—when, namely, the apostles were speaking in the church—the Lord did not reply that this was too much, but enough. Surely he who denies that the temporal sword is in the power of Peter wrongly interprets the word of the Lord when He says: "Put up thy sword in its scabbard." Both swords, the spiritual and the material, therefore, are in the power of the church; the one, indeed, to be wielded for the church, the other by the church; the one by the hand of the priest, the other by the hand of kings and knights, but at the will and sufferance of the priest. One sword, moreover, ought to be under the other, and the temporal authority to be subjected to the spiritual. For when the apostle says "there is no power but of God, and the powers that are of God are ordained," they would not be ordained unless sword were under sword and the lesser one, as it were, were led by the other to great deeds. For according to St. Dionysius the law of divinity is to lead the lowest through the intermediate to the highest things. Not therefore, according to the law of the universe, are all things reduced to order equally and immediately; but the lowest through the intermediate to the highest things. But that the spiritual exceeds any earthly power in dignity and nobility we ought the more openly to confess the more spiritual things excel temporal ones. This also is made plain to our eyes from the giving of tithes, and the benediction and the sanctification; from the acceptation of this same power, from the control over those same things. For, the truth bearing witness, the spiritual power has to establish the early power, and to judge it if it be not good. Thus concerning the church and the ecclesiastical power is verified the prophecy of Jeremiah: "See, I have this day set thee over the nations and over the kingdoms," and the other things which follow. Therefore if the earthly power err it shall be judged by the spiritual power; but if the lesser spiritual power err, by the greater. But if the greatest, it can be judged by God alone, not by man, the apostle bearing witness. A spiritual man judges all things, but he himself is judged by no one. This authority, moreover, even though it is given to man and exercised through man, is not human but rather divine, being given by divine lips to Peter and founded on a rock for him and his successors through Christ himself whom he has confessed; the Lord himself saying to Peter: "Whatsoever thou shalt bind," etc. Whoever, therefore, resists this power thus ordained by God, resists the ordination of God, unless he makes believe, like the Manichean, that there are two beginnings. This we consider false and heretical, since by the testimony of Moses, not "in the beginnings," but "in the beginning" God created the Heavens and the earth. Indeed we declare, announce and define, that it is altogether necessary to salvation for every human creature to be subject to the Roman pontiff. The Lateran, No. 14, in our 8th year. As a perpetual memorial of this matter.

Excerpt from "Unam Sanctam," in *Select Historical Documents of the Middle Ages*, edited by Ernest F. Henderson (London: George Bell and Sons, 1903), 435–37.

The following document records the sort of control that people often assume the pope and Catholic authorities had over writings, art, and even the thoughts of late medieval and early modern people. From the latter half of the sixteenth century, there were indeed serious attempts at that sort of control. However, these efforts always varied in their efficacy and were much rarer and less effective before the mid-1500s. This document pertains to a painting that still exists, the "The Feast in the House of Levi," now in the Accademia Gallery in Venice.

Report of the sitting of the Tribunal of the Inquisition on Saturday July eighteenth, 1573.

This day, July eighteenth, 1573. Called to the Holy Office before the sacred tribunal, Paolo Galliari Veronese, residing in the parish of Saint Samuel, and being asked as to his name and surname replied as above.

Being asked as to his profession:—

Answer. I paint and make figures.

Question. Do you know the reasons why you have been called here?

A. No.

Q. Can you imagine what those reasons may be?

A. I can well imagine.

Q. Say what you think about them.

A. I fancy that it concerns what was said to me by the reverend fathers, or rather by the prior of the monastery of San Giovanni e Paolo, whose name I did not know, but who informed me that he had been here, and that your Most Illustrious Lordships had ordered him to cause to be placed in the picture a Magdalen instead of the dog; and I answered him that very readily I would do all that was needful for my reputation and for the honour of the picture; but that I did not understand what this figure of Magdalen could be doing here; and this for many reasons, which I will tell when occasion is granted me to speak.

Q. What is the picture of which you have been referring?

A. It is the picture which represents the Last Supper of Jesus Christ and with His disciples in the house of Simon.

Q. Where is this picture?

A. In the refectory of the monks of San Giovanni e Paolo.

Q. Is it painted in fresco or on wood or on canvas?

A. It is on canvas.

Q. How many feet does it measure in height?

A. It may measure seventeen feet.

Q. And in breadth?

A. About thirty-nine.

Q. In this Supper of our Lord, have you painted (other) persons?

A. Yes.

Q. How many have you represented? And what is each one doing?

A. First there is the innkeeper, Simon; then, under him, a carving squire whom I supposed to have come there for his pleasure, to see how the service of the table is managed. There are many other figures which I cannot remember, however, as it is a long time since I painted the picture.

Q. Have you painted other Last Suppers besides that one?

A. Yes.

Q. How many have you painted? Where are they?

A. I painted one at Verona for the reverend monks of San Lazzaro; it is in their refectory. Another is in the refectory of the reverend brothers of San Giorgio here in Venice.

Q. But that one is not a Last Supper, and is not even called the Supper of Our Lord.

A. I painted another in the refectory of San Sebastiano in Venice, another at Padua for the Fathers of the Maddalena. I do not remember to have made any others.

Q. In this Supper which you painted for San Giovanni e Paolo, what signifies the figure of him whose nose is bleeding?

A. He is a servant who has a nose-bleed from some accident.

Q. What signify those armed men dressed in the fashion of Germany, with halberds in their hands?

A. It is necessary here that I should say a score of words.

Q. Say them.

A. We painters use the same license as poets and madmen, and I represented those halberdiers, the one drinking, the other eating at the foot of the stairs, but both ready to do their duty, because it seemed to me suitable and possible that the master of the house, who as I have been told was rich and magnificent, should have such servants.

Q. And the one who is dressed as a jester with a parrot on his wrist, why did you put him into the picture?

A. He is there as an ornament, as it is usual to insert such figures.

Q. Who are the persons at the table of Our Lord?

A. The twelve apostles.

Q. What is Saint Peter doing, who is the first?

A. He is carving the lamb in order to pass it to the other part of the table.

Q. What is he doing who comes next?

A. He holds a plate to see what Saint Peter will give him.

Q. Tell us what the third is doing.

A. He is picking his teeth with his fork.

Q. And who are really the persons whom you admit to have been present at this Supper?

A. I believe that there was only Christ and His Apostles; but when I have some space left over in a picture I adorn it with figures of my own invention.

Q. Did some person order you to paint Germans, buffoons, and other similar figures in this picture?

A. No, but I was commissioned to adorn it as I thought proper; now it is very large and can contain many figures.

Q. Should not the ornaments which you were accustomed to paint in pictures be suitable and in direct relation to the subject, or are they left to your fancy, quite without discretion or reason?

A. I paint my pictures with all the considerations which are natural to my intelligence, and according as my intelligence understands them.

Q. Does it seem suitable to you, in the Last Supper of our Lord, to represent buffoons, drunken Germans, dwarfs, and other such absurdities?

A. Certainly not.

Q. Then why have you done it?

A. I did it on the supposition that those people were outside the room in which the Supper was taking place.

Q. Do you not know that in Germany and other countries infested by heresy, it is habitual, by means of pictures full of absurdities, to vilify and turn to ridicule the things of the Holy Catholic Church, in order to teach false doctrine to ignorant people who have no common sense?

A. I agree that it is wrong, but I repeat what I have said, that it is my duty to follow the examples given me by my masters.

Q. Well, what did your masters paint? Things of this kind, perhaps?

A. In Rome, in the Pope's chapel, Michel Angelo has represented Our Lord, His Mother, St. John, St. Peter, and the celestial court; and he has represented all these personages nude, including the Virgin Mary, and in various attitudes not inspired by the most profound religious feeling.

Q. Do you not understand that in representing the Last Judgment, in which it is a mistake to suppose that clothes are worn, there was no reason for painting any? But in these figures what is there that is not inspired by the Holy Spirit? There are neither buffoons, dogs, weapons, nor other absurdities. Do you think, therefore, according to this or that view, that you did well in so painting your picture, and will you try to prove that it is a good and decent thing?

A. No, my most Illustrious Sirs; I do not pretend to prove it, but I had not thought that I was doing wrong; I had never taken so many things into consideration. I had been far from imagining such a great disorder, all the more as I had placed these buffoons outside the room in which Our Lord was sitting.

These things having been said, the judges pronounced that the aforesaid Paolo should be obliged to correct his picture within the space of three months from the date of the reprimand, according to the judgments and decision of the Sacred Court, and altogether at the expense of the said Paolo.

Et ita decreverunt omni melius modo. (And so they decided everything for the best!)

Excerpts from the examination of Paolo Veronese, published in *Gleanings from Venetian History*, edited by Francis Marion Crawford (London: Macmillan, 1907), 458–63.

The Council of Trent confirmed its famous list of forbidden books and first published it in 1559. The list compiled texts that Catholic authorities deemed contrary to the faith. In some cases titles were singled out, while in other cases all the writings of certain authors were forbidden to be read without explicit permission. Individuals caught in possession of those works or printers caught publishing or disseminating them could be punished. In practice, the list had mixed efficacy at best, even in Catholic areas with devoted Catholic rulers, since printers found ways around the index; moreover, Catholic authorities had no sway over printers in Protestant lands. The list was first published in Latin and later updated and revised for centuries. The index was abolished in 1966, after the second Vatican Council. The excerpt that follows contains descriptions of the index and some of its proscribed books from the early twentieth century. Although it is from a later period, the excerpt seeks to provide a sense of the sort of content found in a list like this.

A Summary of the Index

1. Our Duties in Relation to Forbidden Books.

Rule 1. We are not allowed to read any forbidden publication . . .

Rule 2. No one, whether he be the owner or not, is allowed to keep a forbidden book . . .

Rule 3. It is not lawful for a Catholic publisher or printer to issue or print, or reprint forbidden books . . .

2. Forbidden Books

Rule 4. General Rule. Translations of a forbidden book into any language are also forbidden, if they faithfully reproduce the original.

1. The General Decrees Prohibit the Following Publications.

Rule 5.

   a. Books defending heresies, i.e. doctrines contrary to divine revelation.

   b. Books derogatory to God, the Blessed Virgin, the Saints

   c. Books vilifying the sacraments, the clerical or religious state, the hierarchy, the Church.

Rule 6. Books professedly treating of, narrating or teaching lewdness and obscenity.

Rule 7. Books teaching or recommending sorcery, spiritism, Christian Science, or other superstitions.

Rule 8. Books defending as lawful or harmless, Freemasonry, divorce, Socialism, suicide, dueling.

Rule 9. Those *newspapers and periodicals* which not merely now and then, but regularly and of set purpose, attack religion or morality, or propagate anti-Catholic views.

Rule 10. The following classes of publications require the approbation of the bishop of the place where the work is to be published, or of some higher authority, which is to be printed in the beginning or at the end of the work and must be renewed for every new edition.

a. *Books* on theology, Church history, canon law, natural theology and ethics, and all editions of the Bible or parts of it in any language.

b. *Books and pamphlets* of devotion, religious instruction, and practical and mystical piety.

c. *Books, pamphlets and leaflets*, printed or reproduced in any other way, which relate apparitions, visions, revelations, miracles, etc. not yet passed on by the Church; the plea that they are destined for private circulation does not exempt these publications.

d. *Books, pamphlets, and leaflets*, which give catalogues of indulgences or new grants of them; also *all writings* which treat of subjects that are *evidently* of unusual importance for faith or morals at the time being.

> Without ecclesiastical approbation the publications mentioned under **b** and **c** as well as all Bible editions in the vernacular are forbidden, though they may have been issued by most pious and learned men. The failure to obtain the approbation for the rest that fall under rule 10 would be a sin for the author (and publishers), but the works themselves would not be forbidden, provided they are not, on account of their contents, proscribed by other rules.

> An author who is a member of a religious order must add the permission of his "praelatus" to the approbation of the bishop.

. . .

2. Books Forbidden by Particular Decrees . . .

Addison, Jos. Remarks on Several Parts of Italy

. . .

Bacon, Francis. De dignitate et augmentis scientiarum (On the Dignity and Increase of Science)

Balzac, Honoré de. All novels

. . .

Bruno, Giordano. The Conflict of Religion, Morals and Science in Contemporary Education

. . .

D'Annuzio, Gabriele. All novels and dramas. Prose Selections, Milan.

. . .

Descartes, René. Meditations on Original Philosophy.

. . .

Dumas, Alexander (father and son). All novels, except The Count of Montecristo.

. . .

Gibbon, Edward. History of the Decline and Fall of the Roman Empire
Goblet d'Alviella, Eug. The Idea of God
Goldsmith, Oliver. An Abridged History of England, From the Invasion of Julius Caesar to the Death of George II
Graf, Arthur. The Devil
Gregorovius, Ferdinand. History of the City of Rome During the Middle Ages. The Sepulchral Monuments of the Popes. Urban VIII in Opposition to Spain and the Emperor.

. . .

Locke, John. An Essay Concerning Human Understanding. The Reasonableness of Christianity.

. . .

Voltaire, F. M. Arouet. Practically all his works.

. . .

Besides, some more anonymous works were condemned since the first publication of this booklet, also books by the following authors: Palmarini, Lefranc, Gambara, Pulido, Fernandez, Alyos, Prohaszka, Ferrari, Coulevain, Favero, Renzetti, Lasplasas.

Francis S. Betten, excerpts from *The Roman Index of Forbidden Books. Briefly Explained for Catholic Booklovers and Students*, 5th ed. (St. Louis, MO: B. Herder Book, 1917), 51–71.

Two texts—Several Choice Prophecyes of the Incomparable and Famous Dr. Martin Luther as also, the Remarkable Prophecy of the Learned and Reverend Dr. Musculus, collected by R.C. *and* History of the Life, Writings, and Doctrines of Martin Luther, *by J.M.V. Audin—illustrate the biased historical approach sometimes taken to early modern religious topics prior to the latter part of the twentieth century. As seen in the following excerpts, the* Several Choice Prophecyes *text provides a biographical portrait of Martin Luther, depicting him as a protagonist triumphing over his enemies while the second text, written much later by J. M. V. Audin, depicts Luther as wrong to condemn Catholics. These sorts of portrayals and propaganda have led to the creation of stereotypes and myths about both popes and protestant figures.*

Excerpt from *Several Choice Prophecyes of the Incomparable and Famous Dr. Martin Luther:*

Of the Parentage, and Life of Luther.

Martin Luther was the Son of a Farmer, he was born at Isleben, in the County of Mansfield, in the year one thousand foure hundred and eighty three, on the 10th day of November. His Father, his Grand Father, and his Great Grandfather (as he saith himself) were Farmers; His Father abandoning his Farme upon some discontents, and finding some Profitable Imployments at Mansfield, he addressed himself to that place, where he was one of the Miners in the Silver Mines; In the mean time, Luther had his Education in the same Town where he was born, and being fitted for the University at Erfurd, he took there the Degrees of Bachellour, and Master of Arts, and in a short processe of time, he took upon him the Habit and Formality of a Friar, at which his Father was much displeased; But it pleased God by this means to make use of him for the over-throwing of the Power of Antichrist; Luther having found how directly opposite the Supremacy of the Pope was to the Doctrine of the primitive times, there grew on it the first contention, which being bandyed up and down with Animosity, it gave Luther, the occasion more strictly to examine some other Corruptions in the Church of Rome, which he did with so much vigour, that Pope Gregory the 13th, understanding what great hurt and prejudice he received from it, and fearing it might bring a further Contempt upon him, he did exasperate Rodolphus the Second, at that time Emperor of Rome, to publish an Edict throughout the Empire, that all the Books of Martin Luther should be burned, and that it should be Death for any man to keep them in his House, which Edict was not only suddainly put in Execution by himself, but it was continued also by Ferdinand the Second, who was a severe Enemy, and a Persecutor of the Protestant Religion.

Luther, long before this had Esponsed a Virgin, whose Name was Katherine Bora, she had sometimes entred herself into a Cloyster of the Nuns, but disliking many abuses she found therein, before her year of Probation was expired she relinquished it.

This gave an occasion to the Monks and Friars to exclaime against Luther as having broken the Vow of Chastity; but Luther had abandoned the Office of a Friar before; neverthlesse he thus far declared himself, That a Preacher of the Gospel being orderly called thereunto, ought above all things to purify himself before he teacheth others, and if he be able with a good Conscience to live unmarried, it is his safest course to continue so, but in case he cannot abstain, and live chastly, he is then to marry, and to take a wife, for God hath provided such a Remedy for that Infirmity; I could here insert Luther's own Prayer before his Marriage, and the Reason why he took a Wife, which was, as he himself said to upbraid the Devil, and to confound the filthy incontinent life in Popery, which was so odious and abominable, that Pope Leo himself was taken out of the World at that time when he was committing Buggery with a Prostituted Boy. I could here also insert the lamentable Fruits of an unmarried Life in Priests and Nuns, which have been so notorious, that not onely in Rome and Germany, but in England also, and many other Places, there have been found in Ponds and Cellars many thousand heads of Infants, who thus desperately have been thrown away to preserve the Reputation of the Chastity of the Nuns and Friars: But I must returne from whence a little I have digressed.

Luther's Name growing Famous in Germany, for the great overthrows which he gave to many of the chiefest Professors of the Church of Rome, and to the Supremacy of the Pope himself, he was summoned by the Emperour to appear at the Imperial Diet at Worms, which when the Prince Electour of Saxony understood, he did so earnestly diswade him from it, alleaging that he should have the whole Christian world against him; and although he was ready and willing to defend him, yet Luther and he being but two persons, they were unable to oppose so great a Multitude; he there advised him not to undertake so dangerous a Journey, but to be warned by the example of John Hus; who although he had the Emperours Letters of Safe Conduct to preserve him, yet he was surprized there, and consumed by fire to ashes. Luther having heard the Elector to give him this council, made answer to him, that he must confesse, that (as the case now stood) he was too weak to defend him; neverthelesse he was resolved to go, and to defend the Elector; for although (said he) there be in Worms as many Devils as there be Tiles on all the Houses of the City; yet I am resolved to go thither, and to maintain what I have done and undertaken.

Many more suche examples may be given of his Courage, and his Confidence; at the last when he saw that by his endeavours the Gospel began to flourish and to be preached not onely in Germany but other Countryes, and that he had reaped the comfort of his Industry and his Study it pleased God to visit him with sicknesse, at which time, giving thanks unto God who had delivered him from so many Deceits and Assaults of his Merciless Enemies, he composed these following Verses in Latine . . .

Being a little recovered, he was advised to take the Ayre which accordingly he did, on the sixteenth of February in the year, 1546, at what time, he said, when I come again to Wittembergh, I will be lodged in a Coffin, and will surrender to the Worms a fat Luther to feed upon, and so it fell out, for two days afterwards he was translated from this life unto a better, and perceiving himself to grow fainter and draw near unto his end, he called for Pen, Inke, and Paper, and wrote this verse following to lye as it were an Epitaph upon his own Tomb . . .

He lived sixty and three years, and was buried at Isleben (where he was born) on the 19th of February 1546.

Several Choice Prophecyes of the Incomparable and Famous Dr. Martin Luther as also, the Remarkable Prophecy of the Learned and Reverent Dr. Musculus, collected by R. C. (London: Edward Thomas, 1666), 3–6.

Excerpt from *History of the Life, Writings, and Doctrines of Martin Luther*:

. . . The reformation was violent in its principle. Not content with expelling our monks and nuns from their convents, and priests from their presbyteries, it calumniated them in their morals and doctrines, and burned or scattered their books; especially those catholic pamphlets, where the writer—priest, monk, or jurist—contested the mission of Luther, attacked his doctrine, and laid open the privacy of his domestic life—in a word, exhibited him on the same theatre where he had unmercifully sported with so many others. When the drama of the reformation was accomplished, Luther remained alone on the scene, without rivals, and without opponents. To aid us in our appreciation of his adversaries, nothing remains but the writings which he left behind him, and in which he has traced so revolting a picture of the catholic priests; who, according to him, were degraded beings, destitute both of knowledge and discernment; miserable scholars, creeping on the path of Aristotle, whom they knew not how to read; sciolists, whose barbarous Latin would make a village pedant blush. They were Christians without the Gospel, and theologians, who claimed victory as soon as they had retailed a citation of St. Thomas, or of Scotus. In point of morals, they were luxurious and libidinous men, devoted to wine and sensual indulgence, the slaves of their appetites and of their avarice—who were ever ready to say with Judas: "What will you give me, and I will deliver him up." In their contest with Luther you scarcely hear a noble sentiment escape their lips; while their phraseology was confused without being varied, and as grotesque as the appearances of those who spoke. In a word, Luther exhibits them all equally destitute of talent and of morals.

Such, if you believe the reformer, were the men whom God raised up in the sixteenth century, to defend the church of Germany!

The heart sickens when assisting at these debates, in which Luther affects so lofty a tone, and makes his adversaries appear so contemptible. He is a giant; they are miserable dwarfs! His imagination is of fire, while that of his opponents is worn out even to exhaustion! They had at their command those living waters, from which Tertullian, Cyprian, and Lactantius imbibed floods of imagery, and yet, they dared not to approach them! We are ashamed to meet with cowled rhetoricians, who can neither read the Bible nor the Fathers. Faith which transfers mountains, does not unbind their tongues. Is it, then, astonishing that historians who have exclusively acquired a knowledge of the controversies of the sixteenth century from the works of Luther, should have so mean an idea of our doctors, and that they should compare him to St. Paul, and make of him another Arminius—a Roman of the olden time?

Luther drew caricatures, which have, unfortunately, been taken for exact likenesses; but at the time of the reformation, God was no more wanting to the church, than talent to her defenders. History obliges us to constitute ourselves judges of one who judged his brethren with such severity: this is our right. We have said to each of the dead, whom he entombed: "Arise!" We have awakened them from their sleep, and cited them to our tribunal. It will be seen whether their catholic dust does not cover illustrious shades—men of faith and genius, poetic and warm-hearted souls, worthy heirs of the glory of our school. It will be seen if every spark of genius was wanting in these monks whom Luther has misrepresented—if Eck was an ignorant theologian, Aleandro, a vulgar spirit, Cajetan an unskillful diplomatist, and Leo X, the Antichrist foretold by the prophets! It will be seen who sustained the arts, and watched over the ancient monuments of our faith; and if, as Kant has defined it, the beautiful is the symbol of morality, in studying the antagonism of the two creeds, the reader will say, which has best corresponded with the mission of Christ, which is one of civilization and social progress.

There is no writer, either catholic or protestant, who took part in these debates, whom we have not studied. To enable ourselves to judge of the reformer, we visited, one by one, those vast literary cities of the dead, where the remains of catholics and reformers commingle with each other . . .

. . . However high be the column on which they place their Stylite, we defy the apologists of Luther to exalt him to the dignity of affirmation: he was only capable of denying; and to deny is to destroy.

We speak thus, because we have read and studied him. Often has our heart been saddened, at beholding the use this man made of the gifts which God had bestowed on him. We have exposed his continual variations, the impossibilities that he gives for proofs, his prophecies of the downfall of the Roman church, his blasphemies against the chair of St. Peter, his outrages on tradition, and on the splendours of the priesthood and of human nature, and all his wondrous accumulation of gall which he disgorged on whoever did not believe in him. Often will the book be laid down; doubt will be entertained of the fidelity of our recital; but indisposed as the reader may be, he must believe, for our proof is always presented to him; nay more, he must adopt that from which he instinctively recoils, or renounce Luther. It is his language that we produce, and we give it such as it flowed from his pen. For a moment we hesitated, not daring to reproduce images which offend the eye and the ear; but we took courage, when we remembered that we were not to blush for Luther. If there be shame, let it fall on his front; we only regret, that like him, we had not some Latin lexicon or vocabulary at our command.

. . .

A man like Luther lives not only in his works and in the recitals of his adversaries, but wherever his foot has trod, it presses so heavily on the soil, as to leave in it imperishable traces of its passage. The life of the Saxon was at once a combat, and a pilgrimage through Germany. Enthusiastic souls go, now-a-days, to visit the places where the phenomena of the reformation occurred, as formerly our fathers made pilgrimages to the Holy Land. We ourselves have undertaken this journey. We have seen Eissleben, Eisnach, Erfurth, Worms, Spire, Wittenberg, while collecting memorials which might facilitate the understanding of our narration, and occasionally furnish us with useful information. When we are shown, with a degree of respect bordering on idolatry, the glass which the lips of

Luther touched, we ask our adversaries to explain the disdain which they have for the bones of the martyrs of our faith. If the protestant sits with emotion under the tree which sheltered Luther at Oppenheim, may not we be pardoned for kissing the hand of one of our saints, who preferred death to perjury; and when we are shown the drops of ink that fell from the ink-stand, which Luther threw at the head of the Devil, we shall surely have less difficulty in obtaining pardon for the superstitions of some of our plains.

Our history of Luther is a book of conviction and sincerity: let it be judged of in the same spirit in which it has been written.

J. M. V. Audin, excerpt from *History of the Life, Writings, and Doctrines of Martin Luther* (Philadelphia: Michael Kelly, 1841), iii–viii.

What Really Happened

The papacy enjoyed mixed success and varying degrees of power across late medieval and early modern Europe. From a low point in the 900s, the papacy became more ambitious and powerful during the 1000s. Medieval popes began advocating for a concept of papal monarchy which proposed that the pope was the supreme religious and secular ruler of Europe. All other rulers owed allegiance to him. Other rulers, of course, denied and resisted those claims. In what is now Germany, for example, the Holy Roman emperors fought wars against papal allies with both the sword and the pen. The kings of France later picked up similar arguments. At first, the papacy was quite successful. Under Pope Innocent III at the turn of the year 1200, the papacy undoubtedly enjoyed the peak of its power. Innocent deposed the king of England, gained strong control over extensive lands in Italy, became the ward for the child emperor Frederick II, and oversaw a church council to establish greater cohesion in the Christian faith across Europe. After Innocent's death, subsequent popes struggled to maintain his legacy. The emperor and other kings regained their footing. By the year 1300, Pope Boniface VIII attempted the same sorts of arguments and alliances that his predecessor had pursued a century before. Boniface sought to thwart the ambitions of King Philip the Fair of France. Boniface failed. In 1307, the papacy moved its capital from Rome to Avignon, a city owned by the pope but very much under the protection of the king of France.

Popes between 1300 and 1550 would have loved to possess the powers that modern myths contend they had. For example, living in Avignon, the pope's Italian lands fell apart—he could not control his own territories, let alone the rulers of Europe! It took until the mid-1400s for the pope to finally return to Rome permanently. Popes in the 1300s and 1400s had limited control over the writings and even basic religious practices of Europeans. In an age before print, only handwritten manuscripts existed and there would be only a few copies of them. Those manuscripts then circulated in small geographical areas. The pope simply did not have the mechanism to evaluate texts—he had no police force and the famous Inquisition did not gain much power or influence anywhere until the very late 1400s. Theoretically, Christianity was uniform and under the guidance of the pope and church traditions. But in practice, it too was regional and often outside of the pope's control. Many priests themselves lacked the training to know "correct" doctrine from "incorrect" doctrine, and their episcopal superiors may or may not have regularly visited the parishes to check up on them. Some of the more urban areas possessed structures to monitor and enforce general guidelines, but in the vast rural stretches of the European continent communities practiced variations of Christianity that conformed to varying degrees of "official" practice.

The myth of an all-powerful late medieval and early modern pope has its roots in the realities and propaganda of the sixteenth and later centuries. By 1500, the Church had been discussing and implementing reforms for centuries, with varying degrees of success. In addition, the Church, by 1500, had granted various degrees of control over local churches to secular rulers. However, problems continued and so did calls for reform, the most famous and enduring among them being the calls of Martin Luther and his many followers. Writings by these reformers presented an image of the pope, cardinals, monks, and other religious figures as wicked and in possession of more power than they actually had. In response to these challenges from Protestants, the Church doubled down on its long-standing efforts at reform. Many of those reforms focused on ensuring a new emphasis on uniformity in belief. Thus, new institutions were created or old institutions were given new powers and/or new impetus to police the writings and beliefs of people. As with everything else, these changes had mixed success across different Catholic lands. But the image presented by supporters and opponents alike was of a Church with a clear set of beliefs that could be enforced by almost any means necessary. This image was a new development of the later 1500s, and while it did not exactly reflect reality, it has endured in myths to this day.

PRIMARY SOURCE DOCUMENTS

Medieval and early modern arguments about papal supremacy featured strong statements of papal power, such as "Unam sanctam," excerpted earlier in this chapter. However, those texts only present half the story. For every text proclaiming the power of the pope, another text rejects those arguments. These contrary texts argued that the pope's power was subordinate to that of secular rulers like the emperor or king. They usually argued that the pope possessed absolute power in matters of religion, but all matters outside of that limited sphere was under the control of other rulers. The following text, like many others, argues for a limited view of papal power.

Although the proofs of both kinds of law (civil and canon) manifestly declare that the imperial dignity and power proceeded from of old directly through the Son of God, and that God openly gave him laws to the human race through the emperor and the kings of the world; and since the emperor is made true emperor by the election alone of those to whom it pertains, and needs not the confirmation or approbation of any one else, since on earth he has no superior as to the temporal things, but to him peoples and nations are subject, and our Lord Jesus Christ Himself ordered to be rendered unto God the things that are God's, and unto Caesar the things that are Caesar's; because, nevertheless, some, led by the blindness of avarice and ambition, and having no understanding of Scripture, but turning away from the path of right feeling into certain iniquitous and wicked deceptions, and, breaking forth into detestable assertions, do wage war against the prerogatives of the emperors, electors, and other princes, and of the faithful subjects of the empire, falsely asserting that the imperial dignity and power come from the pope and that he who is elected emperor is not true emperor or king unless he be first confirmed and crowned through the pope or the apostolic see; and since, through such wicked assertions and pestiferous dogmas the ancient enemy moves discord, excites quarrels, prepares dissensions and brings about seditions: therefore, for the purpose of averting such evil, by the counsel and consent of the electors and of the other princes of the empire we declare that the imperial dignity and power comes directly from God alone; and that, by the old and approved right and custom of the empire, after any one is chosen as emperor or king by the electors of the empire concordantly, or by the greater part of them, he is, in consequence of the election alone to be considered and called true king and emperor of the

Romans, and he ought to be obeyed by all the subjects of the empire. And he shall have full power of administering the laws of the empire and of doing the other things that pertain to a true emperor; nor does he need the approbation, confirmation, authority or consent of the apostolic see or of any one else.

And therefore we decree by this law, to be forever valid, that he who is elected emperor concordantly or by the majority of the electors, shall, in consequence of the election alone, be considered and regarded by all as the true and lawful emperor; and that he ought to be obeyed by all the subjects of the empire, and that he shall have, and shall be considered and firmly asserted by all to have and to hold, the imperial administration and jurisdiction and the plenitude of power.

Moreover, whatever persons shall presume to assert or say any thing contrary to these declarations, decrees or definitions, or any one of them; or to countenance those who assert or say anything; or to obey their mandates or letters or precepts: we deprive them from now on, and decree them to be deprived by the law and by the act itself, of all the fiefs which they hold from the empire, and of all the favours, jurisdictions, privileges and immunities granted to them by us or our predecessors. Moreover, we decree that they have committed the crime of high treason and are subject to all the penalties inflicted on those committing the crime of high treason. Given in our town of Frankfort on the 8th day of the month of August A.D. 1338.

"The Law 'Licet juris' of the Frankfort Diet of 1338 A.D.," in *Select Historical Documents of the Middle Ages*, edited by Ernest F. Henderson (London: George Bell and Sons, 1903), 437–39.

After about the year 1300, the popes struggled with control on three major fronts. Within the Italian peninsula, the popes lost control over the city of Rome itself as well as the middle part of the Italian peninsula (called the "Papal States"). Within the Church, "conciliarism" presented a major threat to the power of the papacy. Conciliarists argued that a council ought to hold the final say in Church affairs, with even the pope subject to their decisions. The fight against these arguments led to a third problem. Fifteenth-century popes granted increased control over church affairs to different rulers in order to keep their loyalty. Thus, for example, the king of France gained extensive formal powers over the Church in France. The following documents excerpted highlight some of the limitations on and challenges to papal power in late medieval and early modern Europe.

THE DECREE "SACROSANCTA" OF APRIL 6, 1415.

In the name of the Holy and indivisible Trinity; of the Father, Son and Holy Ghost. Amen.

This holy synod of Constance, forming a general council for the extirpation of the present schism and the union and reformation, in head and members, of the Church of God, legitimately assembled in the Holy Ghost, to the praise of Omnipotent God, in order that it may the more easily, safely, effectively and freely bring about the union and reformation of the church of God, hereby determines, decrees, ordains and declares what follows:

It first declares that this same council, legitimately assembled in the Holy Ghost, forming a general council and representing the Catholic Church militant, has its power immediately from Christ, and every one, whatever his state or position, even if it be the Papal dignity itself, is bound to obey it in all those things which pertain to the faith and healing of the said schism, and to the general reformation of the Church of God, in head and members.

It further declares that any one, whatever his condition, station, or rank, even if it be the Papal, who shall contumaciously refuse to obey the mandates, decrees, ordinances or instructions which have been, or shall be issued by this holy council, or by any other general council, legitimately summoned, which concern, or in any way relate to the above mentioned objects, shall, unless he repudiate his conduct, be subject to condign penance and be suitably punished, having recourse, if necessary, to the other resources of the law.

The Decree "Frequens" of Oct. 9, 1417.

A frequent celebration of general councils is an especial means for cultivating the field of the Lord and effecting the destruction of briars, thorns, and thistles, to-wit, heresies, errors and schism, and of bringing forth a most abundant harvest. The neglect to summon these, fosters and develops all these evils, as may be plainly seen from a recollection of the past and a consideration of existing conditions. Therefore, by a perpetual edict, we sanction, decree, establish and ordain that general councils shall be celebrated in the following manner, so that the next one shall follow the close of this present council at the end of five years. The second shall follow the close of that, at the end of seven years and councils shall thereafter be celebrated every ten years in such places as the Pope shall be required to designate and assign, with the consent and approbation of the council, one month before the close of the council in question, or which, in his absence, the council itself shall designate. Thus, with a certain continuity, a council will always be either in session, or be expected at the expiration of a definite time. This term may, however, be shortened on account of emergencies, by the Supreme Pontiff, with the counsel of his brothers, the cardinals of the Holy Roman Church, but it may not be hereafter lengthened. The place, moreover, designated for the future council may not be altered without evident necessity. If, however, some complication shall arise, in view of which such a change shall seem necessary, as, for example, a state of siege, a war, a pest, or other obstacles, it shall be permissible for the Supreme Pontiff, with the consent and subscription of his aid brethren or two-thirds of them (*duarum partium*) to select another appropriate place near one determined upon, which must be within the same country, unless such obstacles, or similar ones, shall exist throughout the whole nation. In that case, the council may be summoned to some appropriate neighboring place, within the bounds of another nation. To this the prelates, and others, who are wont to be summoned to a council, must betake themselves, as if that place had been designated from the first. Such change of place, or shortening of the period, the Supreme Pontiff is required legitimately and solemnly to publish and announce one year before the expiration of the term fixed, that the said persons may be able to come together for the celebration of the council within the term specified.

Excerpts from "The Decrees of 'Sacrosancta' and 'Frequens' of the Council of Constance," in *Translations and Reprints from the Original Sources of European History*, edited by James Harvey Robinson (Philadelphia: University of Pennsylvania Press, 1897), vol. 3, no. 6, pp. 30–32.

PRAGMATIC SANCTION OF BOURGES (1438)

The king declares that, according to the oath taken at their coronation, kings are bound to defend and protect the holy Church, its ministers and its sacred offices, and zealously to guard in their kingdoms the decrees of the holy fathers. The general council assembled at Basel to continue the work begun by the councils of Constance and Siena, and to labor for the reform of the Church, in both its head and members, having had presented to it numerous decrees and regulations, with the request that it accept them and cause them to be observed in the kingdom, the king has convened an assembly composed of prelates and other ecclesiastics representing the clergy of France and of the Dauphiné. He has presided in person over its deliberations, surrounded by his son, the princes of the blood, and the principal lords of the realm. He has listened to the ambassadors of the Pope and the council. From the examination of prelates and the most renowned doctors, and from the thoroughgoing discussions of the assembly, it appears that, from the falling into decay of the early discipline, the churches of the kingdom have been made to suffer from all sorts of insatiable greed; that the *réserve* and the *grâce expectative* have given rise to grievous abuses and unbearable burdens; that the most notable and best endowed benefices have fallen into the hands of unknown men, who do not conform at all to the requirement of residence and who do not understand the speech of the people committed to their care, and consequently are neglectful of the needs of their souls, like mercenaries who dream of nothing whatever but temporal gain; that thus the worship of Christ is declining, piety is enfeebled, the laws of the Church are violated, and buildings for religious uses are falling in ruin. The clergy abandon their theological studies, because there is no hope of advancement. Conflicts without number rage over the possession of benefices, plurality of which is coveted by an execrable ambition. Simony is everywhere glaring; the prelates and other collators are pillaged of their rights and their ministry; the rights of patrons are impaired; and the wealth of the kingdom goes into the hands of foreigners, to the detriment of the clergy.

Since, in the judgment of the prelates and other ecclesiastics, the decrees of the holy council of Basel seemed to afford a suitable remedy for all these evils, after mature deliberation, we have decided to accept them—some without change, others with certain modifications—without wishing to cast doubt upon the power and authority of the council, but at the same time taking account of the necessities of the occasion and of the customs of the nation.

1. General councils shall be held every ten years, in places to be designated by the pope.
2. The authority of the general council is superior to that of the pope in all that pertains to the faith, the extirpation of schism, and the reform of the Church in both head and members.
3. Election is reestablished for ecclesiastical offices; but the king, or the princes of his kingdom, without violating the canonical rules, may make recommendations when elections are to occur in the chapters or the monasteries.
4. The popes shall not have the right to reserve the collation of benefices, or to bestow any benefice before it becomes vacant.

5. All grants of benefices made by the pope in virtue of the *droit d'expectative* are hereby declared null. Those who shall have received such benefices shall be punished by the secular power. The popes shall not have the right to interfere by creation of canonships.
6. Appeals to Rome are prohibited until every other grade of jurisdiction shall have been exhausted.
7. Annates are prohibited.

Excerpts from "The Pragmatic Sanction of Bourges," in *A Source Book of Medieval History*, edited by Frederic Austin Ogg (New York: American Book, 1908), 395–97.

Further Reading

Bauer, Stefan. *The Invention of Papal History. Onofrio Panvinio Between Renaissance and Catholic Reform.* Oxford: Oxford University Press, 2019.

DeSilva, Jennifer Maria. *The Borgia Family. Rumor and Representation.* London: Routledge, 2020.

Eamon Duffy. *Saints and Sinners. A History of the Popes.* 3rd ed. New Haven, CT: Yale University Press, 2006.

Maxson, Brian Jeffrey. "Great Schism." In *The Encyclopedia of Diplomacy.* Hoboken, NJ: Wiley, 2018.

Mayer Thomas F. *The Roman Inquisition. A Papal Bureaucracy and Its Laws in the Age of Galileo.* Philadelphia: University of Pennsylvania Press, 2013.

Moore, John C. *Pope Innocent III (1160/61–1216). To Root Up and to Plant.* Leiden: Brill, 2003.

Murphy, Caroline. *The Pope's Daughter.* Oxford: Oxford University Press, 2005.

O'Brien, Emily. *The "Commentaries" of Pope Pius II (1458–1464) and the Crisis of the Fifteenth-Century Papacy.* Toronto: University of Toronto Press, 2015.

O'Malley, John W. *The Jesuits & the Popes: A Historical Sketch of Their Relationship.* Philadelphia: Saint Joseph's University Press, 2016.

Oxford Bibliographies Online. Available at https://www.oxfordbibliographies .com/ (For individual popes).

Partner, Peter. *The Lands of St. Peter: The Papal State in the Middle Ages and the Early Renaissance.* Berkeley: University of California Press, 1972.

Pattenden, Miles. *Pius IV and the Fall of the Carafa. Nepotism and Papal Authority in Counter-Reformation Rome.* Oxford: Oxford University Press, 2013.

Prodi, Paolo. *The Papal Prince. One Body and Two Souls: The Papal Monarchy in Early Modern Europe.* Translated by Susan Haskins. Cambridge: Cambridge University Press, 1987.

Setton, Kenneth. *The Papacy and the Levant, 1204–1571.* 4 vols. Philadelphia: American Philosophical Society, 1976.

Shea, Artigas, and William R. Shea. *Galileo in Rome.* Oxford: Oxford University Press, 2003.

Tierney, Brian. *The Crisis of Church and State, 1050–1300.* Toronto: University of Toronto Press, 1988.

Von Pastor, Ludwig. *The History of the Popes.* 40 vols. London: Routledge, 1899–1953.

Wright, A. D. *The Early Modern Papacy. From the Council of Trent to the French Revolution, 1564–1789.* London: Routledge, 2000.

6

The Moral Failures of the Catholic Church Made the Reformation Inevitable

What People Think Happened

By the medieval period, the Catholic Church had become all-powerful, corrupt, and concerned far more about its pocketbook than the souls of Christians. The problems began with local priests. These low-ranking, hypocritical members of the Church oppressed and exploited their helpless flocks. Only priests were allowed to read the Latin Bible. However, these men rarely knew Latin and thus they simply made things up or spoke gibberish to the ignorant masses. In theory, priests had to be celibate. In practice, community members were forced to pay to support the priest, his concubine, and their many children. Priests were exempt from secular laws. Church courts and church officials refused to punish one of their own. This resulted in all kinds of unspeakable vices. Immorality was the norm. Virtue was the exception.

The problems grew even worse among other members of the Church. Nuns turned their supposedly pious convents into brothels. Monks preyed upon any young woman unfortunate enough to come under their lecherous gaze. Bishops never visited their dioceses to enforce any sort of moral order. Instead, they collected wealth from people whose souls were in their care but about whom they cared nothing. Cardinals looked only to their own advancement and that of their families. The pope, probably

Woodcut print titled *Traffic in Indulgences*, by 16th-century German artist Hans Holbein the Younger, undated. Popular myth holds that early-modern people became so fed up with the corruption of the Church that they were looking to move on to a new faith. There is abundant evidence of popular discontent about perceived and real shortcomings among Church officials. However, there is also abundant evidence that people tended to separate those actions from their faith itself. The origins and success of the Protestant Reformations is a complicated story that defies easy explanations. (National Gallery of Art)

the worst of all, was little better than Satan himself. At best, he was a political leader concerned only for an increase in church lands. At worst, he drew upon his vast resources to reach ever greater heights of debauchery. Greed, corruption, and all other kinds of vice were committed with complete impunity. Each pope took a different name, but they were all blatantly hypocritical and greedy and this eroded all popular belief in the Church.

In the early sixteenth century, people had finally had enough. A papal representative arrived in northern Europe seeking to sell indulgences. In general terms, he used his forked tongue to cheat the innocent of their hard-earned money. He promised them that, for a price, he could offer, courtesy of the pope, certain salvation or at least a significant reduction in suffering for a deceased loved one. Martin Luther learned of this unprecedented outrage. He condemned it with ninety-five theses. People across Europe flocked to his Protestant banner to take back the salvation of their souls. It took decades, but the people defeated the irredeemable Catholic Church. The Church, in turn, humbled, met at the Council of Trent to try to reform its ways and keep at least some people within the Catholic fold. What emerged was certainly a more pious Catholic Church, but, unfortunately, this newfound piety also ushered in an unprecedented period of censorship and oppression.

How the Story Became Popular

The myth that a fed-up population grew increasingly dissatisfied with Catholicism and rejected its immorality in favor of the new teachings of Martin Luther has its roots in the early modern period itself. The early modern period was in many ways characterized by a violent civil war within Christianity. Many variations of Christianity originated, prospered, languished, or died out during the sixteenth and seventeenth centuries. Conflicts between groups adhering to different Christian denominations were constant, especially between defenders of Catholicism and defenders of other denominations. These fights frequently took on political dimensions. For example, by the latter 1500s England had become a Protestant state, and the king of Spain, a Catholic supporter, attempted to conquer it. Big and small territories and even individual communities fought against each other for the ability to claim lands for one Christian denomination or another.

These political fights coincided with aggressive arguments in print. Martin Luther's original writings often sought to discredit Catholicism while proposing his own vision of the true Christianity. Other writers similarly used the new technology of print to spread their arguments. Soon, literate Christians had access to an unprecedented array of religious arguments. But what about the majority of the population, most of whom were illiterate? They simply could not read theological treatises about predestination or the specific nature of the Eucharist. For them, Catholics and Protestants alike published short texts and broadsheets with blunt pictures. For example, Martin Luther could appear as a humble monk with a halo, whereas the pope and clergy could appear as villains fleecing rather than protecting their flock. Protestant writers, conversely, could be shown dancing with the devil. The consequence was that by around 1600, at the latest, many Europeans already believed in myths about the inevitability of the Reformation in the face of religious dissatisfaction and Catholic corruption.

Another component of this myth assumes that the actions of the early modern Catholic Church were primarily a response to the writings and actions of Protestants. The myth assumes that the Catholic Church remained mostly complacent throughout the late medieval period. That complacence, in turn, led to anger and dissatisfaction among Christians.

It was only after Martin Luther and his fellow reformers began spreading their ideas that the Catholic Church looked inward. The result was the calling of the Council of Trent in 1545. Reformers at Trent, then, finally implemented a number of major improvements. But this "Counter-Reformation," was too little too late.

Subsequent historical scholarship often reinforced these myths. Believers of a particular faith used history to show the righteousness of their own beliefs and the fallibilities of others' beliefs. That is, Catholics tended to write about the history of Catholicism, while Protestants tended to write about the history of their specific denomination. These men and women tended to present versions of the past that glorified their own religious heroes while villainizing others. Typically, they emphasized the good in one's own faith and the bad in someone else's faith, and they downplayed parts of the past that did not fit their narratives. History became as much about defending the actions of people of the past as it was about understanding them. The problem became so well known among specialists that, during the latter part of the twentieth-century, many historians began to openly declare their own religious backgrounds in their books in order to avoid potential criticisms of religious bias. Recent scholarship has begun to better reflect the evidence of a complex past, rather than articulating only what people want to be true. But, after so many centuries, the popular myth—particularly in predominantly Protestant areas—of a wicked Catholicism has long since taken hold.

PRIMARY SOURCE DOCUMENTS

The Decameron *was a collection of a hundred tales published in the mid-1300s. It is considered one of the great examples of early writing in Italian. Even today, some of the stories live up to their reputation for humor and entertainment, even as others very much reflect the period in which they were written. In the* Decameron, *Boccaccio adapted stories from a range of sources. He arranged the stories around a light narrative framework of a group of friends telling stories as they hid in the countryside from the plague. The stories are often bawdy and sometimes shocking. They repeatedly criticize the behaviors of members of the Church. However, the book never criticizes the Christian faith. The following excerpt is a short story taken from near the beginning of the text.*

. . . there was once a great merchant, a large dealer in drapery, a good man, most loyal and righteous, his name Jehannot de Chevigny, between whom and a Jew, Abraham by name, also a merchant, and a man of great wealth, was also most loyal and righteous, there subsisted a very close friendship. Now Jehannot, observing Abraham's loyalty and rectitude, began to be sorely vexed in spirit that the soul of one so worthy and wise and good should perish for want of faith. Wherefore he began in a friendly manner to plead with him, that he should leave the errors of the Jewish faith and turn to the Christian verity, which, being sound and holy, he might see daily prospering and gaining ground, whereas, on the contrary, his own religion was dwindling and was almost come to nothing. The Jew replied that he believed that there was no faith sound and holy except the Jewish faith, in which he was born, and in which he meant to live and die; nor would anything ever turn him therefrom. Nothing daunted, however, Jehannot some days afterwards began again to ply Abraham with similar arguments, explaining to him in such crude fashion as merchants use the reasons why our faith is better than the Jewish. And though the Jew was a great master in the Jewish law, yet, whether it was by reason of his friendship for Jehannot, or that the Holy Spirit dictated the words that the simple merchant used, at any rate the Jew began to be much interested in Jehannot's arguments, though still too staunch in his faith to suffer himself to be converted. But Jehannot was no less assiduous in plying him with argument than he was obstinate in adhering to his law, insomuch that at length the Jew, overcome by such incessant appeals, said: "Well, well, Jehannot, thou wouldst have me become a Christian, and I am disposed to do so, provided I first go to Rome and there see him whom thou callest God's vicar on earth, and observe what manner of life he leads and his brother cardinals with him; and if such it be that thereby, in conjunction with thy words, I may understand that thy faith is better than mine, as thou hast sought to shew me, I will do as I have said: otherwise, I will remain as I am a Jew." When Jehannot heard this, he was greatly distressed, saying to himself: "I thought to have converted him; but now I see that the pains which I took for so excellent a purpose are all in vain; for, if he goes to the court of Rome and sees the iniquitous and foul life which the clergy lead there, so far from turning Christian, had he been converted already, he would without doubt relapse into Judaism." Then turning to Abraham he said: "Nay, but, my friend, why wouldst thou be at all this labour and great expense of travelling from here to Rome? To say nothing of the risks both by sea and by land which a rich man like thee must needs run. Thinkest thou not to find here one that can give thee baptism? And so for any doubts that thou mayst have touching the faith to which I point thee, where wilt thou find greater masters and sages therein than here, to resolve thee of any question thou mayst put to them? Wherefore in my opinion this journey of thine is superfluous. Think that the prelates there are such as thou mayst have seen here, nay, as much better as they are nearer to the Chief Pastor. And so, by my advice thou wilt spare thy pains until some time of indulgence, when I, perhaps, may be able to bear thee company." The Jew replied: "Jehannot, I doubt not that so it is as thou sayst; but once and for all I tell thee that I am minded to go there, and will never otherwise do that which thou wouldst have me and hast so earnestly besought me to do." "Go then," said Jehannot, seeing that his mind was made up, "and good luck go with thee"; and so he gave up the contest because nothing would be lost, though he felt sure that he would never become a Christian after seeing the court of Rome. The Jew took horse, and posted with all possible speed to Rome; where on his arrival he was honourably received by his fellow Jews. He said nothing to any one of the purpose for which he had come; but began circumspectly to acquaint himself with the ways of the Pope and the cardinals and the other prelates and all the courtiers; and from what he saw for himself, being a man of great intelligence, or learned from others, he discovered that without distinction of rank they were all sunk in the most disgraceful lewdness, sinning not only in the way of nature but after the manner of the men of Sodom, without any restraint of remorse or shame, in such sort that, when any great favour was to be procured, the influence of the courtesans and boys was of no small moment. Moreover he found them one and all gluttonous, wine-bibbers, drunkards, and next after lewdness, most addicted to the shameless service of the belly, like brute beasts. And, as he probed the matter still further, he perceived that they were all so greedy and avaricious that human, nay Christian blood, and things sacred of what kind soever, spiritualities no less than temporalities, they bought and sold for money; which traffic was greater and employed more brokers than the drapery trade and all the other trades of Paris put together; open simony and gluttonous excess being glossed under such specious terms as "arrangements" and "moderate use of creature comforts," as if God could not penetrate the thoughts of even the most corrupt hearts, to say nothing of the signification of words, and would suffer Himself to be misled after the manner of men by the names of things. Which matters, with many others which are not to be mentioned, our modest and sober-minded Jew found by no means to his liking, so that, his curiosity being fully satisfied, he was minded to return to Paris; which accordingly he did. There, on his arrival, he was met by Jehannot; and the two made great cheer together. Jehannot expected Abraham's conversion least of all things, and allowed him some days of rest before he asked what he thought of the Holy Father and the cardinals and the other courtiers. To which the Jew forthwith replied: "I think God owes them all an evil recompense: I tell thee, so far as I was able to carry my investigations, holiness, devotion, good works or exemplary living in any kind was nowhere to be found in any clerk; but only lewdness, avarice, gluttony, and the like, and worse, if worse may be, appeared to be held in such honour of all, that (to my thinking) the place is a centre of diabolical rather than of divine activities. To the best of my judgment, your Pastor, and by consequence all that are about him devote all their zeal and ingenuity and subtlety to devise how best and most speedily they may bring the Christian religion to nought and banish it from the world. And because I see that what they so zealously endeavour does not come to pass, but that on the contrary your religion continually grows, and shines more and more clear, therein I seem to discern a very evident token that it, rather than any other, as being more true and holy than any other, has the Holy Spirit for its foundation and support. For which cause, whereas I met your exhortations in a harsh and obdurate temper, and would not become a Christian, now I frankly tell you that I would on no account omit to become such. Go we then to the church, and there according to the traditional rite of your holy faith let me receive baptism." Jehannot, who had anticipated a diametrically opposite conclusion, as soon as he heard him so speak, was the best pleased man that ever was in the world. So taking Abraham with him to Notre Dame he prayed the clergy there to baptise him. When they heard that it was his own wish, they forthwith did so, and Jehannot raised him from the sacred font, and named him Jean; and afterwards he caused teachers of great eminence thoroughly to instruct him in our faith, which he readily learned, and afterwards practised in a good, a virtuous, nay, a holy life.

Giovanni Boccaccio, excerpt from *The Decameron*, vol. 1, translated by J. M. Rigg (London: A. H. Bullen, 1903), 34–37.

Boccaccio's Decameron *is full of stories about monks, nuns, and churchmen acting in immoral and corrupt ways. Upon first reading, the text often suggests to readers that late medieval and early modern Christians were increasingly discontent with the Christianity of the Catholic Church. However, the stories in the* Decameron, *while often critical of various practices or behaviors, rarely criticized the role of the Church in salvation or its centrality to the Christian faith. Boccaccio certainly seems to have looked for reforms in the Church, but he never suggested breaking away from the Church or implied that others should do so. In the story that follows, note that Boccaccio mocks the piety of the nuns but never questions if pious nuns should exist or if pious nuns have a special relationship with God.*

There was formerly in our neighbourhood (and may be still) a convent of nuns, famous for their sanctity. In this convent (which shall be nameless, because I would not lessen the characters of its pious inmates), there were only eight young ladies, with an abbess; there was also a gardener to look after their fine garden, who, not being satisfied with his salary, made up his accounts with their steward, and returned to Lamporecchio, whence he came. Amongst many others who came to welcome him home, was a fine strapping young fellow named Masetto, who inquired of him where he had been to all that time? The honest man (whose name was Nuto) told him. The other inquired again in what capacity he served the convent? "I had the care of the garden," he replied, "and used to go to the wood for faggots; I drew water for them also, with such-like services; but my wages were so small that they would scarcely find me shoes; and besides they are all so young and giddy, that I could do nothing to please them; for when I have been in the garden, one would cry do this, and another do that, and another would take the spade out of my hand, and tell me 'that thing is in the wrong place,' and they have given me so much trouble altogether, that I have left them. The steward desired, at my departure, if I met with a proper person, to send him; but hang me if I do any such thing."

When Massetto heard this, he had a great desire to get among those nuns, guessing from what Nuto had said, that he might be able to gain his ends. But lest his purpose should be defeated, if he let the other into the secret, he said to him, "You did very right to come away: what has a man to do among so many women? He might as well be with as many devils: for it is not once in ten times they know what they would be at." After they had done talking together, Masetto began to contrive what method he should take to get introduced; and being assured that he could do all the work that Nuto had mentioned, he had no fears upon that account: all the danger seemed rather to be in his youth and person: whether he might not be rejected. After much reflection, he reasoned thus with himself: "I live far enough off and nobody knows me: suppose I feign myself dumb, they will certainly receive me then."

Resolved on this, without saying a word to any one about where he was going, he took an axe on his shoulder, and went like a poor man to the convent; and finding the steward in the court-yard, he made signs like a dumb person for a little bread, and that he would cleave wood if they had any occasion. The steward gave him something to eat, and afterwards showed him divers pieces of wood, which Nuto was not able to rend, but which Masetto, in a little time (being very strong), split all to pieces. The steward, having occasion to go to the woods, took him with him; where he made him fell several trees, load the ass with them, and drive it home before him: this Masetto did very well; and the steward wanting him for other things, he continued there for several days, till at length the abbess saw him, and asked the steward what the man did there? "Madam," he replied, "this is a poor man, deaf and dumb, who came the other day to ask charity, which I gave him, and he has done many things for us since: I believe, if he knows anything of gardening and could be prevailed upon to stay, that he might be of good service; for we want such a person, and he is strong, and will do what work we please: besides, there will be no fear of his seducing any of the young ladies."—"Why, truly," quoth the abbess, "you say right: see if he knows how to work, and if so, try to keep him; make much of him, give him a pair of shoes, and an old coat, and let him have his fill of victuals." This the steward promised to do. Masetto, who was at no great distance, but seemed busy in sweeping the court, heard all this, and said merrily to himself, "Yes, if you let me stay here, I'll do your business as it never was done before." The steward, who was aware that he knew how to work, now inquired of him by signs whether he was willing to stay: and Masetto having made signs that he was, the steward took him into the garden, showed him what he wished to have done, and left him there.

Now the nuns used to come every day to tease and laugh at the deaf and dumb gardener, and would say the naughtiest words in the world before him, imagining that he did not hear them: whilst the abbess took no notice of all this, thinking perhaps that as the man could not wag his tongue, he was equally harmless in other respects. One day when he had lain down to rest himself, two nuns, who were walking in the garden, came to the place where he pretended to be asleep: and as they stood looking at him, one, who was a little more forward than the other, said, "Could I be assured of your secrecy, I would tell you of a thought I have often had in my head, which might be of service to yourself." "You may speak safely," said the other, "for I will never disclose it." Then the first nun: "We are kept here in strict confinement, and not a man suffered to come near us, but our steward, who is old, and this dumb man. Now I have many and many a time heard from ladies who have come to see us, that all the other delights in the world are nothing to what a woman enjoys in a man's arms. I have often therefore had it in my mind to try the experiment with this dumb fellow, since no other is to be had; besides he is the fittest in the world for our purpose, being such an idiot, that he cannot expose us if he would; what is your opinion?"—"Alas!" quoth the other, "what is that you say? Do not you know that we have promised our virginity to God?"—"Oh! But sister," she replied, "how many things do we promise every day, which we never perform? If we have promised, there will be others found that shall be more punctual."—"But, if we should be with child, what would become of us then?"—"You think of the worse before it happens: it will be time enough to talk of that when it comes: there are a thousand ways of managing in such a case, that nobody will ever be the wiser, unless we ourselves make the discovery."—"Well, then," said the second nun, who was even more curious than her friend to know what sort of an animal a man might be; "how shall we contrive this matter!"—"You see," replied the other, "it is about mid-day, and I believe our sisters are all asleep; let us look round the garden, and if nobody be in it, what have we to do, but for one of us to lead him into yonder arbour, whilst the other keeps watch. He is such a fool that we can do what we like with him."

Masetto heard all this, and was quite ready to gratify the ladies, but waited until one of them should come and rouse him from his pretended sleep. The two nuns having assured themselves that nobody could see them, she who had been the first to move in the affair went and shook the gardener. He got up, the nun playfully took him by the hand, and led him, grinning and laughing like an idiot, to the arbour, where without giving her much trouble to explain her wishes he did what she wanted. Her curiosity having been satisfied, she made way for her companion, to whom Masetto, fool as he seemed, behaved equally well. Before they left him, each of them repeated the experiment once more, and they agreed in declaring that the result surpassed all that they could have imagined. After this it may easily be guessed how frequent were their visits to the arbour, and how punctually they availed themselves of the fitting hours to take their diversion with the good-natured mute.

It chanced, however, one day that their proceedings were observed by one of the sisterhood, who immediately brought two others to witness them. At first the trio were for informing the lady abbess, but afterwards they changed their minds, entered into an arrangement with the detected pair, and became jointly interested with them in Masetto's services. There now remained but three nuns who were not privy to the secret; but in course of time they too came in various ways to share in it with the rest.

Finally the abbess, who as yet had no notion of these doings, was taking a walk all alone in the garden one very sultry day, and found Masetto stripped to his shirt and asleep on the broad of his back, under an almond tree, having, it seems, not much to do that day, because he had been hard at work all the night before. Just then the wind fluttered the loose end of his single garment, and the Abbess saw what immediately gave her a fit of the complaint then prevalent in the convent. Waking up Masetto she took him to her chamber, where she kept him close for some days, to the great mortification of the nuns, who complained loudly that the gardener did not come to his daily labour. She let him go at last, but often had him back again, and altogether engrossed more than her fair share of his attendance. Masetto began to find it no easy task to please so many mistresses, and was strongly of opinion that things would come to a bad pass with him if he continued dumb much longer. One night then, when he was with the abbess, his tongue was suddenly untied, and said he, "I have often heard say, madam, that one cock can do very well for ten hens, but that ten men can hardly with their best endeavours satisfy one woman, whereas I have to serve nine. I can't stand it any longer. I'm fairly worn out with what I have done already; so please either to let me go my way in God's name, or put this matter to rights somehow."

The abbess was astounded to hear him speak. "Why, how is this?" she said, "I thought you were dumb."—"So I was, madam, but not by nature. I had a long disorder which deprived me of my speech; and it was only this very night, thanks be to God, that I felt it come back to me." The abbess believed this tale, or feigned to do so, and asked him what he meant by saying that he had nine women to satisfy. Masetto explained the whole case to her; and she, like a discreet abbess, instead of sending him away, resolved to come to an understanding with her nuns, and devise with them how they might keep such a good gardener without incurring any scandal. A full and unreserved explanation soon took place between all parties, and the old steward happening to die very opportunely, Masetto was, with his own consent, unanimously chosen to fill the vacant place, and his duties were so apportioned that he could discharge them without inordinate fatigue. At the same time the people of the neighbourhood were made to believe that through the prayers of the sisterhood, and through the merits of the saint to whom the convent was dedicated, the man who had been so long dumb had recovered his speech. Under the new steward's management the convent became a little nursery for the propagation of the monastic order, but everything was so quietly done that there never was any talk about it until after the death of the abbess, when Masetto, being now in years and wealthy, was desirous of returning home.

His desire was readily complied with: and thus, taking no care for his children, but bequeathing them to the place where they were bred and born, he returned a wealthy man to his native place, which he had quitted with nothing but an axe over his shoulder, having had the wit to employ the season of his youth to good purpose.

Giovanni Boccaccio, excerpt from *The Decameron*, translated by Léopold Flameng (Philadelphia: G. Barrie, 1881), 123–27.

People criticized members of the Church hierarchy for not being as pious as they felt they should be. However, most people also believed that no matter how bad a priest or religious figure was, the parish could rest assured that God would let even a sinful person successfully perform the rites of the Church. Thus, for example, a notoriously sinful priest, according to period belief, could still administer the sacrament to his parishioners, hear their confessions, and issue penance. The quality of the chosen vessel did not taint the actions or miracles performed. Some groups, such as the Waldensians, rejected this idea and were deemed heretics. The following passage—from "Against the Waldensians" reveals the common late medieval and early modern Catholic belief about the efficacy of sinful priests. The text was written to attack Waldensian heretics.

Since the sin of adultery does not take from a king the royal dignity, if otherwise he is a good prince who righteously executes justice in the earth, so neither can it take the sacerdotal dignity from the priest, if otherwise he performs the sacraments rightly and preaches the word of God. Who doubts that a licentious king is more noble than a chaste knight, although not more holy? . . . No one can doubt that Nathaniel was more holy than Judas Iscariot; nevertheless Judas was more noble on account of the apostleship of the Lord, to which Judas and not Nathaniel was called.

But thou, heretic, wilt say: "Christ said to his disciples, 'Receive ye the Holy Ghost. Whosesoever sins ye remit, they are remitted unto them'; therefore the priest who does not receive the Holy Ghost because he is wicked cannot absolve." Even if a wicked priest has neither charity nor the Holy Ghost as a private man, nevertheless his priesthood is worthy as far as the efficacy of the sacraments goes, though he himself may be unworthy of the priesthood.

For example, a red rose is equally red in the hands of an emperor or of a dirty old woman; likewise a carbuncle in the hand of a king or of a peasant; and my servant cleans the stable just as well with a rusty iron hoe as with a golden one adorned with gems. No one doubts that in the time of Elijah there were many swans in the world, but the Lord did not feed the prophet by swans, but by a black crow. It might have been pleasanter for him to have had a swan, but he was just as well fed by a crow. And though it may be pleasanter to drink nectar from a golden goblet than from an earthen vessel, the draught intoxicates just the same, wherever it comes from.

Excerpt from "Against the Waldensians," in *Readings in European History*, edited by James Harvey Robinson (Boston: Ginn, 1904), vol. 1, pp. 383–84.

Throughout the 1300s and 1400s, writers frequently criticized the failure of individuals within the Church hierarchy or in holy orders and urged them to live up to Christian morals. Some of the best-known examples of such writers were John Wycliffe, John Huss, and Girolamo Savonarola. Writers during the Protestant Reformation built upon the ideas of these earlier thinkers, even as Protestants introduced novel points of their own and benefited from technological and political changes during the sixteenth century. In the following letter, the humanist Poggio Bracciolini describes the execution of Jerome of Prague—a key ally of John Huss—at the Council of Constance in 1416. The recipient of Poggio's letter, Leonardo Bruni, responded by warning his friend to be careful with his sympathies.

Soon after my return from Baden to Constance, the cause of Jerome of Prague, who was accused of heresy, came to a public hearing. The purport of my present letter is to give you an account of this trial, which must of necessity be a matter of considerable interest, both on account of the importance of the subject, and the eloquence and learning of the defendant. I must confess that I never saw any one who in pleading a cause, especially a cause on the issue of which his own life depended, approached nearer to that standard of ancient eloquence, which we so much admire. It was astonishing to witness with what choice of words, with what closeness of argument, with what confidence of countenance he replied to his adversaries. So impressive was his peroration, that it is a subject of great concern, that a man of so noble and excellent a genius should have deviated into heresy. On this latter point however I cannot help entertaining some doubts. But far be it from me to take upon myself to decide in so important a matter. I shall acquiesce in the opinion of those who are wiser than myself.

Do not however imagine that I intend to enter into the particulars of this cause. I shall only touch upon the more remarkable and interesting circumstances, which will be sufficient to give you an idea of the learning of the man.

Many things having been alleged against the prisoner as proofs of his entertaining heretical notions, and the council being of opinion, that the proof was sufficiently strong to warrant further investigation, it was ordered that he should publicly answer to every particular of the charge. He was accordingly brought before the council. But when he was called upon to give in his answers, he for a long time refused so to do; alleging, that he ought to be permitted to speak generally in his defence, before he replied to the false imputations of his adversaries. This indulgence was however denied him. Upon which, standing up in the midst of the assembly—What gross injustice is this! Exclaimed he, that though for the space of three hundred and forty days, which I have spent in filth and fetters, deprived of every comfort, in prisons situated at the most remote distances from each other, you have been continually listening to my adversaries and slanderers, you will not hear me for a single hour! The consequence of this is, that while on the one hand, every one's ears are open to them, and they have for so long a time been attempting to persuade you that I am a heretic, an enemy of the true faith, a persecutor of the clergy; and on the other hand, I am deprived of every opportunity of defending myself; you have prejudged my cause, and have in your own minds condemned me, before you could possibly become acquainted with my principles. But, says he, you are not Gods, but men, not immortals, but mortals, liable to error, and subject to imperfection. We are taught to believe that this assembly contains the light of the world, the prudent men of the earth. You ought therefore to be unremittingly careful not to do anything rashly, foolishly or unjustly. I indeed, who am pleading for my life, am a man of little consequence; nor do I say what I do say through anxiety for myself (for I am prepared to submit to the common lot of mortality)—but I am prompted by an earnest desire, that the collective wisdom of so many eminent men may not, in my person, violate the laws of justice. As to the injury done to myself, it is comparatively of trifling consequence; but the precedent will be pregnant with future mischief. These and many other observations he made with great eloquence; but he was interrupted by the murmurs and clamours of several of his auditors. It was decreed, that he should first answer to the charges exhibited against him, and afterwards have free liberty of speech. The heads of the accusation were accordingly read from the desk. When, after they had been proved by testimony, he was asked whether he had any remarks to make in his defence, it is incredible with what skill and judgment he put in his answers. He advanced nothing unbecoming a good man; and if his real sentiments agreed with his professions, he was so far from deserving to die, that his principles did not even give just ground for the slightest offence. He denied the whole impeachment, as a fiction invented by the malice of his enemies. Amongst others an article was read, which accused him of being a detractor of the apostolic see, an oppugner of the Roman pontiff, an enemy of the cardinals, a persecutor of prelates, and an adversary of the Christian clergy. When this charge was read, he arose, and stretching out his hands, he said in a pathetic tone of voice, Fathers! to whom shall I have recourse for succour? Whose assistance shall I implore? Unto whom shall I appeal, in protestation of my innocence?—Unto you?—But these my persecutors have prejudiced your minds against me, by declaring that I entertain hostility against all my judges. Thus have they artfully endeavoured, if they cannot reach me by their imputations of error, so to excite your fears, that you may be induced to seize any plausible pretext to destroy your common enemy, such as they most falsely represent me to be. Thus, if you give credit to their assertion, all my hopes of safety are lost. He caused many to smart by the keenness of his wit, and the bitterness of his reproaches. Melancholy as the occasion was, he frequently excited laughter, by turning to ridicule the imputations of his adversaries. When he was asked what were his sentiments concerning the sacrament, he replied, that it was by nature bread; but that at the time of consecration, and afterwards, it was the true body of Christ, &c. according to the strictest orthodoxy. Then some one said, but it is reported that you have maintained, that there remains bread after consecration. True, said Jerome, there remains bread at the baker's. When one of the order of preaching friars was railing against him with uncommon asperity, he said to him— Hold thy peace, hypocrite! When another swore by his conscience, this, said he, is a very safe mode of deceiving. One man, who was particularly inveterate against him, he never addressed but by the title of ass or dog. As, on account of the number and importance of the articles exhibited against him, the cause could not be determined at that sitting, the court adjourned to another day, on which the proofs of each article of impeachment were read over, and confirmed by more witnesses. Then he arose and said, since you have attended so diligently to my adversaries, I have a right to demand that you should also hear me with patience. Though many violently objected to this demand, it was at length conceded to him that he should be heard in his defence. He then began by solemnly praying to God, so to influence his mind, and so to inspire his speech, that he might be enabled to plead to the advantage and salvation of his soul. He then proceeded thus—I know, most learned judges, that many excellent men have been most unworthily dealt with, overborne by false witnesses, and condemned by the most unjust judgements. Illustrating this position by particular instances he began with Socrates. . . . Coming down to the time of John the Baptist and our Saviour, he observed, that all are agreed that they were unjustly condemned, upon false charges, supported by false witnesses. He next quoted the case of Stephen, who was put to death by the priests; and reminded the assembly that all the apostles were condemned to die, as seditious movers of the people, contemners of the gods, and workers of iniquity. He maintained that it was a scandalous thing that one priest should be unjustly condemned by another; that it was still more scandalous that a college of priests should be guilty of this crime; and that it was most scandalous of all, that it should be perpetuated by a general council. Nevertheless he proved from history that these circumstances had actually occurred. Upon these topics he enlarged in so impressive a manner, that every body listened to him with fixed attention. But as the weight of every cause rests upon the evidence by which it is supported, he proved, by various arguments, that no credit was due to the witnesses who deposed against him, more especially as they were instigated to give evidence against him by hatred, malevolence, and envy. He then so satisfactorily detailed the causes of the hatred which he imputed to his prosecutors, that he almost convinced his judges of the reasonableness of his objections against their testimony. His observations were so weighty, that little credit would have been given to the depositions of the witnesses for the prosecution, in any other cause except in a trial for heresy. He moreover added, that he had voluntarily come to the council, in order to defend his injured character; and gave an account of his life and studies, which had been regulated by the laws of duty and of virtue. He remarked, that holy men of old were accustomed to discuss their differences of opinion in matters of belief, not with a view of impugning the faith, but of investigating the truth—that St. Augustine and St. Jerome had thus differed in opinion, and had upon some points even held contrary sentiments, without any suspicion of heresy. All the audience entertained hopes that he would either clear himself by retracting the heresies which were objected to him, or supplicate pardon for his errors. But he maintained that he had not erred, and that therefore he had nothing to retract. He next began to praise John Huss, who had been condemned to the flames, calling him a good, just, and holy man, a man who had suffered death in a righteous cause. He professed that he himself also was prepared to undergo the severest punishment with an undaunted and constant mind, declaring that he submitted to his enemies, and to witnesses who had testified such shameful falsehoods; who would however, on some future day, give an account of what they had said, to a God who could not be deceived. When Jerome made these declarations, the assembly was affected with the greatest sorrow; for every body wished, that a man of such extraordinary talents should repent of his errors and be saved. But he persisted in his sentiments, and seemed to court destruction. Dwelling on the praises of John Huss, he said, that he entertained no principles hostile to the constitution of the holy church, and that he only bore testimony against the abuses of the clergy, and the pride and pomp of prelates: for that since the patrimony of the church was appropriated first to the poor, then to strangers, and lastly to the erection of churches, good men thought it highly improper that it should be lavished on harlots, entertainments, dogs, splendid garments, and other things unbecoming the religion of Christ . . .

Poggio Bracciolini, excerpt from "Letter to Leonardo Bruni," in *The Life of Poggio Bracciolini*, edited by W. M. Shepherd (Liverpool: Harris Brothers, 1837), 69–77.

While crucial for understanding commonly held myths about the Italian Renaissance that are prevalent even today, Jacob Burckhardt's The Civilization of the Renaissance in Italy *had little to say about the sixteenth century and the Reformations. Burckhardt accepted as fact the corruption and dissatisfaction within the Church during the decades before the Reformations. He suggested that, in Italy, movement away from the Church may have been rooted in a new sense of individualism that he argued characterized Italian society and culture during the time. The following excerpt shows Burckhardt's assumptions about the pre-Reformation church, which mirror many current misconceptions, and also points to some of Burckhardt's explanations.*

The morality of a people stands in the closest connection with its consciousness of God, that is to say, with its firmer or weaker faith in the divine government of the world, whether this faith looks on the world as destined to happiness or to misery and speedy destruction. The infidelity then prevalent in Italy is notorious, and whoever takes the trouble to look about for proofs, will find them by the hundred. Our present take, here as elsewhere, is to separate and discriminate; refraining from an absolute and final verdict.

The belief in God at earlier times had its source and chief support in Christianity and the outward symbol of Christianity, the Church. When the Church became corrupt, men ought to have drawn a distinction, and kept their religion in spite of all. But this is more easily said than done. It is not every people which is calm enough, or dull enough, to tolerate lasting contradiction between a principle and its outward expression. But history does not record a heavier responsibility than that which rests upon the decaying Church. She set up as absolute truth and by the most violent means, a doctrine which she had distorted to serve her own aggrandisement. Safe in the sense of her inviolability, she abandoned herself to the most scandalous profligacy, and, in order to maintain herself in this state, she levelled mortal blows against the conscience and the intellect of nations, and drove multitudes of the noblest spirits, whom she had inwardly estranged, into the arms of unbelief and despair.

Here we are met by the question: Why did not Italy, intellectually so great, react more energetically against the hierarchy; why did she not accomplish a reformation like that which occurred in Germany, and accomplish it at an earlier date?

A plausible answer has been given to this question. The Italian mind, we are told, never went further than the denial of the hierarchy, while the origin and vigour of the German Reformation was due to its positive religious doctrines, most of all to the doctrines of justification of faith and of the inefficacy of good works.

It is certain that these doctrines only worked upon Italy through Germany, and this not till the power of Spain was sufficiently great to root them out without difficulty, partly by itself and partly by means of the Papacy, and its instruments. Nevertheless, in the earlier religious movements of Italy, from the Mystics of the thirteenth century down to Savonarola, there was a large amount of positive religious doctrine which, like the very definite Christianity of the Huguenots, failed to achieve success only because circumstances were against it. Mighty events like the Reformation elude, as respects their details, their outbreak and their development, the deductions of the philosophers, however clearly the necessity of them as a whole may be demonstrated. The movements of the human spirit, its sudden flashes, its expansions and its pauses, must for ever remain a mystery to our eyes, since we can but know this or that of the forces at work in it, never all of them together.

The feeling of the upper and middle classes in Italy with regard to the Church at the time when the Renaissance culminated, was compounded of deep and contemptuous aversion, of acquiescence in the outward ecclesiastical customs which entered into daily life, and of a sense of dependence on sacraments and ceremonies. The great personal influence of religious preachers may be added as a fact characteristic of Italy.

That hostility to the hierarchy, which displays itself more especially from the time of Dante onwards in Italian literature and history, has been fully treated by several writers . . .

We have been quoting from an author who wrote in earnest, and who by no means stands alone in his judgment. All the Italian literature of that time is full of ridicule and invective aimed at the begging friars. It can hardly have been doubted that the Renaissance would soon have destroyed these two Orders, had it not been for the German Reformation, and the Counter-Reformation which that provoked. Their saints and popular preachers could hardly have saved them. It would only have been necessary to come to an understanding at a favourable moment with a Pope like Leo X, who despised the Mendicant Orders. If the spirit of the age found them ridiculous or repulsive, they could no longer be anything but an embarrassment to the Church. And who can say what fate was in store for the Papacy itself, if the Reformation had not saved it?

. . .

These modern men, the representatives of the culture of Italy, were born with the same religious instincts as other mediaeval Europeans. But their powerful individuality made them in religion, as in other matters, altogether subjective, and the intense charm which the discovery of the inner and outer universe exercised upon them rendered them markedly worldly. In the rest of Europe religion remained, till a much later period, something given from without, and in practical life egoism and sensuality alternated with devotion and repentance. The latter had no spiritual competitors, as in Italy, or only to a far smaller extent.

Further, the close and frequent relations of Italy with Byzantium and the Mohammedan peoples had produced a dispassionate tolerance which weakened the ethnographical conception of a privileged Christendom. And when classical antiquity with its men and institutions became an ideal of life, as well as the greatest of historical memories, ancient speculation and skepticism obtained in many cases a complete mastery over the minds of Italians.

Since, again, the Italians were the first modern people of Europe who gave themselves boldly to speculations on freedom and necessity, and since they did so under violent and lawless political circumstances, in which evil seemed often to win a splendid and lasting victory, their belief in God began to waver, and their view of the government of the world became fatalistic. And when their passionate natures refused to rest in the sense of uncertainty, they made a shift to help themselves out with ancient, oriental, or mediaeval superstition. They took to astrology and magic.

Finally, these intellectual giants, these representatives of the Renaissance, show, in respect to religion, a quality which is common in youthful natures. Distinguishing keenly between good and evil, they yet are conscious of no sin. Every disturbance of their inward harmony they feel themselves able to make good out of the plastic resources of their own nature, and therefore they feel no repentance. The need of salvation thus becomes felt more and more dimly, while the ambitions and the intellectual activity of the present either shut out altogether every thought of a world to come, or else cause it to assume a poetic instead of a dogmatic form.

When we look on all this as pervaded and often perverted by the all-powerful Italian imagination, we obtain a picture of that time which is certainly more in accordance with truth than are vague declamations against modern paganism. And closer investigation often reveals to us that underneath this outward shell much genuine religion could still survive. . . .

That religion should again become an affair of the individual and of his own personal feeling was inevitable when the Church became corrupt in doctrine and tyrannous in practice, and is a proof that the European mind was still alive . . .

Jacob Burckhardt, excerpt from *The Civilization of the Renaissance in Italy*, translated by S. G. C. Middlemore (London: S. Sonnenschein, 1904), 456–91.

What Really Happened

The causes of the Protestant Reformations were complicated and tied, in part, to the perceived failings of the Church; but the Reformations were not inevitable and were, in fact, part of a long tradition of calls for reform. In the 1000s, people were already targeting corruption and hypocrisy among church officials. By the latter part of the 1100s, new clusters of people had founded new religious groups, like the Franciscan and Dominican orders, which strove to spread piety through preaching and living holy lives. These and other groups enjoyed tremendous success. Many members of new religious orders joined the ranks of Catholic saints. By the fifteenth century, people were concerned that the success of these groups had led them too far from their original missions of poverty, piety, and preaching. Thus, new "observant" groups were founded that sought to reemphasize a strict commitment to a holy life of preaching, piety, and poverty. Beyond new religious orders, church councils had been regularly called to reform church teachings and churchmen. In 1215, for example, the Fourth Lateran Council required all priests to be competent in Latin and to actively practice church teachings so that they could better tend to their spiritual flock. Councils aimed at reform and renewal continued to take place up to the time when Martin Luther famously sparked the Protestant movements.

In addition to formal attempts at reform, ordinary people believed that their existent faith led to salvation. Thus, although many thought that those in the Church should be acting differently, the same people also aimed their complaints at specific people or positions, not at their faith itself. People believed the formal church played an essential role in their salvation. They believed that a priest needed to baptize a baby immediately after birth so that if the baby died, they could still find salvation by entering the essential covenant with God. People believed that the Church played a key role in other parts of their faith. Their local priest possessed the power from God to reenact the Last Supper. He performed the miracle of turning the bread and wine into the body and blood of Christ during the Mass. A church official possessed the power to hear a confession from a parishioner and provide penance to atone for sinful action. As death approached, a priest could perform extreme unction so that the dying person could arrive before God with as clean a soul as possible. There is no doubt that people felt frustration toward religious figures, but they also seem to have separated that frustration from their fundamental belief in their Christian faith and the role of the Church in it.

Finally, many other factors contributed to the success of the Protestant Reformations. These other factors helped ensure that the ideas of Luther spread and took root on a scale that previous heresies had failed to achieve. Some of the heretical movements of the past centuries had been rooted out and destroyed. Others had survived but were largely contained in smaller geographical areas. During those earlier centuries, ideas had spread via word of mouth or handwritten texts. Both these were methods of transmission that moved slowly. By contrast, Martin Luther wrote his ideas in a period when print was beginning to take off in Europe. In previous centuries, even the most popular authors saw, at most, a few hundred copies of their works; Luther's texts, however, numbered in the tens of thousands after only a few years. In addition, politics in sixteenth-century Europe was simply different compared to what it had been in previous centuries: Conflicts were bigger and involved more wide-ranging areas. Consequently, alliances and enmities were broader and far reaching.

Intellectual trends were also different, with a focus on revisiting sources in their original languages. Learned people tried to understand texts as they had originally been written, rather than with the sorts of additions, typos, omissions, and other changes that were inevitable after centuries of handwritten copies. The list could go on. Martin Luther offered a challenge to some of the central tenets of Christianity, and he did so in an age that could transmit those challenges on an unprecedented scale.

PRIMARY SOURCE DOCUMENTS

Abundant evidence exists to document the sincerity and piety of late medieval people in the years before the Protestant Reformations. In addition, Church officials knew about perceived and actual problems with corruption and immorality during the late medieval and early modern periods. Repeatedly, the Church summoned councils that issued decrees condemning various practices and presenting or reconfirming views on how Church officials should act while in office. In the years directly preceding Martin Luther's first publications, the pope summoned a council in Rome. One primary objective of the council was political: the papacy and its political allies wished to render a recent pro-French council moot and to attack the power of the French king. However, the council also addressed areas of reform. The following excerpts provide a sample of decrees aimed at improving the officials and leaders of the Church.

Julius, bishop, servant of servants of God, with the approval of the sacred council, for an everlasting record. The supreme maker of things, the creator of heaven and earth, has willed by his ineffable providence that the Roman pontiff preside over the christian people in the chair of pastoral supremacy, so that he may govern the holy Roman, universal church in sincerity of heart and deeds and may strive after the progress of all the faithful. We may therefore regard it as suitable and salutary that, in the election of the said pontiff, in order that the faithful may look upon him as a mirror of purity and honesty, all stain and every trace of simony shall be absent, that men shall be raised up for this burdensome office who, having embarked in the appropriate manner and order in a due, right and canonical way, may undertake the steering of the barque of Peter and may be, once established in so lofty a dignity, a support for right and good people and a terror for evil people; that by their example, the rest of the faithful may receive instruction on good behaviour and be directed in the way of salvation, that the things which have been determined and established by us for this, in accordance with the magnitude and seriousness of the case, may be approved and renewed by the sacred general council; and that the things so approved and renewed may be communicated, so that the more frequently they are upheld by the said authority, the more strongly they shall endure and the more resolutely they shall be observed and defended against the manifold attacks of the devil. Formerly, indeed, for great and urgent reasons, as a result of important and mature discussion and deliberation with men of great learning and authority, including cardinals of the Roman church, excellent and very experienced persons, a document on the following lines was issued by us . . .

Julius, bishop, servant of the servants of God, for an everlasting record. From a consideration that the detestable crime of simony is forbidden by both divine and human law, particularly in spiritual matters, and that it is especially heinous and destructive for the whole church in the election of the Roman pontiff, the vicar of our lord Jesus Christ, we therefore, placed by God in charge of the government of the same universal church, despite being of little merit, desire, so far as we are able with God's help, to take effective measure for the future with regard to the aforesaid things, as we are bound to, in accordance with the necessity of such an important matter and the greatness of the danger. With the advice and unanimous consent of our brothers, cardinals of the holy Roman church, by means of this our constitution which will have permanent validity, we establish, ordain, decree and define, by apostolic authority and the fullness of our power, that if it happens (which may God avert in his mercy and goodness towards all), after God has released us or our successors from the government of the universal church, that by the efforts of the enemy of the human race and following the urge of ambition or greed, the election of the Roman pontiff is made or effected by the person who is elected, or by one or several members of the college of cardinals, giving their votes in a manner that in any way involves simony being committed—by the gift, promise or receipt of money, goods of any sort, castles, offices, benefices, promises obligations—by the person elected or by one or several other persons, in any manner or form whatsoever, even if the election resulted in a majority of two-thirds or in the unanimous choice of all the cardinals, or even in a spontaneous agreement on the part of all, without a scrutiny being made, then not only is this election or choice itself null, and does not bestow on the person elected or chosen in this fashion any right of either spiritual or temporal administration, but also there can be alleged and presented, against the person elected or chosen in this manner, by any one of the cardinals who has taken part in the election, the charge of simony, as a true and unquestionable heresy, so that the one elected is not regarded by anyone as the Roman pontiff.

A further consequence is that the person elected in this manner is automatically deprived, without the need of any other declaration of his cardinal's rank and of all other honours whatsoever . . . and that the elected person is to be regarded as, and is in fact, not a follower of the apostles but an apostate and, like Simon, a magician and a heresiarch, and perpetually debarred from each and all of the above-mentioned things . . .

[. . .] As we ponder how heavy is the burden and how damaging the loss to the vicars of Christ on earth that counterfeit elections would be, and how great the hurt they could bring to the Christian religion, especially in these very difficult times when the whole Christian religion is being disturbed in a variety of ways, we wish to set obstacles to the tricks and traps of Satan and to human presumption and ambition, so far as it is permitted to us, so that the aforesaid letter shall be better observed the more clearly it is established that it has been approved and renewed by the mature and healthy discussion of the said sacred council, by which it has been decreed and ordained, though it does not need any other approval for its permanence and validity.

. . .

5 May 1514

Leo, bishop, servant of the servants of God, with the approval of the sacred council . . .

. . . When we notice, out of solicitude for our said pastoral office, that church discipline and the pattern of a sound and upright life are worsening, disappearing and going further astray from the right path throughout almost all the ranks of Christ's faithful, with a disregard for law and with exemption from punishment, as a result of the troubles of the times and the malice of human beings, it must be feared that, unless checked by a well-guided improvement, there will be a daily falling into a variety of faults under the security of sin and soon, with the appearance of public scandals, a complete breakdown. We desire, then, as far as it is permitted to us from on high, to check the evils from becoming too strong, to restore a great many things to their earlier observance of the sacred canons, to create with God's help and improvement in keeping with the established practice of the holy fathers, and to give—with the approval of the sacred Lateran council initiated for that reason, among others, by our predecessor of happy memory, pope Julius II, and continued by us— healthy guidance to all these matters.

. . . we rule and establish that henceforward . . . for vacant churches and monasteries . . . the person provided is to be of mature age, learning and serious character. . . and the provision is not to be made at someone's urging, by means of recommendation, direction or enforcement, or in any other way, unless it has seemed right to act differently on the grounds of advantage to the churches, prudence, nobility, uprightness, experience, lengthy contact with the curia (together with adequate learning), or service to the apostolic see . . .

. . .

. . . Since the cardinals of the holy Roman church take precedence in honour and dignity over all the other members of the church after the sovereign pontiff, it is proper and right that they be distinguished beyond all others by the purity of their life and the excellence of their virtues. On that account, we not only exhort and advise them but also decree and order that henceforth each of the cardinals following the teaching of the Apostle, so live a sober, chaste and godly life that he shines out before people as one who abstains not merely from evil but from every appearance of evil. In the first place, let him honour God by his works. Let all of them be vigilant, constant at the divine office and the celebration of masses, and maintain their chapels in a worthy place, as they were wont to do.

Their house and establishment, table and furniture, should not attract blame by display or splendour or superfluous equipment or in any other way, so as to avoid any fostering of sin or excess, but, as is right, let them deserve to be called mirrors of moderation and frugality . . .

. . . They are to visit at least once a year—in person if they have been present in the curia, and by a suitable deputy if they have been absent—the places of their titular basilica. They are, with due care, to keep themselves informed about the clergy and people of the churches subject to their basilica; they are to keep under review the divine worship and the properties of the said churches; above all, let them examine with care the lives of the clergy and their parishioners, and with a father's affection encourage one and all to live an upright and honourable life . . .

. . . Since every generation inclines to evil from its youth, and for it to grow accustomed from tender years towards good is the result of work and purpose we rule and order that those in charge of schools, and those who teach young children and youths, ought not only to instruct them in grammar, rhetoric, and similar subjects but also to teach those matters which concern religion, such as God's commandments, the articles of the faith, sacred hymns and psalms, and the lives of the saints . . .

. . . In order that clerics, especially, may live in continence and chastity according to canonical legislation, we rule that offenders be severely punished as the canons lay down.

. . . So that the stain and disease of abominable simony may be driven out for ever not only from the Roman curia but also from all Christian rule, we renew the constitutions issued by our predecessors, also in sacred councils, against simoniacs of this kind . . .

> Excerpts from "Decrees of the Fifth Lateran Council (1512–1517)," in *Decrees of the Ecumenical Councils*, edited by Norman Tanner (Washington, DC: Georgetown University Press, 1990), vol. 1, pp. 600–602, 614–15, 617–18, 621–23. Copyright held by T&T Clark, an imprint of Bloomsbury Publishing Plc.

Martin Luther's works differed from previous critiques of the Church in that he sought to change many central aspects of the faith. Whereas previous writers had argued matters such as how the priests and the pope needed to be more pious, Luther argued that no fundamental difference existed between people who took religious orders and people who did not. Previous reformers had argued that people needed to be more careful about choosing saints. Luther argued that sainthood was a myth. Previous reformers had argued that the Church needed to rely more on the Bible as well as other holy texts and decrees. Luther claimed that the Bible alone offered insights into the faith. Not everyone agreed with Luther, even in German areas. In 1521, the emperor summoned a council to which Luther was called to defend his teachings. The emperor and his councilors deemed Luther a heretic and confirmed the error of his writings, as the following excerpts from "The Edict of the Diet of the Worms (May, 1521)" reveal.

1. We, Charles V, by God's grace Roman emperor elect . . . salute and tender our gracious good wishes to each and all of our electors, princes . . . and all other beloved and faithful subjects of ours . . . of whatsoever rank they may be, to whom these our imperial letters, or a credible copy certified by a spiritual prelate or a public notary, may come or be announced.

2. Most reverence, honorable, and illustrious friends and relatives, devoted and loyal: as it pertains to our office of Roman emperor, not only to enlarge the bounds of the Holy Roman Empire, which our fathers of the German nation founded for the defense of the Holy Roman and Catholic Church, subduing unbelievers by the sword, through the divine grace, with much shedding of blood, but also, adhering to the rule hitherto observed by the Holy Roman Church, to take care that no stain or

suspicion of heresy should contaminate our holy faith within the Roman Empire, or, if heresy had already begun, to extirpate it with all necessary diligence, prudence, and discretion, as the case might demand;

3. Therefore we hold that if it was the duty of any of our ancestors to defend the Christian name, much greater is the obligation on us, inasmuch the unparalleled goodness of Almighty God has, for the protection and increase of his holy faith, endowed us with more kingdoms and lands and greater power in the Empire than any of our ancestors for many years . . .

4. Whereas, certain heresies have sprung up in the German nation within the last three years, which were formerly condemned by the holy councils and papal decrees, with the consent of the whole Church, and are now drawn anew from hell, should we permit them to become more deeply rooted, or, by our negligence, tolerate and bear with them, our conscience would be greatly burdened, and the future glory of our name would be covered by a dark cloud in the auspicious beginnings of our reign.

5. Since now without doubt it is plain to you all how far these errors and heresies depart from the Christian way, which a certain Martin Luther, of the Augustinian order, has sought violently and virulently to introduce and disseminate within the Christian religion and its established order, especially in the German nation, which is renowned as a perpetual destroyer of all unbelief and heresy; so that, unless it is speedily prevented, the whole German nation, and later all other nations, will be infected by this same disorder, and mighty dissolution and pitiable downfall of good morals, and of the peace and the Christian faith, will result.

. . .

9. And although, after the delivery of the papal bull and final condemnation of Luther, we proclaimed the bull in many places . . . Martin Luther has taken no account of it, nor lessened nor revoked his errors, nor sought absolution from his Papal Holiness or grace from the holy Christian Church; but like a madman plotting the manifest destruction of the holy Church, he daily scatters abroad much worse fruit and effect of his depraved heart and mind through very numerous books, both in Latin and German, composed by himself, or at least under his name, which are full of heresies and blasphemies, not only new ones but also those formerly condemned by holy councils.

10. Therein he destroys, overturns, and abuses the number, arrangement, and use of the seven sacraments, received and held for so many centuries by the holy Church, and in astonishing ways shamefully pollutes the indissoluble bonds of holy matrimony; and says also that holy unction is a mere invention. He desires also to adapt our customs and practice in

the administration of the most holy sacrament of the holy eucharist to the habit and custom of the condemned Bohemians. And he begins to attack confession—most wholesome for the hearts that are polluted or laden with sins—declaring that no profit or consolation can be expected from it. Finally, he threatens to write so much more fully of confession that (if it be allowed) not only will all who read his mad writings venture to say that confession is useless, but most of them declare that one should not confess at all.

11. He not only holds the priestly office and order in contempt, but also urges secular and lay persons to bathe their hands in the blood of priests; and he uses scurrilous and shameful words against the chief priest of our Christian faith, the successor of St. Peter and true vicar of Christ on earth, and pursues him with manifold and unprecedented attacks and invectives. He demonstrates also from the heathen poets that there is no free will, because all things are determined by an immutable decree.

12. And he writes that the mass confers no benefit on him for whom it is celebrated. Moreover he overthrows the custom of fasting and prayer, established by the holy Church and hitherto maintained. Especially does he impugn the authority of the holy fathers, as they are received by the Church, and would destroy obedience and authority of every kind. Indeed, he writes nothing which does not arouse and promote sedition, discord, war, murder, robbery, and arson, and tend towards the complete downfall of the Christian faith. For he teaches a loose, self-willed life, severed from all laws and wholly brutish; and he is a loose, self-willed man, who condemns and rejects all laws; for he has shown no fear or shame in burning publicly the decretals and canon law. And had he feared the secular sword no more than the ban and penalties of the pope, he would have committed much worse offenses against the civil law.

13. He does not blush to speak publicly against holy councils, and to abuse and insult them at will. Especially has he everywhere bitterly attacked the Council of Constance with his foul mouth, and calls it a synagogue of Satan, to the shame and disgrace of the whole Church and of the German nation. . . . And he has fallen into such madness of spirit as to boast that if Huss were a heretic then he is ten times a heretic.

14. But all the other innumerable wickednesses of Luther must, for brevity's sake, remain unreckoned. This fellow appears to be not so much a man as the wicked demon in the form of a man and under a monk's cowl. He has collected many heresies of the worse heretics, long since condemned and forgotten, together with some newly invented ones, in one stinking pool, under pretext of preaching *faith*, which he extols with

so great industry in order that he may ruin the true and genuine faith, and under the name and appearance of evangelical doctrine overturn and destroy all evangelical peace and love, as well as all righteous order and the most excellent hierarchy of the Church . . .

Excerpts from "The Edict of the Diet of Worms (May, 1521)," in *Readings in European History*, edited by James Harvey Robinson (Boston: Ginn, 1906), vol. 2, pp. 83–88.

Further Reading

Arnold, John H. *The Oxford Handbook of Medieval Christianity*. Oxford: Oxford University Press, 2014.

Bamji, Alexandra, Geert H. Janssen, and Mary Laven. *The Ashgate Research Companion to the Counter-Reformation*. Farnham: Ashgate, 2013.

Bossy, John. *Christianity in the West, 400–1700*. Oxford: Oxford University Press, 1985.

Burke, Peter. *Popular Culture in Early Modern Europe*. 3rd ed. Farnham: Ashgate, 2009.

Cameron, Euan. *The European Reformation*. Oxford: Oxford University Press, 1991.

Cameron, Euan. *Enchanted Europe. Superstition, Reason, & Religion, 1250–1750*. Oxford: Oxford University Press, 2010.

Duffy, Eamon. *The Stripping of the Altars. Traditional Religion in England 1400–1580*. 2nd ed. New Haven, CT: Yale University Press, 2005.

Frazier, Alison Knowles. *Possible Lives. Authors and Saints in Renaissance Italy*. New York: Columbia University Press, 2005.

Greengrass, Mark. *Christendom Destroyed. Europe, 1517–1648*. New York: Penguin, 2014.

Johnson, Sherri Franks. *Monastic Women and Religious Orders in Late Medieval Bologna*. Cambridge: Cambridge University Press, 2014.

MacCulloch, Diarmaid. *Reformation: Europe's House Divided 1490–1700*. New York: Penguin, 2003.

Mixson, James D., and Bert Roest. *A Companion to Observant Reform in the Late Middle Ages and Beyond*. Leiden: Brill, 2015.

Muir, Edward. *Civic Ritual in Renaissance Venice*. Princeton, NJ: Princeton University Press, 1981.

Oakley, Francis. *The Western Church in the Later Middle Ages*. Ithaca, NY: Cornell University Press, 1979.

O'Malley, John W. *Trent and All That. Renaming Catholicism in the Early Modern Era*. Cambridge, MA: Harvard University Press, 2000.

Ozment, Steven E. *The Age of Reform, 1250–1550*. New Haven, CT: Yale University Press, 1980.

Salonen, Kirsi, and Jussi Hanska. *Entering a Clerical Career at the Roman Curia, 1458–1471*. Farnham: Ashgate, 2013.

Scribner, R. W. *For the Sake of Simple Folk. Popular Propaganda for the German Reformation*. Cambridge: Cambridge University Press, 1981.

Strocchia, Sharon T. *Nuns and Nunneries in Renaissance Florence*. Baltimore: Johns Hopkins University Press, 2009.

Tanner, Norman. *The Church in the Later Middle Ages*. London: Bloomsbury, 2008.

7

Torture and Superstition Drove the Witch Hunts

What People Think Happened

Deep in a dark, damp dungeon an innocent woman cried out in pain. Dim torches flickered on moss-and-mold-covered rough-hewn bricks as a sadistic churchman calmly repeated his questions: "When did you meet with the devil?"; "How long have you been a witch?"; "Who are your associates?" The woman tried to muster the strength to reply to his questions. She tried to convince him that she was obviously not a witch, that she knew nothing of meetings with the devil nor did she know anyone who did. The churchman sighed and tightened the thumbscrews, or possibly the boot (a device that crushed one's foot), or perhaps some other means of torture meant to inflict maximum pain. The woman could take it no longer, and so began a familiar tale. She had met with the devil for a couple of years. The devil wore a black hat. Three associates in town had accompanied her. These were their names. The churchman nodded his head, already planning to seize the three new people the following day. It was obvious that they were all witches. The Church would find them, torture out a confession, and burn each of them.

This fictional story seeks to highlight some of the most common assumptions about the so-called early modern witch hunts. People, usually women, were accused of witchcraft for the most ludicrous of reasons. An accusation easily led to a conviction because courts were all too ready to accept even the most outlandish accusations, including orgies, dances

Title page of *Witches Apprehended...* showing a witch being dunked in a river, printed in London, 1613. Popular myth holds that an appalling legal system, misogyny, and a backwards way of thinking about the natural world brought about the witch hunts of the early modern period. Early-modern legal systems could indeed be cruel; misogyny was common; and early-modern people often did believe in very different things than people today. However, the causes, scope, continuation, and end of the witch hunts are both complicated and contested among historians. (Wellcome Library, London)

with the devil, and magic potions. To make matters worse, court officials, usually churchmen, always resorted to torture to ensure that a person confessed their so-called crimes. With confession in hand, the courts forced their captives to implicate even more innocent people. The acts of terror then moved to a stake on a public platform where the convicted witches were burned alive. This craze over witches seized Europe during the sixteenth and seventeenth centuries. Eventually, according to the myth, science progressed enough for people to realize the error of their ways. They realized that witchcraft was not real, and thus to accuse—let alone convict—another person of the crime was nonsense.

How the Story Became Popular

Much of what people think about early modern magic, witchcraft, and the so-called witch hunts derives from a combination of increasingly secular history writers and twentieth-century popular culture and literature. During the late seventeenth century and the eighteenth century, the early-modern witch hunts became a foil against which writers could show their enlightened rationality. They argued that the new skepticism toward old authorities and the birth of new empirical studies made it impossible to believe accusations of witchcraft. Now, the natural sciences showed that the world worked like a machine. Thus, all forces in nature had to have a place in that rational structure: witchcraft and spirits simply did not fit the new model. Those who still believed in them were viewed more with pity than with fear; the witch trials of previous centuries fell to the triumphant progress of science. People began to reject torture and to believe that the accused deserved to know their alleged crimes. They created new, enlightened legal systems to match these new beliefs. Then, they presented the older systems and beliefs as irrational, immoral, and infested with all sorts of horrors.

By the turn of the twentieth century, people already assumed that the witch trials were the height of religious fanaticism, irrationality, and barbaric cruelty. The 1900s then popularized some of the stereotypes that we associate with the witch trials. In 1939, for example, the classic movie *The Wizard of Oz* frightened viewers with the "Wicked Witch of the West" who largely conforms to modern stereotypes of "witch." There, actress Margaret Hamilton wore a long black garment that matched her wide-brimmed, black, pointed hat. Her hands clutched a broom. Her green skin continues to influence depictions of witches to this day. Other witches portrayed in the media added familiar variations, like a wart on their overly large noses or, perhaps, buckled shoes. In the 1970s and 1980s, the stereotypical image could even be applied to a male: In the animated TV series *The Smurfs*, for example, the warlock Gargamel has a large nose, wears all-black with patches on his garments, and keeps a bald head instead of wearing the common witch's hat.

Popular media has also linked unfair social and political persecution with the early modern witch hunts. The publication of Arthur Miller's play *The Crucible* has been particularly influential in this regard and turned the witch-craze in Salem, Massachusetts, into a common story. Writing in the early 1950s, Miller was responding to and commenting upon the attempts by the U.S. government to identify and prosecute communists. Like in the early modern witch trials, individuals were viewed as being in the league of an enemy of society (the devil in early modern witch trials and the USSR in the early 1950s) and often assumed to be guilty prior to their trial. The popularity of Miller's text brought these parallels to the attention of the American public. In another often-cited work, Margaret Murray claimed that the European witch hunts may have reflected the survival of an underground, uninterrupted devotion to ancient pagan gods. However, Murray's arguments for the continuation of hidden pagan cults from Antiquity into the early modern period have not held up to scholarly scrutiny. No evidence has come to light that the witch trials responded to widespread pagan practices of early modern people.

PRIMARY SOURCE DOCUMENTS

Belief in witchcraft and magic predated the early modern period. One particularly influential medieval text on the subject was a compilation of Arabic writings called Picatrix. It was translated as part of a broader trend of translating Arabic works into Latin, sometimes called the Twelfth-Century Renaissance. Picatrix proved influential for later readers and writers, especially those who were interested in using mysterious natural forces in the world toward practical ends. Much later, writers during the first half of the twentieth century, inspired by works like Picatrix, identified these sorts of inquiries by medieval people into the natural world as helping to lay the foundation for modern science. Lynn Thorndike wrote an influential work, A History of Magic and Experimental Science—During the First Thirteen Centuries of Our Era, *along these lines. The following excerpts come from Thorndike's discussions of magic in Picatrix.*

Picatrix divides into four books and is accompanied in the manuscripts by tables of contents which, however, are not as helpful as might be expected, since the work really has no plan and the division into books and chapters is quite arbitrary. In short, the work is a confused compilation of extracts from occult writings and a hodgepodge of innumerable magical and astrological recipes. The author states that he "has compiled this book," that he intends to set forth "in simple language" what past sages have concealed in cryptic words, and that he has spent some six years in reading two-hundred-and-twenty-four books by "ancient sages" . . .

. . . At the close of the first of its four books we are told that its contents are "the roots of the magic art" and that "without them one cannot become perfect in such arts." Throughout all four books such phrases are used as "magic works," "magic effects," "magical sciences," and "the operator of magic," and books of magic are cited by Abrarem (Abraham?), Geber, and Plato. It is true that the term necromancy is also employed frequently and a chapter devoted to its definition, and that astrological images and invocations of demons are the subjects most discussed. So in a way the work is primarily a treatise of astrological necromancy. But it is said on the supposed authority of Aristotle that the first man to work with such images and to whom spirits appeared was Caraphrebim, the inventor of the magic art. It is also affirmed that the science of the stars is the root of magic, that the forms of the planets or astronomical images "have power and marvelous effects in magic operations"; while after announcing his intention of listing "the secrets of ancient sages in the magic art," the first thing that our author divulges is that the influence of Saturn exceeds the influence of the moon. Evidently little distinction is made between astrology and magic. On the whole then, although magic is not defined at length in *Picatrix*, it seems justifiable to apply it as a general term covering the contents of the book, and to regard astronomical images and invocations of demons as two leading features of the magic art.

Picatrix regards magic as a science, as a superior branch of learning, to excel in which one must first master many other studies. He believes that the greatest philosophers of antiquity, such as Plato and Aristotle, have written books of magic. Hermes is also cited frequently. Our author also has a high appreciation of science which in his first chapter he declares to be God's greatest gift to man. "It always is making acquisitions and never diminishes; it ever elevates and never degenerates; it is always clear and never conceals itself."

Much use of natural objects is made in the various recipes of *Picatrix*. Here is one brief example: Adam the prophet says that if you take fourteen grains of the fruit of the laurel tree, dry them well and pulverize them and put the powder in a very clean dish in vinegar, and beat it with a twig from a fig tree, you can make anyone you wish possessed of demons by giving them this powder to drink. One chapter is especially devoted to "the virtues of certain substances produced from their own peculiar natures," and the author further explains that "in this section we shall state the marvelous properties of simple things, as well of trees as of animals and of minerals." Hermes is quoted as saying that there are many marvels for necromancy in the human body, and various parts thereof are often employed by Picatrix. Thus in making a magic mirror a suffumigation is employed of several products of the human body, namely, tears, blood, ear-wax, spittle, *sperma, stercus, urina*. Indeed, vile and obscene substances are in great demand for purposes of magic throughout the book. Picatrix, like the *De mirabilibus mundi*, considers heat an important force in magic and mentions both elemental and natural heat, the former referring to the use of the element fire in sacrifice, suffumigation, and the preparation of magic compounds, the latter designating the heat of digestion when samples or mixtures must be eaten to take effect.

Although we have found one chapter devoted to the virtues of simples, in actual magical procedure several things are generally combined, as in a suffumigation with fourteen dead bats and twenty-four mice, to give a comparatively simple example. On the supposed authority of Aristotle in a book written to Alexander, detailed instructions are given how to make four "stones" of great virtue and of elaborate composition by procedure more or less alchemistic. Indeed, there are listed all sorts of "confection," compounds, and messes, either to burn or to sacrifice or to eat or to drink or to smell of or to anoint oneself with, in order to bring various wonders to pass. The ingredients employed include different oils and drugs, butter, honey, wine, sugar, incense, aloes, pepper, mandragora, twigs, branches, adamant, lead, sulphur, gold, the brains of a hare, the blood of a wolf, the urine of an ass, the filth of a leopard, and various portions of such further animals as apes, cats, bears, and pigs. Besides the actual ingredients all sorts of receptacles and material paraphernalia are called into requisition: vessels, jars, vases, braziers, crosses, candles, crowns, and so on.

Much is said of the magician himself as well as of the materials which he employs. He should have faith in his procedure, put himself into an expectant and receptive mood, be diligent and solicitous. . . . It has already been implied that great stress is laid upon procedure in *Picatrix*. Extensive use is made of images of the person or thing concerned. . . . Ritual also plays an important part in the invocation of spirits. . . . Throughout *Picatrix* planets and spirits are closely associated. . . . Finally *Picatrix* devotes much space to astronomical images, which, engraved preferably upon gems in accordance with the aspect of the sky at some instant when the constellations are especially favorable, are supposed to receive the celestial influences at their maximum and store them up for future use. . . . Some of the results attributed to images and characters are to drive away mice, free captives, throw an army into a town, either render buildings safe and stable or impede the erection of them, the acquisition of wealth, making two persons fall in love, making men loyal to their lord, making the king angry with someone, curing a scorpion's sting, walking on water, assuming any animal form, causing rain in dry weather and preventing it in rainy weather, making the stars fall or sun and moon appear divided into many parts. The possessor of such images can further ascend into the air and take on the form of a falling star, or speak with the dead, or destroy an enemy or city, or traverse great distances in the twinkling of an eye. The aims of incantations, invocations, and recipes are similar, as has already been indicated in several cases. Ten "confections" are listed that stop evil tongues; eight, that generate discord and enmity; six, that cure impotency, if taken in food; seven, that induce a sleep like unto death; ten, that induce a sleep from which one never wakes. Others prevent dogs from barking at you, produce green tarantulas or red snakes, remove bothersome frogs from pools, cause water to burn and appear red, enable you to see small objects a long way off, make the winds and tempests obey you, deprive others of memory or sense or speech or sight or healing, and so on through a long list. The aims are infinitely varied, and are sometimes good, sometimes evil.

Lynn Thorndike, excerpts from *A History of Magic and Experimental Science—During the First Thirteen Centuries of Our Era* (New York: Macmillan, 1923), vol. 2, pp. 814–21.

Although the persecution of witches is often associated with the early modern "witch hunts," accusations of witchcraft had been around for centuries. Late medieval governments often took such accusations very seriously and both investigated and prosecuted those accused. At times, witchcraft accusations were used as a tool to settle scores with disliked neighbors or feuding family members. In such cases, it is impossible to evaluate the inner sincerity or beliefs of the people involved, but often there is no reason to doubt that historical people believed that somebody dabbling in mysterious diabolical powers had caused their problems. The excerpt below—taken from a text written in the mid-1400s—reveals some aspects of witch hunts that became more common a hundred years later.

I will relate to you some examples, which I have gained in part from the teachers of our faculty, in part from the experience of a certain upright secular judge, worthy of all faith, who from the torture and confession of witches and from his experiences in public and private has learned many things of this sort—a man with whom I have often discussed this subject broadly and deeply—to wit, Peter, a citizen of Bern, in the diocese of Lausanne, who has burned many witches of both sexes, and has driven others out of the territory of the Bernese. I have moreover conferred with one Benedict, a monk of the Benedictine order, who, although now a very devout cleric in a reformed monastery at Vienna, was a decade ago, while still in the world, a necromancer, juggler, buffoon, and strolling player, well-known as an expert among the secular nobility. I have likewise heard certain of the following things from the Inquisitor of Heretical Pravity at Autun, who was a devoted reformer of our order in the convent at Lyons, and has convicted many of witchcraft in the diocese of Autun.

Relating then two or three anecdotes derived from these sources, the theologian closes his answer with this one:

The same procedure was more clearly described by another young man, arrested and burned as a witch, although, as I believe, truly, penitent, who had earlier, together with his wife, a witch invincible to persuasion, escaped the clutches of the aforesaid judge, Peter. The aforesaid youth, being again indicted at Bern, with his wife, and placed in a different prison from hers, declared: "If I can obtain absolution for my sins, I will freely lay bare all I know about witchcraft, for I see that I have death to expect." And when he had been assured by the scholars that, if he should truly repent, he would certainly be able to gain absolution for his sins, then he gladly offered himself to death, and disclosed the methods of the primeval infection.

The ceremony, he said, of my seduction was as follows: First, on a Sunday, before the holy water is consecrated, the future disciple with his masters must go into the church, and there in their presence must renounce Christ and his faith, baptism, and the church universal. Then he must do homage to the *magisterulus,* that is, to the little master (for so, and not otherwise, they call the Devil). Afterward he drinks from the aforesaid flask; and, this done, he forthwith feels himself to conceive and hold within himself an image of our art and the chief rites of this sect. After this fashion was I seduced; and my wife also, whom I believe of so great pertinacity that she will endure the flames rather than confess the least whit of the truth; but, alas, we are both guilty. What the young man had said was found in all respects the truth. For, after confession, the young man was seen to die in great contrition. His wife, however, though convicted by the testimony of witnesses, would not confess the truth even under the torture or in death; but, when the fire was prepared for her by the executioner, uttered in most evil words a curse upon him, and so was burned.

Nider, excerpts from "Formicarius," ca. 1476, in *Translations and Reprints from the Original Sources of European History*, edited and translated by George L. Burr (Philadelphia: University of Pennsylvania Press, 1908), vol. 3, no. 4, pp. 6–7.

"The Hammer of Witches" was published by two churchmen around the year 1486, and it became a handbook for people responsible for interrogating and prosecuting accused witches. The text originated in a misogynistic society, but its prejudices against women were extreme even for the late fifteenth century. The work describes in detail the danger posed by witches, their usual traits, and how individuals charged with combatting them should proceed. In the excerpt below, the authors offer some instructions for using torture in the interrogations of people accused of witchcraft.

The method of beginning an examination by torture is as follows: First, the jailers prepare the implements of torture, then they strip the prisoner (if it be a woman, she has already been stripped by other women, upright and of good report). This stripping is lest some means of witchcraft may have been sewed into the clothing—such as often, taught by the Devil, they prepare from the bodies of unbaptized infants, [murdered] that they may forfeit salvation. And when the implements of torture have been prepared, the judge, both in person and through other good men zealous in the faith, tries to persuade the prisoner to confess the truth freely; but, if he will not confess, he bids attendants make the prisoner fast to the strappado or some other implement of torture. The attendants obey forthwith, yet with feigned agitation. Then, at the prayer of some of those present, the prisoner is loosed again and is taken aside and once more persuaded to confess, being led to believe that he will in that case not be put to death.

Here it may be asked whether the judge, in the case of a prisoner much defamed, convicted both by witnesses and by proofs, nothing being lacking but his own confession, can properly lead him to hope that his life will be spared—when, even if he confess his crime, he will be punished with death.

It must be answered that opinions vary. Some hold that even a witch of very ill repute, against whom the evidence justifies violent suspicion, and who, as a ringleader of the witches, is accounted very dangerous, may be assured her life, and condemned instead to perpetual imprisonment on bread and water, in case she will give sure and convincing testimony against other witches; yet this penalty of perpetual imprisonment must not be announced to her, but only that her life will be spared, and that she will be punished in some other fashion, perhaps by exile. And doubtless such notorious witches, especially those who prepare witch-potions or who by magical methods cure those bewitched, would be peculiarly suited to be thus preserved, in order to aid the bewitched or to accuse other witches, were it not that their accusations cannot be trusted, since the Devil is a liar, unless confirmed by proofs and witnesses.

Others hold, as to this point, that for a time the promise made to the witch sentenced to imprisonment is to be kept, but that after a time she should be burned.

A third view is, that the judge may safely promise witches to spare their lives, if only he will later excuse himself from pronouncing the sentence and will let another do this in his place . . .

But if, neither by threats nor by promises such as these, the witch can be induced to speak the truth, then the jailers must carry out the sentence, and torture the prisoner according to the accepted method, with more or less of severity as the delinquents' crime may demand. And, while he is being tortured, he must be questioned on the articles of accusation, and this frequently and persistently, beginning with the lighter charges—for he will more readily confess the lighter than the heavier. And, while this is being done, the notary must write down everything in his record of the trial—how the prisoner is tortured, on what points he is questioned, and how he answers.

And note that, if he confesses under the torture, he must afterward be conducted to another place, that he may confirm it and certify that it was not due alone to the force of the torture.

But, if the prisoner will not confess the truth satisfactorily, other sorts of tortures must be placed before him, with the statement that, unless he will confess the truth, he must endure these also. But, if not even thus he can be brought into terror and to the truth, then the next day or the next but one is to be set for a *continuation* of the tortures—not a *repetition*, for they must not be repeated unless new evidences be produced.

The judge must then address to the prisoners the following sentence: We, the judge, etc., do assign to you,   , such and such a day for the continuation of the tortures, that from your own mouth the truth may be heard, and that the whole may be recorded by the notary.

And during the interval, before the day assigned, the judge, in person or through approved men, must in the manner above described try to persuade the prisoner to confess, promising her (if there is aught to be gained by this promise) that her life shall be spared.

The judge shall see to it, moreover, that throughout this interval guards are constantly with the prisoner, so that she may not be left alone; because she will be visited by the Devil and tempted into suicide.

Excerpt from "The Witch-Hammer," in *Translations and Reprints from the Original Sources of European History*, edited and translated by George L. Burr (Philadelphia: University of Pennsylvania Press, 1908), vol. 3, no. 4, pp. 11–13.

The following heartbreaking passage records the examination of an accused witch in what is now Germany. The record is particularly striking because it also contains a note from the accused, Johannes Junius, to his daughter, in which he describes the process by which authorities extracted his false confession. This excerpt comes from real historical sources and conforms to many modern stereotypes about the early-modern witch hunts. Horrible incidents of this sort of witch hysteria did take place in early modern Europe. Some aspects of our modern myth, thus, have some truth, even though the myth tends to focus on extreme cases like this one.

. . . On Wednesday, June 28, 1628, was examined without torture Johannes Junius, Burgomaster at Bamberg, on the charge of witchcraft: how and in what fashion he had fallen into that vice. Is fifty-five years old, and was born at Niederwaysich in the Wetterau. Says he is wholly innocent, knows nothing of the crime, has never in his life renounced God; says that he is wronged before God and the world, would like to hear of a single human being who has seen him at such gatherings [as the witch-sabbaths].

Confrontation of Dr. Georg Adam Haan. Tells him to his face he will stake his life on it [*er wolle darauf leben und sterben*] that he saw him, Junius, a year and a half ago at a witch-gathering in the electoral council-room, where they ate and drank. Accused denies the same wholly.

Confronted with Hopffens Else. Tells him likewise that he was on Haupts-moor at a witch-dance; but first the holy wafer was desecrated. Junius denies. Hereupon he was told that his accomplices had confessed against him and was given time for thought.

On Friday, June 30, 1628, the aforesaid Junius was again without torture exhorted to confess, but again confessed nothing, whereupon, . . . since he would confess nothing, he was put to the torture, and first the *Thumb-screws* were applied. Says he has never denied God his Saviour nor suffered himself to be otherwise baptized; will again stake his life on it; feels no pain in the thumb-screws.

Leg-screws. Will confess absolutely nothing; knows nothing about it. He has never renounced God; will never do such a thing; has never been guilty of this vice; feels likewise no pain.

Is stripped and examined; on his right side is found a bluish mark, like a clover leaf, is thrice pricked therein, but feels no pain and no blood flows out.

Strappado. He has never renounced God, God will not forsake him; if he were such a wretch he would not let himself be so tortured; God must show some token of his innocence. He knows nothing about witchcraft . . .

On July 5, the above named Junius is without torture, but with urgent persuasions, exhorted to confess, and at last begins and confesses:

When in the year 1624 his law-suit at Rothweil cost him some six hundred florins, he had gone out, in the month of August, into his orchard at Friedrichsbronnen; and, as he sat there in thought, there had come to him a woman like a grass-maid, who had asked him why he sat there so sorrowful; he had answered that he was not despondent, but she had led him by seductive speeches to yield him to her will. . . . And thereafter this wench had change into the form of a goat, which bleated and said, "Now you see with whom you have had to do. You must be mine or I will forthwith break your neck." Thereupon he had been frightened, and trembled all over for fear. Than the transformed spirit had seized him by the throat and demanded that he should renounce God Almighty, whereupon Junius said, "God forbid," and thereupon the spirit vanquished through the power of these words. Yet it came straightway back, brought more people with it, and persistently demanded of him that he renounce God in Heaven and all the heavenly host, by which terrible threatening he was obliged to speak this formula. "I renounce God in Heaven and his host and will henceforward recognize the Devil as my God."

After the renunciation he was so far persuaded by those present and by the evil spirit that he suffered himself to be otherwise baptized in the evil spirit's name. The Morhauptin had given him a ducat as dower-gold, which afterward became only a potsherd.

He was then named Krix. His paramour he had to call Vixen. Those present had congratulated him in Beezlebub's name and said that they were now all alike. At this baptism of his there were among others the aforesaid Christiana Morhauptin, the young Geiserlin, Paul Glaser, [and others]. After this they had dispersed.

At this time his paramour had promised to provide him with money, and from time to time to take him to other witch-gatherings.

. . . Whenever he wished to ride forth [to the witch-sabbath] a black dog had come before his bed, which said to him that he must go with him, whereupon he had seated himself upon the dog and the dog had raised himself in the Devil's name and so had fared forth.

About two years ago he was taken to the electoral council-room, at the left hand as one goes in. Above at a table were seated the Chancellor, the Burgomaster Neydekher, Dr. George Haan, [and many others]. Since his eyes were not good, he could not recognize more persons.

More time for consideration was now given him. On July 7, the aforesaid Junius was again examined, to know what further had occurred to him to confess. He confesses that about two months ago, on the day after an execution was held, he was at a witch-dance at the Black Cross, where Beelzebub had shown himself to them all and said expressly to their faces that they must all be burned together on this spot, and had ridiculed and taunted those present . . .

Of crimes. His paramour had immediately after his seduction demanded that he should make away with his younger son Hans Georg, and had given him for this purpose a gray powder, this, however, being too hard for him, he had made away with his horse, a brown, instead.

His paramour had also often spurred him on to kill his daughter, . . . and because he would not do this he had been maltreated with blows by the evil spirit.

Once at the suggestion of his paramour he had taken the holy wafer out of his mouth and given it to her . . .

A week before his arrest as he was going to St. Martin's church the Devil met him on the way, in the form of a goat, and told him that he would soon be imprisoned, but that he should not trouble himself—he would soon set him free. Besides this, by his soul's salvation, he knew nothing further but what he had spoken was the pure truth on that he would stake his life. On August 6, 1628, there was read to the aforesaid Junius this his confession, which he then wholly ratified and confirmed, and was willing to stake his life upon it. And afterward he voluntarily confirmed the same before the court.

[So ended the trial of Junius, and he was accordingly burned at the stake. But it so happens that there is preserved in Bamberg a letter, in quivering hand, secretly written by him to his daughter while in the midst of his trial (July 24, 1628)]:

Many hundred thousand good-nights, dearly beloved daughter Veronica. Innocent have I come into prison, innocent have I been tortured, innocent must I die. For whoever comes into the witch prison must become a witch or be tortured until he invents something out of his head and—God pity him—bethinks him of something. I will tell you how it has gone with me. When I was the first time put to the torture, Dr. Braun, Dr. Kötzendörffer, and two strange doctors were there. Then Dr. Braun asks me, "Kinsman, how come you here?" I answer, "Through falsehood, through misfortune." "Hear you," he says, "you are a witch; will you confess it voluntarily? If not, we'll bring in witnesses and the executioner for you." I said "I am no witch, I have a pure conscience in the matter; if there are a thousand witnesses, I am not anxious, but I'll gladly bear the witnesses." Now the chancellor's son was set before me . . . and afterward Hoppfen Elss. She had seen me dance on Haupts-moor . . . I answered: "I have never renounced God, and will never do it—God graciously keep me from it. I'll rather bear whatever I must." And then came also—God in highest Heaven have mercy—the executioner, and put the thumb-screws on me, both hands bound together, so that the blood ran out at the nails and everywhere, so that for four weeks I could not use my hands, as you can see from the writing. . . . Thereafter they first stripped me, bound my hands behind me, and drew me up in the torture. Then I thought heaven and earth were at an end; eight times did they draw me up and let me fall again, so that I suffered terrible agony . . .

And this happened on Friday, June 30, and with God's help I had to bear the torture. . . . When at last the executioner led me back into the prison, he said to me: "Sir, I beg you, for God's sake confess something, whether it be true or not. Invent something, for you cannot endure the torture which you will be put to; and, even if you bear it all, yet you will not escape, not even if you were an earl, but one torture will follow after another until you say you are a witch. Not before that," he said, "will they let you go, as you may see by all their trials, for one is just like another." . . .

And so I begged, since I was in wretched plight, to be given one day for thought and a priest. The priest was refused me, but the time for thought was given. Now, my dear child, see in what hazard I stood and still stand.

I must say that I am a witch, though I am not, must now renounce God, though I have never done it before. Day and night I was deeply troubled, but at last there came to me a new idea. I would not be anxious, but, since I had been given no priest with whom I could take counsel, I would myself think of something and say it. It were surely better that I just say it with mouth and words, even though I had not really done it; and afterwards I would confess it to the priest, and let those answer for it who compel me to do it. . . . And so I made my confession, as follows; but it was all a lie.

Now follows, dear child, what I confessed in order to escape the great anguish and bitter torture, which it was impossible for me longer to bear.

[Here follows his confession, substantially as it is given in the minutes of his trial. But he adds:]

Then I had to tell what people I had seen [at the witch-sabbath]. I said that I had not recognized them. "You old rascal, I must set the executioner at you. Say—was not the Chancellor there?" So I said yes. "Who besides?" I had not recognized anybody. So he said: "Take one street after another; begin at the market, go out on one street and back on the next." I had to name several persons there. Then came the long street. I knew nobody. Had to name eight persons there. Then the Zinkenwert—one person more. Then over the upper bridge to the Georgthor, on both sides. Knew nobody again. Did I know nobody in the castle—whoever it might be, I should speak without fear. And thus continuously they asked me on all the streets, though I could not and would not say more. So they gave me to the executioner, told him to strip me, shave me all over, and put me to the torture. "The rascal knows one on the market-place, is with him daily, and yet won't name him." By that they meant Dietmeyer: so I had to name him too.

Then I had to tell what crimes I had committed. I said nothing. . . . "Draw the rascal up." So I said that I was to kill my children, but I had killed a horse instead. It did not help. I had also taken a sacred wafer, and had desecrated it. When I had said this, they left me in peace.

Now, dear child, here you have all my confession, for which I must die. And they are sheer lies and made-up things, so help me God. For all this I was forced to say through fear of the torture which was threatened beyond what I had already endured. For they never leave off with the torture till one confesses something; be he never so good, he must be a witch. Nobody escapes, though he were an earl. . . .

Dear child, keep this letter secret so that people do not find it, else I shall be tortured most piteously and the jailers will be beheaded. So strictly is it forbidden. . . . Dear child, pay this man a dollar . . . I have taken several days to write this: my hands are both lame. I am in a sad plight . . .

Good night, for your father Johannes Junius will never see you more, July 24, 1628.

[And on the margin of the letter he adds:]

Dear child, six have confessed against me at once: the Chancellor, his son, Neudecker, Zaner, Hoffmaisters Ursel, and Hoppfen Els—all false, through compulsion, as they have all told me, and begged my forgiveness in God's name before they were executed. . . . They know nothing but good of me. They were forced to say it, just as I myself was . . .

"The Witch-Persecution at Bamberg," in *Translations and Reprints from the Original Sources of European History*, edited and translated by George L. Burr (Philadelphia: University of Pennsylvania Press, 1908), vol. 3, no. 4, pp. 23–38.

What Really Happened

Popular myths about the early modern witch hunts tend to emphasize the most extreme examples, like the trial of Johannes Junius excerpted earlier. As such, they oversimplify the past. It is true that accusations of witchcraft were taken seriously throughout the early modern period. It is also true that thousands of individuals were convicted of the crime and executed for it. Torture could be a part of the interrogations of faultless people. But early modern people did work to try to root out obvious flaws in their judicial proceedings. They knew, for example, that people would confess to just about anything when tortured. Thus, they used torture in specific scenarios and required a second, uncoerced confession at a later time. Torture was rarely their first method of inquiry. Obviously, such a system remains abhorrent to modern senses of justice and due process. Obviously, an individual who confessed under torture could, and often did, confess later without torture simply to avoid the prospect of more pain. But to early modern sensibilities, physical pain was sometimes the only way to arrive at the truth. The stakes were high for early modern people. They thought that there were ways to tap into mysterious forces in the natural world to make things happen. The line between religion and magic, or between acceptable and unacceptable magical forces, was blurred, contested, and varied across social groups in early modern Europe. During the sixteenth and seventeenth centuries, some people became terrified that the devil was seeking worldly power by recruiting people to do his bidding. But when was a person part of Satan's legions and when was a person simply using the natural forces of the world?

Early modern people knew that some individuals abused the legal system by accusing their enemies of nefarious crimes or by blaming town outcasts for broken equipment or bad harvests. Consequently, officials tried to weed out false accusations or misplaced blame even as they took the existence and charge of witchcraft very seriously. It is a strange idea in our modern world, but for early modern people the threat of witches was very real: both Protestants and Catholics believed that witches were among us and could use the power of demons toward absolutely terrible ends. The fight against witches was a fight against the devil himself and his demonic minions. Historical systems and beliefs that are so different from our contemporary ones are easy to characterize and view with disdain and difficult to resituate into their historical contexts. It is hard to imagine the very real terror that people felt at the prospect that Satan was gathering an army of demons and witches who were difficult to identify without taking the most extreme measures.

Certainly, some aspects of the myths about witchcraft have elements of truth, even as the myth exaggerates or misconstrues the historical record. For example, modern stereotypes assume witches were women. The stereotypical witch cackles when she laughs, dresses in black, and probably has a cauldron sequestered in a secret part of her dank lair. Indeed, extensive scholarship over the past decades has confirmed that most people in most places in early modern Europe who were accused of witchcraft were women. However, this was not always the case. In parts of France and Scandinavia, for example, more men were accused than women. Thousands of people during the sixteenth and early seventeenth centuries were executed as convicted witches. But thousands more were accused and acquitted in the period by the judicial system. Stereotypes like a pointed black hat or a broomstick do not necessarily conform to early modern assumptions about witches. Early modern people did think that witches could possess a physical mark that revealed a pact with a demon. They thought witches could fly through the air, often by means of a pitchfork or an animal. People tended to think that witches used their flight as a means to convene at a social gathering known as a witch's sabbath. At that event, witches performed sacrilegious acts and the devil appeared often wearing a black hat.

The idea that the Scientific Revolution rooted out the superstitious belief in witches simply does not agree with the facts. Traditional historical thinking dates the start of the Scientific Revolution to people like Copernicus in Astronomy or Harvey in Biology, for example. But rather than putting an end to magical superstitions, changes in the natural sciences were contemporaneous with the explosion of accusations of witchcraft. Indeed, all men and women praised for their scientific innovations during the 1500s and 1600s lived in a world where witchcraft and magic and witch crazes and witch hunts were simply a part of life. Many of these individuals would have, like their contemporaries, accepted the existence of demons and devils, the dangerous and forbidden means of accessing their power, and accepted that witches needed to be stopped.

To twenty-first-century readers, such ideas may seem absurd, but in this and in so many other ways, people 400, 500, and 600 years ago thought about the world differently than we do. Early modern people believed that the Christian Bible depicts a God very much involved in the daily progression of people's lives. It also describes attempts by wicked forces to tempt the pious and to intervene directly in human affairs. People witnessed the power of rituals every day: In church services, they saw priests go through prescribed actions and say specific words and thus turn ordinary bread and wine into the actual body and blood of Christ. Such rituals were less pronounced in Protestant faiths, but the emphasis upon the literal truth of biblical passages similarly showed that demons were a force that could be summoned, controlled, and combatted. Knowing—*assuming*—that such things were real meant that pious and responsible people had a duty to root out the devil's henchmen. It was, in their minds, difficult and dangerous work: people could falsely accuse others; witches worked in secret; the devil was a powerful adversary.

Historians have offered numerous reasons for what may have caused accusations of witchcraft to eventually, more or less, die out. For one thing, witch crazes thrived in places of local control. When external powers came to town and took over trials and investigations, accusations and executions generally slowed and stopped. By the latter part of the 1600s, centralized political structures had increased in strength to the point that external forces more closely policed local judicial proceedings. By the eighteenth century, people too were beginning to replace old assumptions about the world with new ones. It was much harder to find educated people who viewed the devil and demons as an existential threat. Whereas people had once agreed upon real magical forces, they increasingly began to distance themselves from such "superstitious" beliefs. An accusation of witchcraft changed from being a grave concern into something best dismissed as nonsense. Yet, even today some traces of the old assumptions remain. Popular culture continues to tell stories about demons and pacts with the devil. Many Christian denominations continue to accept the reality and danger of demons. The power of the stars and astrology still holds credibility among many people.

One other, final myth is the belief that the early modern witch hunts reveal evidence of an unbroken tradition of pagan beliefs stretching back to Antiquity. The myth claims that accusations of witchcraft revealed, to some degree, accurate descriptions of widespread actions by practicing pagans. Those practices were built upon beliefs that had been passed down orally for 1,000 years. Through much of the twentieth century, historians looked into the accuracy of this claim. However, in recent decades historians have dismissed this argument because there simply is no evidence to support it. It is certainly true that parts of Europe, even as late as the early 1700s, retained some rituals and beliefs seemingly at odds with the then mainstream forms of Christianity. But the most straightforward and plausible explanation for these kinds of practices probably lies in the medieval and early modern periods themselves, rather than in ancient religions. Moreover, it is true that many confessions and accusations about witchcraft have similar descriptions and themes. Yet, this was probably because early modern people spoke with one another about witchcraft and educated people were taught to look for similar sorts of things.

PRIMARY SOURCE DOCUMENTS

In 1486, Giovanni Pico della Mirandola proposed 900 theses that he argued could unify knowledge and remove apparent contradictions among different historical thinkers. He published a preface to this work, which scholars have called "On the Dignity of Man." In this preface, Pico argued that humans had the ability, through their way of life and their studies, to either sink to the level of rocks or rise temporarily to unity with God. Pico used his preface to introduce some of the types of authors and works included in his 900 theses. One section of his work focused on the knowledge of magicians. The following excerpts help to show just how differently people in early modern Europe viewed the world. Pico assumed that magical forces were woven into the world. They came in two varieties. There was a natural, acceptable kind of magic and an unacceptable type that used dangerous forces. These different assumptions, rather than an irrationality, naivete, or "simple" nature, help explain how and why people accepted the existence and danger of witches in early modern Europe and were willing to use extreme measures like torture to try to root them out.

I have also proposed theorems dealing with magic, in which I have indicated that magic has two forms, one of which depends entirely on the work and authority of demons, a thing to be abhorred, so help me the God of truth, and a monstrous thing. The other, when it is rightly pursued, is nothing else than the utter perfection of natural philosophy. While the Greeks make mention of both of them, they call the former γοητεία, in no way honoring it with the name of magic; the latter they call by the characteristic and fitting name of μαγεία, as if it were a perfect and most high wisdom. For, as Porphyry says, in the Persian tongue *magus* expresses the same idea as "interpreter" and "worshiper of the divine" with us. Moreover, Fathers, the disparity and unlikeness between these arts is great, nay, rather, the greatest possible. The former not only the Christian religion but all religions and every well-constituted state condemn and abhor. The latter all wise men, all peoples devoted to the study of heavenly and divine things, approve and embrace. The former is the most deceitful of arts; the latter a higher and more holy philosophy. The former is vain and empty; the latter, sure, trustworthy, and sound. Whoso has cherished the former has ever dissembled, because it is a shame and a reproach to an author; but from the latter the highest renown and glory of letters was derived in ancient days, and almost always has been. No man who was a philosopher and eager to study the good arts has ever been a student of the former; but Pythagoras, Empedocles, Democritus, and Plato all traveled to study the latter, taught it when they returned, and esteemed it before all others in their mysteries. As the former is approved by no reasonable arguments, so is it not by established authors; the latter, honored by the most celebrated fathers, as it were, has in particular two authors: Zamolxis, whom Abaris and Hyperborean copied, and Zoroaster, not him of whom perhaps you are thinking but him who is the son of Oromasius.

If we ask Plato what the magic of both these men was, he will reply, in his *Alcibiades,* that the magic of Zoroaster was none other than the science of the Divine in which the kings of the Persians instructed their sons, to the end that they might be taught to rule their own commonwealth by the example of the commonwealth of the world. He will answer, in the *Charmides,* that the magic of Zamolxis was that medicine of the soul through which temperance is brought to the soul as through temperance health is brought to the body. In their footsteps Charondas, Damigeron, Apollonius, Osthanes, and Dardanus thereafter persevered. Homer persevered, whom I shall sometime prove, in my *Poetic Theology,* to have concealed this philosophy beneath the wanderings of his Ulysses, just as he had concealed all others. Eudoxus and Hermippus persevered. Almost all who have searched through the Pythagorean and Platonic mysteries have persevered. Furthermore, from among the later philosophers I find three who have scented it out—the Arabian al-Kindi, Roger Bacon, and William of Paris. Plotinus also mentions it when he demonstrates that a *magus* is the servant of nature and not a contriver. This very wise man approves and maintains this magic, so hating the other that, when he was summoned to the rites of evil spirits, he said that they should come to him rather than that he should go to them; and surely he was right. For even as the former makes man the bound slave of wicked powers, so does the latter make him their ruler and their lord. In conclusion, the former can claim for itself the name of neither art nor science, while the latter, abounding in the loftiest mysteries, embraces the deepest contemplation of the most secret things, and at last the knowledge of all nature. The latter, in calling forth into the light as if from their hiding-places the powers scattered and sown in the world by the loving-kindness of God, does not so much work wonders as diligently serve a wonder-working nature. The latter, having more searchingly examined into the harmony of the universe, which the Greeks with greater significance called συμπάθεια, and having clearly perceived the reciprocal affinity of natures, and applying to each single thing the suitable and peculiar inducements (which are called the ἴυγγες of the magicians) brings forth into the open the miracles concealed in the recesses of the world, in the depths of nature, and in the storehouses and mysteries of God, just as if she herself were their maker; and, as the farmer weds his elms to vines, even so does the *magus* wed earth to heaven, that is, he weds lower things to the endowments and powers of higher things. Whence it comes about that the latter is as divine and as salutary as the former is unnatural and harmful; for this reason especially, that in subjecting man to the enemies of God, the former calls him away from God, but the latter rouses him to the admiration of God's works which is the most certain condition of a willing faith, hope, and love. For nothing moves one to religion and to the worship of God more than the diligent contemplation of the wonders of God; if we have thoroughly examined them by this natural magic we are considering, we shall be compelled to sing, more ardently inspired to the worship and love of the Creator: "The heavens and all the earth are full of the majesty of thy glory." And this is enough about magic. I have said these things about it, for I know there are many who, just as dogs always bark at strangers, in the same way often condemn and hate what they do not understand.

Giovanni Pico della Mirandola, excerpts from "On the Dignity of Man," in *The Renaissance Philosophy of Man*, edited by Ernst Cassirer and others (Chicago: University of Chicago Press, 1948), 246–49.

Further Reading

Ankarloo, Bengt, Stuart Clark, and William Monter. *Witchcraft and Magic in Europe: The Period of the Witch Trials*. Philadelphia: University of Pennsylvania Press, 2002.

Briggs, Robin. *Witches and Neighbors*. New York: Penguin, 1996.

Cameron, Euan. *Enchanted Europe. Superstition, Reason, & Religion, 1250–1750*. Oxford: Oxford University Press, 2010.

Cohen, Thomas V., and Elizabeth S. *Words and Deeds in Renaissance Rome: Trials before the Papal Magistrates*. Toronto: University of Toronto Press, 1993.

Copenhaver, Brian, ed. *The Book of Magic. From Antiquity to the Enlightenment*. New York: Penguin, 2015.

Del Col, Andrea, ed. *Domenico Scandella Known as Menocchio. His Trials Before the Inquisition (1583–1599)*. Translated by John & Anne C. Tedeschi. Binghamton, NY: Medieval & Renaissance Texts and Studies, 1996.

Ginzburg, Carlo. *The Cheese and the Worms*. New York: Penguin, 1980.

Ginzburg, Carlo. *The Night Battles: Witchcraft and Agrarian Cults in the Sixteenth Century*. Baltimore: Johns Hopkins University Press, 1983.

Godbeer, Richard. *The Salem Witch Hunt. A Brief History with Documents*. 2nd ed. Boston: Bedford/St. Martin's, 2018.

Greene, Heather. *Bell, Book and Camera. A Critical History of Witches in American Film and Television*. Jefferson, NC: McFarland, 2018.

Kieckhefer, Richard. *Forbidden Rites: A Necromancer's Manual of the Fifteenth Century*. University Park: Pennsylvania State University Press, 1997.

Kieckhefer, Richard. *Magic in the Middle Ages*. Cambridge: Cambridge University Press, 1990.

Kors, Alan Charles, and Edward Peters. *Witchcraft in Europe, 400–1700*. 2nd ed. Philadelphia: University of Pennsylvania Press, 2001.

Levack, Brian, ed. *Articles on Witchcraft, Magic, and Demonology: A Twelve Volume Anthology of Scholarly Articles*. New York: Garland, 1992.

Levack, Brian, ed. *The Oxford Handbook of Witchcraft in Early Modern Europe and Colonial America*. Oxford: Oxford University Press, 2013.

Levack, Brian, *The Witch-Hunt in Early Modern Europe*. 4th ed. London: Routledge, 2016.

Levack, Brian, ed. *The Witchcraft Sourcebook*. New York: Routledge, 2004.

Morton, Peter A., ed. *The Trial of Tempel Anneke*. Translated by Barbara Dähms. 2nd ed. Toronto: University of Toronto Press, 2017.

Parish, Helen, ed. *Superstition and Magic in Early Modern Europe: A Reader*. London: Bloomsbury, 2015.

Seitz, Jonathan. *Witchcraft and Inquisition in Early Modern Venice*. Cambridge: Cambridge University Press, 2011.

Thorndike, Lynn. *A History of Magic and Experimental Science*. 8 vols. New York: Columbia University Press, 1923–58.

8

A Few Geniuses Sparked the Scientific Revolution

What People Think Happened

In the Dark Ages, people lived primitive lives of subsistence. Their lives were short and without joy. The world was drab. After Antiquity, technology had reverted to being primitive. The ring of a hammer hitting hot iron rang through the mud-choked streets of disease-filled towns. Horses provided the means of transportation. Color was largely absent, except for the dresses of women. Knowledge stood still; life stood still; it was as if time itself stood still. The major reason for this was that the Church had strangled out the creation of new knowledge. The Church had declared a handful of authorities to be infallible and punished anyone who might even think about challenging something these authorities said. Even things that contradicted common sense and basic sensory experience were deemed irrefutable: If the Church judged something to be true then it was true. A citation to an authority ended any conversation; ended any debate; and ended all technological, social, and cultural progress.

During the Renaissance and early modern periods, people finally began to challenge these so-called authorities. Despite grave personal risks, a few brave geniuses printed their radical findings about the world around them. Men like Copernicus argued valiantly that the earth circled around the sun, not the other way round. Galileo dared to suggest that Copernicus was correct. Then he used a telescope to prove that some planets had moons and that the sun had sunspots. Churchmen,

Popular myth holds that a few early-modern geniuses progressively improved science after the darkness of the Middle Ages. Moreover, at times those men did so at great personal risk. It is true that some people, like Galileo, undeniably made major contributions to scientific understanding and were prosecuted, at least in part, for their ideas. However, the history of early modern science encompasses a far greater number and variety of people than popular myth suggests, and changes to accepted scientific thought happen in far less linear paths than is often assumed. (*Allegorie op Galileo Galilei*, Carlo Lasinio, after Rafaël, 1769–1838, Rijksmuseum)

predictably, refused to even look through Galileo's instrument and placed him under permanent house arrest. They stopped just short of burning him at the stake. To take another example, William Harvey finally proved to incredulous contemporaries that blood circulated through the body. Isaac Newton provided a basic, natural explanation for gravity, rather than relying upon spirits or other supernatural causes. In each scientific discipline, one great man followed another great man as they removed the blinders of ignorance and superstition from the progress of civilization. Today, according to the myth, modern scientists stand on the shoulders of these geniuses to add their own new findings about the real world. Scientific scholarship progressively fills out the puzzle that is nature, using mathematics as an unchanging, universal, and objective language. With the primitive darkness of the authority-bound Middle Ages behind us, new technologies continue the march of scientific progress in the modern world.

How the Story Became Popular

Myths about the history of science date mostly to the eighteenth, nineteenth, and twentieth centuries. During the eighteenth century, the idea became popular that the study and application of science could help society progress from a primitive to an advanced state. People began to believe that Renaissance thinkers had started this progress by rediscovering classical learning. Traits like secularism and individualism were identified as taking root. Apart from these accomplishments, natural scientists, especially after 1500, began to reveal the workings of the natural world. They argued that nature worked like a machine: that is, irrespective of whether or not God had created the machine, the machine now worked in predictable ways that they could observe and explain. In other words, God was like a clockmaker who created existence and then allowed it to work on its own.

In the eighteenth and nineteenth centuries, these ideas about progress spread to many other areas of society. The belief was that people could fashion a progressively better world by creating new machines. These new machines, in turn, increased leisure time and productivity while decreasing the time people needed to spend at work. When people looked back in time, they pointed to the Scientific Revolution for the origin of progress. Science textbooks told stories about the heroes of their disciplines. The narrative might start with the first individuals, usually men during the 1500s, 1600s, or 1700s, who presented ideas similar to what people today still believe. The narrative then continued from person to person as each scientist progressively created the discipline as it exists today. The life and work of each historical individual was shimmied down into a paragraph or two that identified his greatest teleological triumphs. The effect is a narrative of continued progress in the discipline: In the distant past, the discipline did not exist. Now, after the singular accomplishments of specific geniuses, the discipline has reached the present. In such stories, the past itself, the context of each individual, how each person viewed his or her own experiments, how they were viewed, and even the accuracy of crediting things to a specific individual gets lost under the construction of a narrative of disciplinary progress.

PRIMARY SOURCE DOCUMENTS

Myths about the Scientific Revolution emphasize the triumphs of individual geniuses squaring off against superstitious authorities. No example is better known than that of Galileo and his run-ins with the Catholic Church. The story goes that Galileo used new techniques and instruments to try to show his contemporaries new things about the world and about outer space. The Catholic Church rejected those arguments because they contradicted accepted dogma. Then, they punished Galileo for daring to question them. Galileo, however, had the last laugh because subsequent scientific geniuses built upon Galileo's work and continued the march of scientific progress toward modernity. While part of this story is accurate, it also leaves out the context in which Galileo worked, the personalities involved, and the stakes for everyone. It also picks and chooses from the past. By leaving out less appealing and strange parts of the past, a false narrative going in a straight line from past to present can be created. The following excerpts from several different documents reveal some of the complexities of the debates between Galileo and his opponents during the 1600s.

August 19, 1610: Galileo to Johannes Kepler: You are the first and almost the only person who, even after but a cursory investigation, has, such is your openness of mind and lofty genius, given entire credit to my statements. . . . We will not trouble ourselves about the abuse of the multitude, for against Jupiter even giants, to say nothing of pigmies, fight in vain. Let Jupiter stand in the heavens, and let the sycophants bark at him as they will. . . . In Pisa, Florence, Bologna, Venice, and Padua many have seen the planets; but all are silent on the subject and undecided, for the greater number recognize neither Jupiter nor Mars and scarcely the moon as planets. At Venice one man spoke against me, boasting that he knew for certain that my satellites of Jupiter, which he had several times observed, were not planets because they were always to be seen with Jupiter, and either all or some of them, now followed and now preceded him. What is to be done? Shall we side with Democritus or Heraclitus? I think, my Kepler, we will laugh at the extraordinary stupidity of the multitude. What do you say to the leading philosophers of the faculty here, to whom I have offered a thousand times of my own accord to show my studies, but who with the lazy obstinacy of a serpent who has eaten his fill have never consented to look at planets, nor moon, nor telescope? Verily, just as serpents close their ears, so do these men close their eyes to the light of truth. These are great matters; yet they do not occasion me any surprise. People of this sort think that philosophy is a kind of book like the Aeneid or the Odyssey, and that the truth is to be sought, not in the universe, not in nature, but (I use their own words) *by comparing texts!* How you would laugh if you heard what things that first philosopher of the faculty of Pisa brought against me in the presence of the Grand Duke, for he tried, now with logical arguments, now with magical adjurations, to tear down and argue the new planets out of the heavens.

. . .

Friday, the 26th [1616].—At the Palace, the usual residence of the Lord Cardinal Bellarmine, the said Galileo having been summoned and brought before the said Lord Cardinal, was, in presence of the Most Revd. Michael Angelo Segnezzio, of the order of preachers, Commissary-General of the Holy Office, by the said Cardinal warned of the error of the aforesaid opinion, and admonished to abandon it; and immediately thereafter, before me and before witnesses, the Lord Cardinal Bellarmine being still present, the said Galileo was by the said Commissary commanded and enjoined, in the name of His Holiness the Pope, and the whole congregation of the Holy Office, to relinquish altogether the said opinion that the sun is the centre of the world and immovable, and that the earth moves; nor henceforth to hold, teach, or defend it in any way whatsoever, verbally or in writing; otherwise proceedings would be taken against him in the Holy Office; which injunction the said Galileo acquiesced in and promised to obey. Done in Rome . . .

. . .

May, 1618: With this I [that is, Galileo] send a treatise on causes of the tides, which I wrote rather more than two years ago at the suggestion of his Eminence Cardinal Orsini, at Rome, at the time when the theologians were thinking of prohibiting Copernicus's book and the doctrine denounced therein of the motion of the earth, which I then held to be true, until it pleased those gentlemen to prohibit the work, and to declare that opinion to be false and contrary to Scripture. Now, knowing as I do, that it behoves us to obey the decisions of the authorities, and to believe them, since they are guided by a higher insight than any to which my humble mind can of itself attain, I consider this treatise which I send you merely to be a poetical conceit, or a dream, and desire that your Highness may take it as such, inasmuch as it is based on the double motion of the earth, and indeed contains one of the arguments which I have adduced in confirmation of it. But even poets sometimes attach a value to one or other of their fantasies, and I likewise attach some value to this fancy of mine. Now, having written the treatise, and having shown it to the Cardinal above-mentioned, and a few others, I have also let a few exalted personages have copies, in order that in case any one not belonging to our Church should try to appropriate my curious fancy, as has happened to me with many of my discoveries, these personages, being above all suspicion, may be able to bear witness that it was I who first dreamed of this chimera. What I now send is but a fugitive performance; it was written in haste, and in the expectation that the work of Copernicus would not be condemned as erroneous eighty years after its publication. I had intended at my convenience, and in the quiet, to have gone more particularly into this subject, to have added more proofs, to have arranged the whole anew, and to have put it into a better form. But a voice from heaven has aroused me, and dissolved all my confused and tangled fantasies in mist. May therefore your highness graciously accept it, ill arranged as it is. And if Divine love ever grants that I may be in a position to exert myself a little, your Highness may expect something more solid and real from me.

. . .

Papal opinion on Galileo, June 7, 1624: We have observed in him not only the literary distinction, but also the love of religion and all the good qualities worthy of the papal favour. When he came to congratulate us on our accession, we embraced him affectionately, and listened with pleasure to his learned demonstrations which add fresh renown to Florentine eloquence. We desire that he should not return to his native country without having received by our generosity manifold proofs of our papal favour. . . . And that you may fully understand to what extent he is dear to us, we wish to give this brilliant testimony to his virtues and piety. We are anxious to assure you that we shall thank you for all the kindness that you can show him, by imitating or even surpassing our fatherly generosity.

. . .

January 15, 1633: I [that is, Galileo] am sorry that the two books of Morin and Fromond did not reach me till six months after the publication of my "Dialogues," because otherwise I should have had an opportunity of saying much in praise of both, and of giving some consideration to a few particular points, especially to one in Morin and to another in Fromond. I am quite astonished that Morin should attach so great a value to astrology, and that he should pretend to be able, with his conjectures (which seem to me very uncertain) to establish its truth. It will really be a wonderful thing, if, as he promises, he raises astrology by his acuteness to the first rank among human science, and I await such a startling novelty with great curiosity. As to Fromond, who proves himself to be a man of much mind, I could have wished not to see him fall into, in my opinion, a grave though wide-spread error; namely, in order to refute the opinions of Copernicus, he first hurls scornful jests at his followers, and then (which seems to me still more unsuitable), fortifies himself by the authority of Holy Scripture, and at length goes so far as to call those views on these grounds nothing less than heretical. That such a proceeding is not praiseworthy seems to me to admit of very easy proof. For if I were to ask Fromond, who made the sun, the moon, the earth, and the stars, and ordained their order and motions, I believe he would answer, they are the creations of God. If asked who inspired Holy Scripture, I know he would answer, the Holy Spirit, which means God likewise. The world is therefore the work and the Scriptures are the word of the same God. If asked further, whether the Holy spirit never uses words which appear to be contrary to things as they really are, and are only so used to accommodate them to the understandings of rude, uncultivated people, I am convinced that he would reply, in agreement with the holy fathers, that such is the usage of Scripture, which, in a hundred passages, says things for the above reason, that if taken literarily, are not only heresies, but blasphemies, since they impute to God, anger, repentance, forgetfulness, etc. But if I were to ask Fromond, whether God, in order to accommodate Himself to the understanding of the multitude, ever alters His creations, or whether nature, which is God's handmaid, and is not changeable at man's desire, has not always observed, and does not still maintain, her usual course in respect to motion, form, and relative positions of the various parts of the universe—I am certain that he would answer, the moon has always been spherical, although for a long period the people thought she was flat; he would say, in fine, that nothing ever changes in nature to accommodate itself to the comprehension or notions of men. But if it be so, why, in our search for knowledge of the various parts of the universe, should we begin rather with the words than with the works of God? Is the work less noble or less excellent than the word? If Fromond, or anyone else, had settled that the opinion that the earth moves is a heresy, and if afterwards demonstration, observation, and necessary concatenation should prove that it does move, into what embarrassment he would have brought himself and the holy Church. But if, on the contrary, the works are indisputably proved to vary from the literal meaning of the words, and we give the Scriptures the second place, no detriment to Scripture results from this. Since, in order to accommodate themselves they often ascribe, even to God Himself, entirely false conditions, why should we suppose that in speaking of the earth or the sun they should keep to such strict laws, as not to attribute conditions to these creations, out of regard for the ignorance of the masses, which are opposed to fact. If it be true that the earth moves and the sun stands still, it is no detriment to Holy Scripture, since it speaks of things as they appear to the people . . .

. . .

Galileo to Geri Boccineri, February 25, 1632: We (Niccolini and Galileo) hear at last that the many and serious accusations are reduced to one, and that the rest have been allowed to drop. Of this one I shall have no difficulty in getting rid when the grounds of my defense have been heard, which are meanwhile being gradually brought, in the best way that circumstances allow, to the knowledge of some of the higher officials, for these are not at liberty to listen freely to intercession, and still less to open their lips in reply. So that in the end a favourable issue may be hoped for . . .

Francesco Niccolini to Andrea Cioli, February 27, 1632: Although I am unable to say precisely what stage Galileo's affair has reached, or what may happen next, as far as I can learn the main difficulty consists in this— that these gentlemen maintain that in 1616 he was ordered neither to discuss the question nor to converse about it. He says, on the contrary, that those were not the terms of the injunction, which were that *that doctrine was not to be held nor defended.* He considers that he has the means of justifying himself, because it does not at all appear from his book that he does hold or defend the doctrine, nor that he regards it as a settled question, as he merely adduces the reasons *hinc hinde.* The other points appear to be of less importance and easier to get over.

. . .

Vincenzo Maccolani da Firenzuola to Cardinal Francesco Barberini, April 28, 1633: In compliance with the commands of his Holiness, I yesterday informed the most eminent Lords of the Holy Congregation of Galileo's cause, the position of which I briefly reported. Their Eminences approved of what has been done thus far, and took into consideration, on the other hand, various difficulties with regard to the manner of pursuing the case, and of bringing it to an end. More especially as Galileo has in his examination denied what is plainly evident from the book written by him; since in consequence of his denial there would result the necessity for greater rigour of procedure and less regard to the other considerations belonging to this business. Finally I suggested a course, namely, that the Holy Congregation should grant me permission to treat extra-judicially with Galileo, in order to render him sensible of his error, and bring him, if he recognizes it, to a confession of the same. This proposal appeared at first sight too bold, not much hope being entertained of accomplishing this object by merely adopting the method of argument with him; but upon my indicating the grounds upon which I had made the suggestion, permission was granted me. That no time might be lost, I entered into discourse with Galileo yesterday afternoon, and after many arguments and rejoinders had passed between us, by God's grace I attained my object, for I brought him to a full sense of his error, so that he clearly recognized that he had erred, and had gone too far in his book. And to all these he gave expression in words of much feeling, like one who experienced great consolation in the recognition of his error, and he was also willing to confess it judicially. He requested, however, a little time in order to consider the form in which he might most fittingly make the confession, which, as far as its substance is concerned, will, I hope, follow in the manner indicated.

I have thought it my duty at once to acquaint your Eminence with this matter, having communicated it to no one else; for I trust that his Holiness and your Eminence will be satisfied that in this way the affair is being brought to such a point that it may soon be settled without difficulty. The court will maintain its reputation: it will be possible to deal leniently with the culprit; and whatever the decision arrived at, he will recognize the favour shown him, with all the other consequences of satisfaction herein desired. To-day I think of examining him in order to obtain the said confession; and having, as I hope, received it, it will only remain to me further to question him with regard to his intention, and to impose the prohibitions upon him; and that done, he might have the house assigned to him as a prison, as hinted to me by your Eminence, to whom I offer my most humble reverence.

. . .

[*Galileo did confess, a but trial nevertheless ensued in May 1633 with the following sentence issued*]

. . . Whereas you, Galileo, son of the late Vincenzo Galilei, Florentine, aged seventy years, were in the year 1615 denounced to this Holy Office for holding as true the false doctrine taught by many, that the sun is the centre of the world and immovable, and that the earth moves, and also with a diurnal motion; for having disciples to whom you taught the same doctrine; for holding correspondence with certain mathematicians of Germany concerning the same; for having printed certain letters, entitled "On the Solar Spots," wherein you developed the same doctrine as true; and for replying to the objections from the Holy Scriptures, which from time to time were urged against it, by glossing the said Scriptures according to your own meaning: and whereas there was thereupon produced the copy of a document in the form of a letter, purporting to be written by you to one formerly your disciple, and in this divers propositions are set forth, following the hypothesis of Copernicus, which are contrary to the true sense and authority of Holy Scripture:

This Holy Tribunal being therefore desirous of proceeding against the disorder and mischief thence resulting, which went on increasing to the prejudice of the Holy Faith, by command of his Holiness and of the most eminent Lords Cardinals of this supreme and universal Inquisition, the two propositions of the stability of the sun and the motion of the earth were by the theological "Qualifiers" qualified as follows:

The proposition that the sun is the centre of the world and does not move from its place is absurd and false philosophically and formally heretical, because it is expressly contrary to the Holy Scripture.

The proposition that the earth is not the centre of the world and immovable, but that it moves, and also with a diurnal motion, is equally absurd and false philosophically, and theologically considered, at least erroneous in faith.

But whereas it was desired at that time to deal leniently with you, it was decreed at the Holy Congregation held before his Holiness on the 25th February, 1616, that his Eminence the Lord Cardinal Bellarmine should order you to abandon altogether the said false doctrine, and, in the event of your refusal, that an injunction should be imposed upon you by the Commissary of the Holy office, to give up the said doctrine, and not to teach it to others, nor to defend it, nor even discuss it; and failing your acquiescence in this injunction, that you should be imprisoned. And in execution of this decree, on the following day, at the palace, and in the presence of his Eminence, the said Lord Cardinal Bellarmine, after being gently admonished by the said Lord Cardinal, the command was intimated to you by the Father Commissary of the Holy Office for the time before a notary and witnesses, that you were altogether to abandon the said false opinion, and not in future to defend or teach it in any way whatsoever, neither verbally nor in writing; and upon your promising to obey you were dismissed.

And in order that a doctrine so pernicious might be wholly rooted out and not insinuate itself further to the grave prejudice of Catholic truth, a decree was issued by the Holy Congregation of the Index, prohibiting the books which treat of this doctrine, and declaring the doctrine itself to be false and wholly contrary to sacred and divine Scripture.

And whereas a book appeared here recently, printed last year at Florence, the title of which shows that you were the author, this title being: "Dialogue of Galileo Galilei on the Two Principal Systems of the World, the Ptolemaic and the Copernican"; and whereas the holy Congregation was afterwards informed that through the publication of the said book, the false opinion of the motion of the earth and the stability of the sun was daily gaining ground; the said book was taken into careful consideration, and in it there was discovered a patent violation of the aforesaid injunction that had been imposed upon you, for in this book you have defended the said opinion previously condemned and to your face declared to be so, although in the said book you strive by various devices to produce the impression that you leave it undecided, and in express terms as probable: which however is a most grievous error, as an opinion can in no wise be probable which has been declared and defined to be contrary to Divine Scripture:

Therefore by our order you were cited before this Holy Office, where, being examined upon your oath, you acknowledge the book to be written and published by you. You confessed that you began to write the said book about ten or twelve years ago, after the command had been imposed upon you as above; that you requested license to print it, without however intimating to those who granted you this license that you had been commanded not to hold, defend, or teach in any way whatever the doctrine in question.

You likewise confessed that the writing of the said book is in various places drawn up in such a form that the reader might fancy that the arguments brought forward on the false side are rather calculated by their cogency to compel conviction than to be easy of refutation; excusing yourself for having fallen into an error, as you alleged, so foreign to your intention, by the fact that you had written in dialogue, and by the natural complacency that every man feels in regard to his own subtleties, and in showing himself more clever than the generality of men, in devising, even on behalf of false propositions, ingenious and plausible arguments.

And a suitable term having been assigned to you to prepare your defence, you produced a certificate in the handwriting of his Eminence the Lord Cardinal Bellarmine, procured by you, as you asserted, in order to defend yourself against the calumnies of your enemies, who gave out that you had abjured and had been punished by the Holy Office; in which certificate it is declared that you had not abjured and had not been punished, but merely that the declaration made by his Holiness and published by the Holy Congregation of the Index, had been announced to you, wherein it is declared that the doctrine of the motion of the earth and the stability of the sun is contrary to the Holy Scriptures, and therefore cannot be defended or held. And as in this certificate there is no mention of the two articles of the injunction, namely, the order not "to teach" and "in any way," you represented that we ought to believe that in the course of fourteen or sixteen years you had lost all memory of them; and that this was why you said nothing of the injunction when you requested permission to print your book. And all this you urged not by way of excuse for your error, but that it might be set down to a vainglorious ambition rather than to malice. But this certificate produced by you in your defence has only aggravated your delinquency, since although it is there stated that the said opinion is contrary to Holy Scripture, you have nevertheless dared to discuss and defend it and to argue its probability; nor does the licence artfully and cunningly extorted by you avail you anything, since you did not notify the command imposed upon you.

And whereas it appeared to us that you had not stated the full truth with regard to your intention, we thought it necessary to subject you to a rigorous examination, at which (without prejudice, however, to the matters confessed by you, and set forth as above, with regard to your said intention) you answered like a good Catholic. Therefore, having seen and maturely considered the merits of this your cause, together with your confessions and excuses above mentioned, and all that ought justly to be seen and considered, we have arrived at the underwritten final sentence against you:

Invoking, therefore, the most holy name of our Lord Jesus Christ and of His most glorious Mother, and ever Virgin Mary, by this our final sentence, which sitting in judgment, with the counsel and advice of the Reverend Masters of sacred theology and Doctors of both laws, our assessors, we deliver in these writings, in the cause and causes presently before us between the magnificent Carlo Sinceri, doctor of both laws, Proctor Fiscal of his Holy office, of the one part, and you Galileo Galilei, the defendant, here present, tried and confessed as above, of the other part, we say, pronounce, sentence, declare, that you, the said Galileo, by reason of the matters adduced in process, and by you confessed as above, have rendered yourself in the judgment of this Holy office vehemently suspected of heresy, namely, of having believed and held the doctrine – which is false and contrary to the sacred and divine Scriptures—that the sun is the centre of the world and does not move from east to west, and that the earth moves and is not the centre of the world; and that an opinion may be held and defended as probable after it has been declared and defined to be contrary to Holy Scripture; and that consequently you have incurred all the censures and penalties imposed and promulgated in the sacred canons and other constitutions, general and particular, against such delinquents. From which we are content that you be absolved, provided that first, with a sincere heart, and unfeigned faith, you abjure, curse, and detest the aforesaid errors and heresies, and every other error and heresy contrary to the Catholic and Apostolic Roman Church in the form to be prescribed by us.

And in order that this your grave and pernicious error and transgression may not remain altogether unpunished, and that you may be more cautious for the future, and an example to others, that they may abstain from similar delinquencies—we ordain that the book of the "*Dialogues of Galileo Galilei*" be prohibited by public edict. We condemn you to the formal prison of this Holy Office during our pleasure, and by way of salutary penance, we enjoin that for three years to come you repeat once a week the seven penitential Psalms. Reserving to ourselves full liberty to moderate, commute, or take off, in whole or in part, the aforesaid penalties and penance. And so we say, pronounce, sentence, declare, ordain, condemn and reserve, in this and any other better way and form which we can and may lawfully employ.

So we the undersigned Cardinals pronounce . . .

. . .

[Galileo's recantation after]: I, Galileo Galilei, son of the late Vincenzo Galilei, Florentine, aged seventy years, arraigned personally before this tribunal, and kneeling before you, most Eminent and Reverend Lord Cardinals, inquisitors general against heretical depravity throughout the whole Christian Republic, having before my eyes and touching with my hands, the holy Gospels—swear that I have always believed, do now believe, and by God's help will for the future believe, all that is held, preached, and taught by the Holy Catholic and Apostolic Roman Church. But whereas—after an injunction had been judicially intimated to me by this Holy Office, to the effect that I must altogether abandon the false opinion that the sun is the centre of the world and immovable, and that the earth is not the centre of the world, and moves, and that I must not hold, defend, or teach in any way whatsoever, verbally or in writing, the said doctrine, and after it had been notified to me that the said doctrine was contrary to Holy Scripture—I wrote and printed a book in which I discuss this doctrine already condemned, and adduce arguments of great cogency in its favour, without presenting any solution of these; and for this cause I have been pronounced by the Holy Office to be vehemently suspected of heresy, that is to say, of having held and believed that the sun is the centre of the world and immovable, and that the earth is not the centre and moves.

Therefore, desiring to remove from the minds of your Eminences, and of all faithful Christians, this strong suspicion, reasonably conceived against me, with sincere heart and unfeigned faith I abjure, curse, and detest the aforesaid errors and heresies, and generally every other error and sect whatsoever contrary to the said Holy Church; and I swear that in future I will never again say or assert, verbally or in writing, anything that might furnish occasion for a similar suspicion regarding me; but that should I know any heretic, or person suspected of heresy, I will denounce him to this Holy Office, or to the Inquisitor and ordinary of the place where I may be. Further, I swear and promise to fulfil and observe in their integrity all penances that have been, or that shall be, imposed upon me by this Holy Office. And, in the event of my contravening, (which God forbid!) any of these my promises, protestations, and oaths, I submit myself to all the pains and penalties imposed and promulgated in the sacred canons and other constitutions, general and particular, against such delinquents. So help me God, and these His holy Gospels, which I touch with my hands.

I, the said Galileo Galilei, have abjured, sworn, promised, and bound myself as above; and in witness of the truth thereof I have with my own hand subscribed the present document of my abjuration, and recited it word for word at Rome, in the Convent of Minevra, this twenty-second day of June, 1633 . . .

> Documents related to Galileo, as found in excerpts from Karl von Gebler, *Galileo Galilei and the Roman Curia from Authentic Sources*, translated by George Sturge (London: C. Kegan Paul & Col, 1879), 26, 78, 100, 188–89, 194, 213–14, 231–34, 243–44.

Myths about the history of science emphasize that individual geniuses, over time, have progressively and consecutively improved the knowledge about the world. In these stories, each genius adds a new block to the artifice of scientific understandings. But that is just not how the past works. Picking out a handful of writings from a handful of people creates an illusion of linearity. In reality, people exist in their own times and respond to those times. Some things people believed and wrote about in the past may appeal to us. Other things may seem strange and very different. When we only focus on the parts of the past that we like, the result is caricatures of people and their writings that veer far from historical truth. Historians study change over time. They situate people in their past contexts. The goal is to understand the past on its own terms, whether or not that past links to the present. The excerpts that follow provide a narrative about the Scientific Revolution that emphasizes individual and progressive accomplishments over time. This narrative conforms to myths about the history of science, but veers away from how specialists now understand their subject.

An attempt has been made in these pages to trace the evolution of intellectual thought in the progress of astronomical discovery, and, by recognising the different points of view of the different ages, to give due credit even to the ancients. . . . The progress of human knowledge is measured by the increased habit of looking at facts from new points of view, as much as by the accumulation of facts. The mental capacity of one age does not seem to differ from that of other ages; but it is the imagination of new points of view that gives a wider scope to that capacity. And this is cumulative, and therefore progressive. Aristotle viewed the solar system as a geometrical problem; Kepler and Newton converted the point of view into a dynamical one. Aristotle's mental capacity to understand the meaning of facts or to criticise a train of reasoning may have been equal to that of Kepler or Newton, but the point of view was different. Then, again, new points of view are provided by the invention of new methods in that system of logic which we call mathematics. . . . No one recognises more than the mathematical astronomer this feebleness of the human intellect, and no one is more conscious of the limitations of the logical process called mathematics. . . . These reflections, arising from the writing of this History, go to explain the invariable humility of the great mathematical astronomers. Newton's comparison of himself to the child on the seashore applies to them all. As each new discovery opens up, it may be, boundless oceans for investigation, for wonder, and for admiration, the great astronomers, refusing to accept mere hypotheses as true, have founded upon these discoveries a science as exact in its observation of facts as in theories. So it is that these men, who have built up the most sure and most solid of all the sciences, refuse to invite others to join them in vain speculation . . .

Book I: The Geometrical Period
I. Primitive Astronomy and Astrology
. . . Even if the scientific spirit of observation and deduction (astronomy) has sometimes led to erroneous systems for predicting terrestrial events (astrology), we owe to the old astronomer and astrologers alike the deepest gratitude for their diligence in recording astronomical events. For, out of the scanty records which have survived the destructive acts of fire and flood, of monarchs and mobs, we have found much that has helped to a fuller knowledge of the heavenly motions than was possible without these records . . .

There are other reasons why we must be tolerant of the crude notions of the ancients. The historian, wishing to give credit wherever it may be due, is met by two difficulties. Firstly, only a few records of very ancient astronomy are extant, and the authenticity of many of these is open to doubt. Secondly it is very difficult to divest ourselves of present knowledge, and to appreciate the originality of thought required to make the first beginnings . . .

Great progress was made when systematic observations began, such as following the motion of the moon and planets among the stars, and the inferred motion of the sun among the stars. . . . To not one of the above important steps in the progress of astronomy can we assign the author with certainty. . .

. . . Ptolemy (130 A.D.) wrote the Suntaxis, or Almagest, which includes a cyclopaedia of astronomy, containing a summary of knowledge at that date. . . . The cumbrous system advocated by Ptolemy answered its purpose, enabling him to predict astronomical events approximately. He improved the lunar theory considerably, and discovered minor inequalities which could be allowed for by the addition of new epicycles. We may look upon these epicycles of Apollonius, and the eccentric of Hipparchus, as the responses of these astronomers to the demand of Plato for uniform circular motions. Their use became more and more confirmed, until the seventeenth century, when the accurate observations of Tycho Brahe enabled Kepler to abolish these purely geometrical makeshifts, and to substitute a system in which the sun became physically its controller . . .

George Forbes, excerpts from *History of Astronomy* (New York: G. P. Putnam's Sons, 1909), iii–v, 3–4, 6, 8, and 27–29.

What Really Happened

Historians have argued for nearly seventy years that any narrative of the history of science based upon a succession of increasingly correct breakthroughs is inaccurate. Past scientists, instead, were products of their times. They wrote about all kinds of things, some of which we find familiar, some of which we find strange. All their writings and arguments, both novel and mundane, respond to other writings and arguments of their times. All that is innovative, and all that is not innovative, is part of a process of exchange of ideas among contemporaries. In the early modern world, people from all walks of life contributed to what people knew about the natural world. Women as well as men participated in those conversations. Ideas that we like and ideas that we don't like coexisted and were passed down to future writers and thinkers. Isaac Newton was a physicist, but he was also an alchemist. Galileo was an astronomer, but he was also a man who could intentionally provoke and insult people who disagreed with him. The historical context establishes the worlds in which—and the people with whom—scientists worked and lived, rather than a succession of great men building progressively on the ideas of previous geniuses.

All of these processes, and many others, combine to complicate popular ideas about historical progress and its relationship with science. Before the early modern period, people used religion as their key metric to measure progress. For them, things were progressively getting worse as events moved further and further from the time when Christ walked the earth. For example, after the first encounters with native populations in the North and South American continents, some Europeans argued that those Amerindians were superior to Europeans because they lived in a state closer to the Garden of Eden. During the early modern period, technology and science and other factors joined together to create different ideas about progress. In these new conceptualizations, religious assumptions became less significant than secularism, experiments, and machines. Ideas about progress could lead to innovations, but ideas about progress could also be used to justify things like slavery and imperialism. In recent years, our own ideas about the relationships between science, technology, and progress may be changing yet again. During the twentieth century, fantasies about the future usually focused on technological marvels and utopias. Yet, by the 2020s, a lot of people imagine the future as a dystopia. Ideas about the future are becoming, for some, less about the promises of technological and scientific innovations and more to do with questions about what progress is and how it relates to science and other parts of our modern world.

PRIMARY SOURCE DOCUMENTS

Myths about the Scientific Revolution assume that great individuals built upon the studies of previous geniuses to create better science. However, that myth creates an inaccurate view of the past. In early modern Europe, people assumed various things about the world. They built their hypotheses and conclusions upon those assumptions. Men and women collaborated together and discussed scientific questions and problems. Sometimes those collaborations resulted in conclusions that still seem relatively accurate. But more often than not, their conclusions were relevant only to early modern Europeans. All of history can only be understood by situating its actors and their writings into their specific contexts. In the following excerpts, Margaret Cavendish, a woman better known for her literary works, corresponds with a contemporary about the fascinating "Rupert's Drop." The hypotheses here are generally inaccurate, but the letters attest to the collaborative nature of early modern science based upon early modern assumptions about the world.

Constantijn Huygens to Margaret Cavendish: "I had the honour to heare so good solutions given by your Excellencie upon divers questions . . . I am . . . humbly beseeching your Ex.cie . . . to instruct me about the natural reason of these wonderfull glasses, which, as I told you, Madam, will fly into powder, if one breakes but the least top of their tailes, whereas without that way they are hardly to be broken by any waight or stength. The King of France is as yet unresolved in the question, notwithstanding he hath been curious to moove it to an assemblie of the best philosophers of Paris. . . . Your Ex.cie hath no cause to apprehend the cracking blow of these little innoxious gunnes. If you did, Madam, a servant may hold them close in his fists, and yourselfe can break the little end of their taile without the least danger. But, as I was bold to tell your Ex.cie, I should bee loth to beleeve, any female feare should reigne amongst so much over-masculine wisdeom as the world doth admire in her . . ."

. . .

Margaret Cavendish to Huygens: . . . As for your request concerninge my opinion of the glasses, you have done mee the favor to sende mee . . . for itt were a presumtion to give my oppinion after these famous and lerned phylosophers, as those which are in France . . . but to myne outward sense these glasses doe appeare to have on the head, body or belly a liquid and oyly substance, which may be the oyly spirrits or essences of sulpher; alsoe the glasses doe appeare to my senses like the nature or arte of guns and the spirrit of sulpher as the powder; where although they are charged, yet untill they bee discharged, gives no report or sound; the discharging of these glasses is by the breakeinge of a piece or part or end of the tailes, where the discharging of guns are by much firelockes, scrues or the like, which setts fire or gives vent to the powder, but these sulpherousse spirrits, having as it seemes a more forceable nature, it doth viollently thurst itselfe out, where itt findes vent, like as wind, but rather like fire, being of a firy nature, and may have the effects of bright shineing fire, which, when it has noe vent, lyes as dead, but as soone as it can ease out a passage, or findes a vent, it breakes forth in a violent crack or thundering noisse. I doe not saye, the effects of these spirritts are to flame or to burne after your way, but only it hath the like effects as to break, dispersse and spread abroad as bright shineing fire doth, for oylye sulphur, vittral spirritts and the like firy natures are those which are called a cold dead fire, that is the exterior part is colde and dull, although the interior is hott and active. As for the woounder, how this liquid matter should be putt into the this glasse, for it is vissible, a liquid matter is therein, which to my sense itt must be first putt into the matter or substance that makes the glasses, and when the glasse is blowne, the liquer runs or crouds to the most hollowest and largest place it can get into, like as wind will blow the watter into a crowd or heape togeither and fill all hollow places it can gett into, as ditches, pitts or the like; soe doth the breath of the glassemaker blow that oyly essences or spirritts into the belly of the glasse, where, before it can have soe much tyme to retire back, the end of the little porus taile is soathred up, where aftterwards, when the soadred part is broke of, the spirritts findeing vent strugles and strives to gett forth, wherin the strife it breakes the glasse to pieces, wherwith itt makes a noise or report like a gun, or rather as a fired house or the like . . .

Huygens to Margaret Cavendish

. . . In ordre of your Ex.cies determination, I did conceave, if the matter inclosed in the hollow parts of these bottels should be a sulphureous liquid gunpowder, that without quest fire would worke upon it, and make it active. But, madam, I found myself so farre short of my opinion, that firing one of these bottels to the reddest hight of heat, I have not onely seene it without any effect, but also beeing cooled again, I have wondred to see all his vertue spent and spoiled, so that I could break of the whole taile by peeces even to the belly, without any motion more than you would see in an ordinarie peece of glasse. Having alsoe broke the belly asunder and wel observed the little hollow bubles within it, I have not found the least appearance of any liquor or oyly substance should have been inclosed therein. If your Ex.cie thinketh it worth her paynes to consider of these circumstances, it may bee degrees she will bring herself to the true notice of the mysterie. . .

Margaret Cavendish to Huygens

I have received your second letter by Mr. Dewerts, wherin I find your dissatisfaction of the opinion of those little glasses. Truly arts are as obscure and hard to finde out by those that are unlerned in them, as natures workes; but to cleer my opinion, or rather to answer yours desires, I shall argue something more of them, though my arguments may be as weake as my opinions, and my opinions as weake as my judgement, and my judgement as weake as want of knowlledge can make it.—As for your liquor, you say in your letter, that if it were a sulphurous liquor, or a liquid gunpowder—as I said—I thought it might bee, doubtlesse it would be active by the help of fire; I answer for that, fire hath severall active effects both in ittselfe and uppon other substances, or subjects, wherfore, if the liquor had be[e]n dry powder, it might be subject to that effect of fire, as to flash, flame, or bounce, but if the powder were wett, the fire could worke noe such effects; but as the substance is a liquor, fire is as subject to that substance or matter, as that substance or matter is to fire, for all liquors, although strong with spirritts and hott in operation, will quench fire as sudenly, as fire shall evapporate liquor; take quantity for quantity, and it is probable, that the high fire, you did applye to the glasse, did eveporat out the liquor in the glasse, which might be the weakening and changing or altering the former effects. Alsoe you say, you cannot perceive the buble to be a licquor. I answer, that it is probable, the licquor, if any be therin, was evaporated out either by the fire, you applyed, or by the vent of passage, which may soon turn itt into vapor, by reason of the little quantity that is in in a glasse; thus it might be wasted before the truth could possible be found out; for certainly to my sense, as alsoe to my reason, a liquor apeared to be in those glasses, you sent me; but if there be noe licquor in those glasses, then it is probable, it might be pent up ayre eclosed therin, which having vent was the cause of the sound or report, which those glasses gave.—Thus, Sir, you may perceive by my argueings, I strive to make my former opinion or sense good, allthough I doe not binde myselfe to opinions, but truth; and the truth is, that, though I cannot finde out the truth of the glasses, yet in truth I am . . .

Excerpts from "Correspondence Between Margaret Cavendish and Constantijn Huygens," in *Constantijn Huygens, De Briefwisseling*, edited by J. A. Worp (The Hague: Martinus Nijhoff, 1916), vol. 5, pp. 284–86.

In the following excerpt, Robert Hooke also describes the phenomenon of the Rupert's Drop. Hooke is famous today for his use of the microscope. But in early modern Europe, he was a part of a broader community of men and women using early modern assumptions to explore the natural world. Rather than a narrative of great men continually and progressively building on the findings of the past, scientific change is muddy, multifaceted, full of error, full of things that we today view as appealing, and full of things we today view as odd. Sometimes, people drew conclusions based on empirical evidence, but sometimes they simply believed another person because of his or her social reputation. The excerpts that follow seek to situate Hooke within broader conversations about the natural world around him, conversations involving women and men from many different walks of life.

Observ. VII. Of some *phaenomena* of glass drops

These glass drops are small parcels of coarse green glass taken out of the pots that contain the metal (as they call it) in fusion, upon the end of an iron pipe; and being exceeding hot, and thereby of a kind of sluggish fluid consistence, are suffered to drop from thence into a bucket of cold water, and in it to lye till they be grown sensibly cold.

Some of these I broke in the open air, by snapping off a little of the small item with my fingers, others by crushing it with a small pair of plyers; which I had no sooner done, then the whole bulk of the drop flew violently, with a very brisk noise, into multitudes of small pieces, some of which were as small as dust, though in some there were remaining pieces pretty large, without any flaw at all, and others very much flaw'd, which by rubbing between ones fingers was easily reduced to dust; these dispersed every way so violently, that some of them pierced my skin. I could not find, either with my naked eye, or a microscope, that any of the broken pieces were of a regular figure, nor any other like another, but for the most part those that flaw'd off in large pieces were prettily branched.

The ends of others of these drops I nipt off whilst all the bodies and ends of them lay buried under the water, which, like the former, flew all to pieces with as brisk a noise, and as strong a motion.

Others of these I tried to break, by grinding away the blunt end, and though I took a seemingly good one, and had ground away neer two thirds of the ball, yet would it not fly to pieces, but now and then some small rings of it would snap and fly off, not without a brisk noise and quick motion, leaving the surface of the drop whence it flew very prettily branched or creased, which was easily discoverable by the microscope. This drop, after I had thus ground it, without at all impairing the remnant that was not ground away, I caused to fly immediately all into sand upon the nipping of the very tip of its slender end.

Another of these drops I began to grind away at the smaller end, but had not worn away on the stone above a quarter of an inch before the whole drop flew with a brisk crack into sand or small dust; nor would it have held so long, had there not been a little flaw in the piece that I ground away, as I afterwards found.

Several others of these drops I covered over with a thin but very tuff skin of *Icthyocolla,* which being very tough and very transparent, was the most convenient substance for these tryals that I could imagine . . .

. . . The cause of all which Phaenomena I imagine to be no other then this, that the parts of the glass being by the excessive heat of the fire kept off and separated one from another, and thereby put into a kind of sluggish fluid consistence, are suffered to drop off with that heat or agitation remaining in them, into cold water; by which means the outsides of the drop are presently cool'd and crusted, and are thereby made of a loose texture, because the parts of it have not time to settle themselves leisurely together, and so to lie very close together: And the innermost parts of the drop, retaining still much of their former heat and agitations, remain of a loose texture also, and, according as the cold strikes inwards from the bottom and sides, are quenched, as it were, and made rigid in that very posture wherein the cold finds them. For the parts of the crust being already hardened, will not suffer the parts to shrink any more from the outward surface inward; and though it shrink a little by reason of the small parcels of some aerial substances dispersed through the matter of the glass, yet that is not neer so much as it appears (as I just now hinted;) nor if it were, would it be sufficient for to consolidate and condense the body of glass into a tuff and close texture, after it had been so excessively rarified by the heat of the glass furnace.

But that there may be such an expansion of the aerial substance contained in those little blebbs or bubbles in the body of the drop, this following experiment will make more evident.

Take a small glass-cane about a foot long . . .

Robert Hooke, excerpts from "Observ. VII Of some Phaenomena of Glass drops," in *Micrographia* (London: Jo. Martyn and Ja. Allestry, 1665), 33–36.

Early modern people who studied the natural world believed and were interested in things that modern readers often find strange. One of the most famous examples is Isaac Newton's fascination with alchemy, writing of which he filled numerous notebooks. When we remove early modern people from their historical contexts and focus only on the aspects of the past that we like, the result is the illusion that successive breakthroughs characterize the Scientific Revolution and the history of science in general: Some great men seem to have somehow risen above the superstitions and falsehoods of their times. But, more accurately, early modern people wrote things that we like and things that we don't like. They had ideas that we find familiar and others that we don't.

In the excerpts below, William Whiston, a student of Isaac Newton, details his predictions for the end times based upon astrology. Benjamin Franklin mocked Whiston's predictions. But Franklin was only one person. Whiston corresponded with most of the best scientists of his day and was a professor of mathematics at Cambridge University for a time.

I shall here add an epitome of my VI lectures preparatory to the Restoration of the Jews to the rebuilding of their temple, and the commencement of the millennium.

. . .

I.   A Preliminary Demonstration, to ascertain the chronology of the world to a single year, according to my XXX chronological tables . . .

. . .

II. A Demonstration from Ptolemy's canon, and the eclipses of the sun and moon, that the state of the four monarchies, and of the Jews under them, has been all along the same that the scripture prophecies foretold . . .

. . .

III. That fifteen eminent scripture prophecies have been all along rightly understood, and their remarkable events all along foretold from them, and have been already fulfilled accordingly. . .

. . . Mr. Whiston, from the same prophecies, still foretells the sudden destruction of the Turkish Empire; of the House of Austria; and afterwards of the German Emperors, and Popes of Rome. The sudden Ascension also of the witnesses, or vaudois; the restoration of the Jews; the rebuilding their temple, and the commencement of the mellennium; and these four by A.D. 1766 . . .

IV. That, according to the same scripture prophecies, the Jews are to be restored to their own country, and rebuild their Temple, and the millennium to commence by A.D. 1766.

This is demonstrated.

. . .

3.   From the remarkable astronomical signals that are to alarm mankind of what is coming.

1.   Those mentioned in my astronomical year 1736. Especially the northern lights, since 1715, with six comets at the Protestant Reformation, in four years, 1530, 1531, 1533, 1534. Page 25

compar'd with the seven comets already seen in these last eleven years 1737, 1739, 1742, 1743, 1744, 1746, and the last 1748 . . .

. . .

Lecture II. March 8, the Day of the second earthquake at London.

An account of the fulfilling of those signals whose times are already past.

Prediction: 1. That a general curse should, in these very last days, be on the earth, and a dissolution of its former state.

Completion 1: This seems now to be fulfilling, by all proper symptoms of such a curse and dissolution.

Prediction 2: That the horrid wickedness of men should precede these sore judgments.

Completion 2: This horrid wickedness of the present age, is almost too evident to need any particular proofs. However, such proofs will be pro-duc'd abundantly in my IIId lecture.

. . .

Prediction 6: That terrible meteors are to come upon mankind from the air.

Completion 6: It is to be observed, that the first of our modern remark-able meteors, or northern lights, came in the year 1715, (as did the great eclipse of the sun come the same year) the very year when the period of the outer court of the temple trodden down by the gentile first ended; immediately after which Christ foretold these tokens should come, as we have seen. Which sort of meteors were so common after 1715, for about twenty-one years, till the second of those years 1736 (the great year for eclipses also) as to be at length little regarded. Altho' they have since been remarkably revived; especially by that red or bloody canopy that encom-pas'd the sky almost round every way, Jan. 23, 1749–50, at night, which I saw myself at Lyndon . . .

. . .

Prediction 20: The King of the North was to come against the Roman Empire, with great forces and success.

Completion 20: This King of the North is plainly the Turkish Sultan, or Ottoman Emperor, who came or sent vast armies against the same empire from Turcomania, in the northern parts of the world, being the sixth trumpet, or second woe, in the Revelation.

Prediction 21: The same King of the North was to conquer many coun-tries belonging to the Roman Empire.

Completion 21: This was exactly true of the Turks.

Prediction 22: The same King of the North was to get possession of Judea, and the neighbouring countries.

Complete 22: This was exactly true of the Turks . . .

. . .

Prediction 30: This King of the North was at length to go out with great fury to destroy many.

Completion 30: This the Turk did, in a terrible manner, at the siege and taking of Belgrade, 1736.

Prediction 31: This King of the North is to plant his royal pavilion between the Mediterranean and Dead Seas in a glorious holy Mountain of Judea.

Completion 31: This is justly and speedily to be expected of the Turk.

Prediction 32: Yet is he there and then to come to his end, without any means of avoiding it.

Completion 32: This is justly and speedily to be expected of the Turks: Till which avoidance the Jews cannot peaceably settle themselves in their own country of Judea.

. . .

Prediction 43: This rebuilding of the Jewish Temple is to be after a grand Week of Years, when the seventh millenary is beginning.

Completion 43: This seventh millenary will begin 1766, as has been already demonstrated, pag. 608, 609. But as to the Times of the Completion of these last six predictions, it is evident that they are not fully come, although I believe they are very soon approaching.

William Whiston, excerpts from *Memoirs of the life and writings of Mr. William Whiston* (London: J. Whiston and B. White, 1753), vol. 1, pp. 602–8 and vol. 2, pp. 46–88.

Astrology is one of the most ancient Sciences, held in high Esteem of old, by the Wise and Great. Formerly, no Prince would make War or Peace, nor any General fight a Battle, in short, no important Affair was undertaken without first consulting an Astrologer, who examined the Aspects and Configurations of the heavenly Bodies, and mark'd the *lucky Hour*. Now the noble Art (more Shame to the Age we live in!) is dwindled into Contempt; the Great neglect us, Empires make Leagues, and Parliaments Laws, without advising with us; and scarce any other Use is made of our learned Labours, than to find the best Time of cutting Corns, or gelding Pigs. This Mischief we owe in a great measure to ourselves: The

Ignorant Herd of Mankind, had they not been encourag'd to it by some of us, would never have dared to depreciate our sacred Dictates; but *Urania* has been betray'd by her own Sons; those whom she had favour'd with the greatest Skill in her divine Art, the most eminent Astronomers among the moderns, the *Newtons*, *Halleys*, and *Whistons*, have wantonly contemn'd and abus'd her, contrary to the Light of her own Consciences.

Of these, only the last nam'd, *Whiston*, has liv'd to repent, and speak his Mind honestly. In his former Works he had treated *Judiciary Astrology* as a Chimera, and asserted, That not only the fixed Stars, but the planets (Sun and Moon excepted) were at so immense a Distance, as to be incapable of any Influence on this Earth, and consequently nothing could be foretold from their Positions: but now in the Memoirs of his Life, publish'd 1749, in the 82d year of his age, he foretels, Page 607, the sudden Destruction of the *Turkish* Empire, and of the House of *Austria*, *German* Emperors, etc and *Popes* of *Rome*; the Restoration of the *Jews*, and Commencement of the *Millennium*; all by the Year 1766; and this not only from Scripture Prophecies; but (take his own Words) - "From the remarkable *astronomical* signals that are to Alarm Mankind of what is coming; viz. The *Northern Lights* since 1715; the six Comets at the Protestant Reformation in four years, 1530, 1531, 1533, 1534, compar'd with the seven Comets already seen in these last eleven Years 1737, 1739, 1742, 1743, 1744, 1746, and 1748. - From the great Annular Eclipse of the sun, *July* 14, 1748, whose Center pass'd through all the four Monarchies, from *Scotland* to the *East Indies*. From the Occultation of the *Pleiades* by the Moon each periodical Month, after the Eclipse last *July*, from above three Years, visible to the whole *Roman* Empire; as there was a like Occultation of the *Hyades* from A. 590, to A. 595, for six Years foretold by *Isaiah*. From the Transit of *Mercury* over the *Sun*, April 25, 1753, which will be visible thro' that Empire. From the comet of A.D. 1456, 1531, 1607, and 1682, which will appear again about 1757 ending, or 1758 beginning, and will also be visible thro' that Empire. From the transit of *Venus* over the *Sun*, *May* 26, 1761, which will be visible over the same Empire: and lastly from the annular Eclipse of the *Sun*, *March* 11, 1764, which will be visible over the same Empire." From these *Astronomical Signs* he foretels those great Events, That with 16 Years from this Time, "The *Millennium* or 1000 years Reign of Christ shall begin, there shall be a *new Heavens*, and *a new Earth*; there shall be no more an Infidel in *Christendom*, Page 398, nor a Gaming-Table at Tunbridge!"

When these Predictions are accomplished, what glorious Proofs they will be of the Truth of our Art? And if they happen to fail, there is no doubt but so profound an Astronomer as Mr. *Whiston*, will be able to see *other*

Signs in the Heavens, foreshowing that the Conversion of Infidels was to be postponed, and the *Millennium* adjorun'd. After these great Things can any Man doubt our being capable of predicting a little Rain or Sun-shine?

Reader, Farewell, and make the best Use of your Years and your Almanacks, for you see, that according to *Whiston*, you may have at most, but sixteen more of them.

R. Saunders

Patowmack, July 30, 1750

Benjamin Franklin, excerpts from *The Writings of Benjamin Franklin*, collected and edited by Albert Henry Smyth, vol. 3, 1750–1759 (New York: Macmillan, 1907), 9–12.

Further Reading

Burns, William E. *The Scientific Revolution: An Encyclopedia*. Santa Barbara, CA: ABC-CLIO, 2001.

Burns, William E. *The Scientific Revolution in Global Perspective*. Oxford: Oxford University Press, 2016.

Butterfield, Herbert. *The Origins of Modern Science*. Rev. ed. New York: Free Press, 1965.

Davis, Natalie Zemon. *Women on the Margins. Three Seventeenth-Century Lives*. Cambridge, MA: Harvard University Press, 1995.

Findlen, Paula. *Possessing Nature: Museums, Collecting, and Scientific Culture in Early Modern Italy*. Berkeley: University of California Press, 1996.

Grafton, Anthony. *Defenders of the Text: The Traditions of Scholarship in an Age of Science, 1450–1800*. Cambridge, MA: Harvard University Press, 1994.

Hellyer, Marcus. *The Scientific Revolution: The Essential Readings*. London: Blackwell, 2003.

Jacob, Margaret C. *The Scientific Revolution. A Brief History with Documents*. Boston: Bedford/St. Martins, 2010.

Jardine, Lisa. *Ingenious Pursuits: Building the Scientific Revolution*. New York: Anchor Books, 2000.

Kuhn, Thomas. *The Structure of Scientific Revolutions*. 4th ed. Chicago: University of Chicago Press, 2012.

Linden, Stanton J., ed. *The Alchemy Reader. From Hermes Trismegistus to Isaac Newton*. Cambridge: Cambridge University Press, 2003.

Machamer, Peter. *The Cambridge Companion to Galileo*. Cambridge: Cambridge University Press, 1998.

Newman, William R. *Newton the Alchemist: Science, Enigma, and the Quest for Nature's "Secret Fire."* Princeton, NJ: Princeton University Press, 2019.

Osler, Margaret J., ed. *Rethinking the Scientific Revolution.* Cambridge: Cambridge University Press, 2000.

Park, Katharine, and Lorraine Daston, eds. *The Cambridge History of Science.* Vol. 3. *Early Modern Science.* Cambridge: Cambridge University Press, 2003.

Project Vox team. (2019). "Margaret Cavendish, Duchess of Newcastle-upon-Tyne." *Project Vox.* Duke University Libraries. https://projectvox .org/cavendish-1623-1673/

Ray, Meredith K. *Daughters of Alchemy: Women and Scientific Culture in Early Modern Italy.* Cambridge, MA: Harvard University Press, 2015.

Robin, Diana. "Women on the Move: Trends in Anglophone Studies of Women in the Italian Renaissance." *I Tatti Studies in the Italian Renaissance* 16, nos. 1/2 (2013): 13–25.

Shapin, Steven. *A Social History of Truth.* Chicago: University of Chicago Press, 1994.

Shapin, Steven. *The Scientific Revolution.* 2nd ed. Chicago: University of Chicago Press, 2018.

Smith, Pamela H. *The Body of the Artisan: Art and Experience in the Scientific Revolution.* Chicago: University of Chicago Press, 2004.

Smith, Pamela H. "Science on the Move: Recent Trends in the History of Early Modern Science." *Renaissance Quarterly* 62 (2009): 345–75.

Strocchia, Sharon. *Women and the Pursuit of Health in Late Renaissance Italy.* Cambridge, MA: Harvard University Press, 2019.

9

The Crusades Ended
in the Middle Ages

What People Think Happened

In 1095, Pope Urban II announced the First Crusade to knights at the Council of Clermont. The men in attendance raised their swords in jubilation. After some preparations, heavily armored men marched through Islamic lands before arriving at the doors of Jerusalem. Soon the city fell and the Holy Land returned to Christian hands. However, European successes did not last for long; and a series of distinct armies descended upon the Middle East from Europe. Today, these distinct armies are known as the numbered crusades. Some of them are still famous. In the Third Crusade, for example, King Richard of England fought against noble Saladin. Their mutual military brilliance made gains difficult on either side, but their stalemate led to a surprising, even unprecedented respect between the Christian king and the Islamic sultan. Back in England, Robin Hood helped ensure the well-being of the English and the security of Richard's throne during the king's absence.

The myth goes that the Crusades consisted of nine distinct events spread out over a bit more than 200 years of history. Over time, it became clear that the land route from Europe to the Holy Land was not working. Thus, Crusaders began sailing to Egypt and then trying the shorter land passage to Jerusalem. These different Crusades often sought both to retake lands from Islam and to provide aid to the Crusader Kingdoms established after the First Crusade. Those Crusader Kingdoms were Christian

Scenes from the Eighth Crusade of King Louis IX of France and his troops arriving in Tunis, and then being attacked by Muslims, from *Chroniques de France ou de St Denis*, mid-13th century. Popular myth holds that the Crusades were a series of distinct, numbered events, fought between the West and the East, with a clear beginning and clear ending during the medieval period. However, historians debate what made the Crusades different from other kinds of warfare and pilgrimage. The same kinds of wars and calls to crusade continued throughout the early modern period. Clear lines between religions could define conflicts and daily life, but wars and daily life also could defy such clear boundaries. (The British Library)

bulwarks in Islamic lands. Each heavily fortified kingdom fought never-ending wars against bellicose people who simply viewed the world differently than they did. The fall of the last Christian outposts at Acre in 1291 ended the Crusades. From that point onward, Europeans lacked a foothold in the east. Additionally, their conflicts became simply different than the Crusades had been. During the Crusades, according to the myth, big armies had fought huge campaigns aimed at conquering the Holy Land. They had adopted the Cross as their symbol. They had fought for religious purposes. The myth goes that all of that ended in 1291. Armies stopped seeking the Holy Land or wearing the cross. A stalemate began between the Islamic East and the Christian West.

How the Story Became Popular

The idea that the Crusades began in 1095 at the Council of Clermont and ended in 1291 at Acre had already been established by the 1700s. In that century, authors like Voltaire and David Hume presented the Crusades as something focused exclusively on the Holy Land. Moreover, the Crusades were part of a distant, superstitious past. Enlightenment writers sought to show that the Crusades had ended and were yet another example of medieval darkness dispelled by recent rationalism. During the 1800s, these Enlightenment ideas combined with European imperialism: The Crusades were an example of a past when Europeans had fought for and conquered faraway lands. One of the most influential writers of this period was the novelist Walter Scott. For example, Scott popularized the still common idea of the enlightened Sultan Saladin. By the time World War I started in the early twentieth century, the Crusades had offered national heroes like Richard the Lionhearted.

Many modern assumptions about the Crusades were further popularized in Steven Runciman's three-volume *History of the Crusades*, published in the 1950s. Runciman structured his book around the idea of numbered conflicts that began with Clermont and ended with the fall of Acre in 1291. He also argued many points that people still assume are true. For example, Runciman claimed that money, not religion, actually motivated medieval Crusaders. Runciman proposed that second and later sons faced uncertain financial futures. Thus, they might have said they were fighting for religion, but in truth they decided to take the cross to seize lands for themselves. Thus Crusaders, for Runciman, became proto-modern, would-be colonizers, who were motivated by greed and who had little, financially speaking, at home to lose.

In more recent decades, the Crusades have become enmeshed into broader ideas about the "West." In this line of thinking, the Crusades serve as a key early example of warfare between two fundamentally different ways of viewing the world: A Christian West and an Islamic East. Arguments for the incompatibility of these worldviews became especially popular after the September 11, 2001, attacks on the United States. In the months that followed, the clash of civilization rhetoric led some individuals to declare that U.S. efforts in Afghanistan and the Middle East were parts of a new "crusade." Such rhetoric was not limited to Americans: Writers in the Middle East also took a new interest in the Crusades. Islamic writers had largely ignored the history of the Crusades until the end of the nineteenth century. Then, in the twentieth century, they too began to draw connections between the Crusades of the past and the imperialism of the present. Their modern relations with states like Britain, the United States, and Israel became parts of modern "crusades."

PRIMARY SOURCE DOCUMENTS

Most myths about the Crusades declare that they began after Pope Urban II's call for what became the First Crusade in 1095. No transcription of Urban's speech survives. Thus, historians have tried to piece together exactly what the pope urged and what he promised from four different accounts of the speech. Each account of the speech differs from the others and each has its own strengths and weaknesses as an historical source. For historians interested in using 1095 as the start of the Crusades, it is important to know how Urban's words differed from those of previous holy wars and spiritual promises. What, in short, made the Crusades unique?

In 1095 a great council was held in Auvergne, in the city of Clermont. Pope Urban II, accompanied by cardinals and bishops, presided over it. It was made famous by the presence of many bishops and princes from France and Germany. After the council had attended to ecclesiastical matters, the pope went out into a public square, because no house was able to hold the people, and addressed them in a very persuasive speech, as follows: "O race of the Franks, O people who live beyond the mountains [that is, reckoned from Rome], O people loved and chosen of God, as is clear from your many deeds, distinguished over all other nations by the situation of your land, your catholic faith, and your regard for the holy church, we have a special message and exhortation for you. For we wish you to know what a grave matter has brought us to your country. The sad news has come from Jerusalem and Constantinople that the people of Persia, an accursed and foreign race, enemies of God, 'a generation that set not their heart aright, and whose spirit was not steadfast with God' [Ps. 78:8], have invaded the lands of those Christians and devastated them with the sword, rapine, and fire. Some of the Christians they have carried away as slaves, others they have put to death. The churches they have either destroyed or turned into mosques. They desecrate and overthrow the altars. They circumcise the Christians and pour the blood from the circumcision on the altars or in the baptismal fonts. Some they kill in a horrible way by cutting open the abdomen, taking out a part of the entrails and tying them to a stake; they then beat them and compel them to walk until all their entrails are drawn out and they fall to the ground. Some they use as targets for their arrows. They compel some to stretch out their necks and then they try to see whether they can cut off their heads with one stroke of the sword. It is better to say nothing of their horrible treatment of the women. They have taken from the Greek empire a tract of land so large that it takes more than two months to walk through it. Whose duty is it to avenge this and recover that land, if not yours? For to you more than to other nations the Lord has given the military spirit, courage, agile bodies, and the bravery to strike down those who resist you. Let your minds be stirred to bravery by the deeds of your forefathers, and by the efficiency and greatness of Karl the Great, and of Ludwig his son, and of the other kings who have destroyed Turkish kingdoms, and established Christianity in their lands. You should be moved especially by the holy grave of our Lord and Saviour which is now held by unclean peoples, and by the holy places which are treated with dishonour and irreverently befouled with their uncleanness.

O bravest of knights, descendants of unconquered ancestors, do not be weaker than they, but remember their courage. If you are kept back by your love for your children, relatives, and wives, remember what the Lord says in the Gospel: 'He that loveth father or mother more than me is not worthy of me' [Matt. 10:37]; 'and everyone that hath forsaken houses, or brothers, or sisters, or father, or mother, or wife, or children, or lands for my name's sake, shall receive a hundred-fold and shall inherit everlasting life' [Matt. 19:29]. Let no possessions keep you back, no solicitude for your property. Your land is shut in on all sides by the sea and the mountains, and is too thickly populated. There is not much wealth here, and the soil scarcely yields enough to support you. On this account you kill and devour each other, and carry on war and mutually destroy each other. Let your hatred and quarrels cease, your civil wars come to an end, and all your dissensions stop. Set out on the road to the holy sepulchre, take the land from that wicked people, and make it your own. That land which, as the Scripture says, is flowing with milk and honey, God gave to the children of Israel. Jerusalem is the best of all lands, more fruitful than all others, as it were a second Paradise of delights. This land our Saviour made illustrious by his birth, beautiful with his life, and sacred with his suffering; he redeemed it with his death and glorified it with his tomb. This royal city is now held captive by her enemies, and made pagan by those who know not God. She asks and longs to be liberated and does not cease to beg you to come to her aid. She asks aid especially from you because, as I have said, God has given more of the military spirit to you than to other nations. Set out on this journey and you will obtain the remission of your sins and be sure of the incorruptible glory of the kingdom of heaven."

When Pope Urban had said this and much more of the same sort, all who were present were moved to cry out with one accord, "It is the will of God, it is the will of God." When the pope heard this he raised his eyes to heaven and gave thanks to God, and commanding silence with a gesture of his hand, he said: "My dear brethren, today there is fulfilled in you that which the Lord says in the Gospel, 'Where two or three are gathered together in my name, there am I in the midst' [Matt. 18:20]. For unless the Lord God had been in your minds you would not all have said the same thing. For although you spoke with many voices, nevertheless it was one and the same thing that made you speak. So I say unto you, God, who put those words into your hearts, has caused you to utter them. Therefore let these words be your battle cry, because God caused you to speak them. Whenever you meet the enemy in battle, you shall all cry out, 'It is the will of God, it is the will of God.' And we do not command the old or weak to go, or those who cannot bear arms. No women shall go without their husbands, or brothers, or proper companions, for such would be a hindrance rather than a help, a burden rather than an advantage. Let the rich aid the poor and equip them for fighting and take them with them. Clergymen shall not go without the consent of their bishop, for otherwise the journey would be of no value to them. Nor will this pilgrimage be of any benefit to a layman if he goes without the blessing of his priest. Whoever therefore shall determine to make this journey and shall make a vow to God and shall offer himself as a living sacrifice, holy, acceptable to God [Rom. 12:1], shall wear a cross on his brow or on his breast. And when he returns after having fulfilled his vow he shall wear the cross on his back. In this way he will obey the command of the Lord, 'Whosoever doth not bear his cross and come after me is not worthy of me'" [Luke 14:27]. When these things had been done, while all prostrated themselves on the earth and beat their breasts, one of the cardinals, named Gregory, made confession for them, and they were given absolution for all their sins. After the absolution, they received the benediction and the permission to go home.

> Excerpts from the "Speech at the Council of Clermont" by Pope Urban II, Robert the Monk version, published in *A Source Book for Mediaeval History*, edited by Oliver J. Thatcher and Edgar McNeal (New York: Charles Scribner's Sons, 1905), 518–21.

Modern myths about the Crusades often involve stories about King Richard the Lionheart and his battles against Saladin. Such stories repeat that both men modeled honor and chivalry. The two men greatly respected each other and their religious differences. These tales are often the result of nineteenth- and twentieth-century fictions. Moreover, the myths of Robin Hood also tie into these stories. Stories about Robin Hood speak of the adventures of outlaw

Robin fighting to keep the English Kingdom for Richard, who was away in the Holy Land. Robin opposed Richard's wicked brother John and his evil henchmen. Like many myths, parts of these stories are accurate while much of them are not. Various political figures did try to take control over Richard's territory in his absence; Saladin did benefit from favorable writings among Christians. However, the myths take those historical facts out of context and exaggerate them, while creating heroes and villains out of complex historical actors. In the following excerpt, a chronicler presents an account of Richard in the Holy Land that largely conforms to common modern assumptions about the Crusades.

John, the king's brother, who alone of the sons of his mother, queen Eleanor, survived his brother, besides the earldom of Mortain, which, by his father's gift, he had long enjoyed, was so greatly enriched and increased in England by his brother, that both privately and publicly it was affirmed by many that the king had no thoughts of returning to the kingdom, and that his brother, already no less powerful than himself, if he should not restrain his innate temper, would, impelled by the desire of sovereignty, endeavor to drive him vanquished from the realm.

Sect. 9. The time of commencing his journey pressed hard upon King Richard, as he, who had been first of all the princes on this side the Alps in the taking up of the cross, was unwilling to be last in setting out. A king worthy of the name of king, who, in the first year of his reign, left the kingdom of England for Christ, scarcely otherwise than if he had departed never to return. So great was the devotion of the man, so hastily, so quickly and so speedily did he run, yea fly, to avenge the wrongs of Christ. However, whilst he kept the greater matter in his mind, giving himself in some little measure to deliberation for the kingdom, having received power from the pope that he might withdraw the cross from such of his own subjects, as he should desire, for the government of his kingdom, he first appointed Hugh Pudsey, bishop of Durham, to be chief justice of the whole realm . . .

. . .

Sect. 86. The King of the English, Richard, had already completed two years in conquering the region around Jerusalem, and during all that time there had no aid been sent to him from any of his kingdoms. Nor yet were his only and uterine brother, John, Earl of Mortain, nor his justiciaries, nor his other nobles, observed to take any care to send him any part of his revenues; but they did not even think of his return. However, prayer was made without ceasing by the church to God for him. The king's army was decreased daily in the Land of Promise, and besides those who were slain with the sword, many thousands of the people perished every month by the too sudden extremities of the nightly cold and the daily heat. When it appeared that they would all have to die there, every one had to choose whether he would die as a coward or in battle. On the other side, the strength of the Gentiles greatly increased, and their confidence was strengthened by the misfortunes of the Christians; their army was relieved at certain times by fresh troops; the weather was nature to them; the place was their native country; their labour, health; their frugality, medicine . . .

. . .

Sect. 87. The king was extremely sick, and confined to his bed; his fever continued without intermission; the physicians whispered that it was an acute semitertian. And as they despaired of his recovery even from the first, terrible dismay was spread from the king's abode through the camp. There were few among the many thousands who did not meditate on flight, and the utmost confusion of dispersion or surrender would have followed, had not Hubert of Walter, bishop of Salisbury, immediately assembled the council. He obtained by forcible allegations that the army should not break up until a truce was demanded of Saladin. . . .

. . .

Sect. 88. In the meantime, a certain Gentile, called Saffatin, came down to see the king, as he generally did; he was a brother of Saladin, an ancient man of war of remarkable politeness and intelligence, and one whom the king's magnanimity and munificence had charmed even to the love of his person and favour of his party. The king's servants greeting him less joyfully than they were accustomed, and not admitting him to an interview with the king, "I perceive," said he by his interpreter, "that you are greatly afflicted; nor am I ignorant of the cause. My friend, your king, is sick, and therefore you close his doors to me." And falling into tears, with his whole heart exclaimed, "O God of the Christians, if thou be a God, do not suffer such a man, so necessary to thy people, to fall so suddenly!" He was intrusted with their avowal, and thus spoke on: "In truth I forewarn you, that if the king should die while things stand as they are at present, all you Christians will perish, and all this region will in time to come be ours without contest. Shall we at all dread that stout king of France, who before he came into battle was defeated, whose whole strength, which three years had contributed, the short space of three months consumed? Hither will he on no account return anymore; for we always esteem this as a sure token (I am not speaking craftily, but simply), that those whom at first we think cowardly, we ever after find worse. But that king, of all the princes of the Christian name whom the round circle of the whole world encompasses, is alone worthy of the honour of a captain and the name of a king, because he commenced well, and went on better, and will be crowned by the most prosperous result, if only he shall remain with you a short time . . .”

Excerpts from the “Itinerary of the Pilgrims and Deeds of Richard,” in J. A. Giles, *Chronicles of the Crusades*, edited by H. G. Bohn (London: Henry G. Bohn, 1848), 5, 55–57.

The idea of breaking Crusades into numbered expeditions was already popular by the eighteenth century. This numbering system was based upon the belief that serious fighting in the east began after Clermont and ended after the fall of Acre in 1291. Part of this interpretation was rooted in broader assumptions about European history: the medieval past was religious and the Crusades were a part of that. The Renaissance period was secular and thus religious Crusades simply did not fit in. The fall of Acre as an endpoint worked because Acre was the last major stronghold of the older Crusader kingdoms. It also worked because it conveniently happened just before the Renaissance supposedly began. In the following excerpt, a nineteenth-century writer relates what historians of the period simply assumed well into the second half of the twentieth century.

Eighth and last Crusade, 1270.—Chiefs: Saint Louis, Charles of Anjou, and prince Edward of England. Under the pontificate of Clement IV.

The progress of Bibars, the solicitations of the Khan of the Moguls, and above all the desire of liberating the Christian prisoners, determined Saint Louis to undertake a second crusade. The interested suggestions of the king of Sicily, and the hope of converting the king of Tunis, induced him to sail towards Africa. The French army, landing near the ruins of Carthage, laid siege to Tunis; but a contagious disorder devastating the camp, carried off the French monarch, who met his death with the courage of a hero, and the pious resignation of a Christian. Terms of peace were now concluded by Philip the Hardy, and Charles of Anjou, with Mohammed Mostanser, and the renunciation of the expedition to the Holy Land was agreed on. Fresh disasters attended the French during their return, and characterized the termination of the crusades.

End of the Christian Dominion in Syria, 1270–91.—The ruin of the last Christian colonies of the East, already foreseen by the general council of Lyons in 1274, and which had only been retarded by the incursions of the Moguls and the death of Bibars, was at length consummated by the loss of Tripoli and Acre, which fell into the power of Khalil-Ascraf, the Sultan of Egypt, in 1291.

The Hospitalers, Templars, and Teutonic knights, the last defenders of the Holy Land, withdrew to the isle of Cyprus. In 1310, the Hospitallers fixed their residence at Rhodes. The Templars were finally established in 1312; and the Teutons, in 1300, transferred the seat of their order into Courland, where they already possessed some influence, and where they long continued powerful . . .

T. G. Jones, excerpt from *A Manual of the History of the Middle Ages* (London: D. Nutt, 1841), 208–9.

What Really Happened

What seems like a very straightforward topic masks a very complicated and sometimes confusing historical reality. The idea of a series of clearly defined numbered crusades setting out from Europe to conquer Jerusalem requires scholars to be able to clearly define what made a Crusade different from other types of warfare. It also assumes that each Crusade had similar goals—goals that basically ended by the year 1300. The problem is that historians have a hard time identifying any characteristics that were both common to all Crusades and that made them different from other sorts of warfare. Historians debate about whether such unifying characteristics even existed.

In the late 1000s, there was clearly an initial call for mostly French nobles to set out on what historians have dubbed the "First Crusade." It is also clear that medieval people did not initially view the call as something different from past practice. The motivation behind the call was in part to assist the Byzantine emperor, who ruled over parts of what is now Greece and Turkey. The pope had made similar requests in the past. Moreover, the idea of the church being involved in warfare had a long history. Additionally, the idea that people would travel long distances to reap spiritual rewards was long established through the practice of religious pilgrimage. The idea of a "plenary indulgence," that is, a full removal of the taint of sin in exchange for some action, would have been a novel idea, but it is not clear if that was the offer initially made by church leaders.

The union of warfare, pilgrimage to the Holy Land, and papal sanction does appear to have been viewed as novel, but that specific union only really fits the so-called First Crusade. In some instances, for example, people clearly perceived warfare within Europe itself along the same lines as they thought about Crusades aimed at Jerusalem. Already, by the time of the so-called Second Crusade, crusaders were eligible for the same sorts of spiritual rewards if they fought against Islam on the Iberian Peninsula as they would receive if they traveled to the Holy Land. By the end of the twelfth century, crusading rewards were available for individuals who fought against other Christians in Europe. In the so-called Fourth Crusade, a crusader army fought against a Christian city that had rebelled against Venice. The crusaders then eventually conquered Constantinople—another Christian city. In another example, crusading rewards were offered for Christian rulers who warred against Albigensian heretics in southern France.

Another significant problem with the myths about the Crusades is that Latin Christians continued to preach for crusades and crusades in fact continued to happen for centuries after 1291. In the 1400s, for example, Pope Eugenius IV oversaw a crusade featuring over 10,000 people. The crusading army eventually was defeated at Varna. Writers throughout Europe wrote dozens of texts advocating for a new crusade after Constantinople fell to the Islamic armies of the Ottoman Turks in 1453. Pope Pius II, pope from 1458 to 1464, made a new crusade the central tenet of his papacy. In 1459, he called a Europe-wide council to gain support for the idea and then died as his army and ships assembled to travel to the east—an army he had planned to personally lead. None of these crusades during the late medieval and early modern periods were successful in their goals of retaking Jerusalem or Constantinople, but in practice and conception they varied little from the numbered crusades of the twelfth and thirteenth centuries.

The concept and application of the term "crusade" continues to be much debated among scholars. If historians expand the purview of the crusades beyond 1291 then it becomes extremely difficult to determine what falls within the study of the crusades versus what falls into the general history of religion, politics, or warfare in late medieval and early modern Europe. Thus, some argue the traditional purview of the crusades up to 1291 can remain a segmented area of study. They claim that, although events aimed at other places or occurring in later centuries certainly carry similarities with earlier events, things like the Latin Kingdoms in the east had ended. Then, only less frequent, smaller armies moved across those areas in later decades. Others disagree and see more similarities than differences between late medieval and early modern crusades. It is a myth that the "crusades" ended in the thirteenth century, but what the crusades were and whether the medieval crusades were distinct from later ones is still a point of scholarly debate.

PRIMARY SOURCE DOCUMENTS

The following excerpt presents a second, different account (compared to the one excerpted earlier in this chapter) of Pope Urban's speech at the Council of Clermont in 1095. The major difference between the sources highlights some of the challenges and complexities that historians of the Crusades have to take into account in their interpretations. In addition, this account highlights aspects of the speech that people probably found both traditional and new. Here, Urban pushes for religious reform and calls for aid for Christian allies. Neither was unusual during the eleventh century. Urban also offers something new, a full remission of sins for joining the Crusade. Texts like the one excerpted below defy myths about what the Crusades were, what they aimed for, and how long they lasted.

"Most beloved brethren: Urged by necessity, I, Urban, by the permission of God chief bishop and prelate over the whole world, have come into these parts as an ambassador with a divine admonition to you, the servants of God. I hoped to find you as faithful and as zealous in the service of God as I had supposed you to be. But if there is in you any deformity or crookedness contrary to God's law, with divine help I will do my best to remove it. For God has put you as stewards over his family to minister to it. Happy indeed will you be if he finds you faithful in your stewardship. You are called shepherds, with your crooks always in your hands. Do not go to sleep, but guard on all sides the flock committed to you. For if through your carelessness or negligence a wolf carries away one of your sheep, you will surely lose the reward laid up for you with God. And after you have been bitterly scourged with remorse for your faults, you will be fiercely overwhelmed in hell, the abode of death. For according to the gospel you are the salt of the earth [Matt. 5:13]. but if you fall short in your duty, how, it may be asked, can it be salted? O how great the need of salting! It is indeed necessary for you to correct with the salt of wisdom this foolish people which is so devoted to the pleasures of this world, lest the Lord, when He may wish to speak to them, find them putrefied by their sins, unsalted and stinking. For if He shall find worms, that is, sins, in them, because you have been negligent in your duty, He will command them as worthless to be thrown into the abyss of unclean things. And because you cannot restore to Him His great loss, He will surely condemn you and drive you from His loving presence. But the man who applies this salt should be prudent, provident, modest, learned, peaceable, watchful, pious, just, equitable, and pure. For how can the ignorant teach others? How can the licentious make others modest? And how can the impure make others pure? If anyone hates peace, how can he make others peaceable? Or if anyone has soiled his hands with baseness, how can he cleanse the impurities of another? We read also that if the blind lead the blind, both will fall into the ditch [Matt. 15:14]. But first correct yourselves, in order that, free from blame, you may be able to correct those who are subject to you. If you wish to be the friends of God, gladly do the things which you know will please Him. You must especially let all matters that pertain to the church be controlled by the law of the church. And be careful that simony does not take root among you, lest both those who buy and those who sell [church offices] be beaten with the scourges of the Lord through narrow streets and driven into the place of destruction and confusion. Keep the church and the clergy in all its grades entirely free from the secular power. See that the tithes that belong to God are faithfully paid from all the produce of the land; let them not be sold or withheld. If anyone seizes a bishop let him be treated as an outlaw. If anyone seizes or robs monks, or clergymen, or nuns, or their servants, or pilgrims, or merchants, let him be anathema [that is, cursed]. Let robbers and incendiaries and all their accomplices be expelled from the church and anathematized. If a man who does not give a part of his goods as alms is punished with the damnation of hell, how should he be punished who robs another of his goods? For thus it happened to the rich man in the gospel [Luke 16:19]; for he was not punished because he had stolen the goods of another, but because he had not used well the things which were his.

"You have seen for a long time the great disorder in the world caused by these crimes. It is so bad in some of your provinces, I am told, and you are so weak in the administration of justice, that one can hardly go along the road by day or night without being attacked by robbers; and whether at home or abroad, one is in danger of being despoiled either by force or fraud. Therefore it is necessary to reenact the truce, as it is commonly called, which was proclaimed a long time ago by our holy fathers. I exhort and demand that you, each, try hard to have the truce kept in your diocese. And if anyone shall be led by his cupidity or arrogance to break this truce, by the authority of God and with the sanction of this council he shall be anathematized."

After these and various other matters had been attended to, all who were present, clergy and people, gave thanks to God and agreed to the pope's proposition. They all faithfully promised to keep the decrees. Then the pope said that in another part of the world Christianity was suffering from a state of affairs that was worse than the one just mentioned. He continued:

"Although, O sons of God, you have promised more firmly than ever to keep the peace among yourselves and to preserve the rights of the church, there remains still an important work for you to do. Freshly quickened by the divine correction, you must apply the strength of your righteousness to another matter which concerns you as well as God. For your brethren who live in the east are in urgent need of your help, and you must hasten to give them the aid which has often been promised them. For, as the most of you have heard, the Turks and Arabs have attacked them and have conquered the territory of Romania [the Greek empire] as far west as the shore of the Mediterranean and the Hellespont, which is called the Arm of St. George. They have occupied more and more of the lands of those Christians, and have overcome them in seven battles. They have killed and captured many, and have destroyed the churches and devastated the empire. If you permit them to continue thus for a while with impunity, the faithful of God will be much more widely attacked by them. On this account I, or rather the Lord, beseech you as Christ's heralds to publish this everywhere and to persuade all people of whatever rank, foot-soldiers and knights, poor and rich, to carry aid promptly to those Christians and to destroy the vile race from the lands of our friends. I say this to those who are present, it is meant also for those who are absent. Moreover, Christ commands it.

All who die by the way, whether by land or by sea, or in battle against the pagans, shall have immediate remission of sins. This I grant them through the power of God with which I am invested. O what a disgrace if such a despised and base race, which worships demons, should conquer a people which has the faith of omnipotent God and is made glorious with the name of Christ! With what reproaches will the Lord overwhelm us if you do not aid those who, with us, profess the Christian religion! Let those who have been accustomed unjustly to wage private warfare against the faithful now go against the infidels and end with victory this war which should have begun long ago. Let those who, for a long time, have been robbers, now become knights. Let those who have been fighting against their brothers and relatives now fight in a proper way against the barbarians. Let those who have been serving as mercenaries for small pay now obtain the eternal reward. Let those who have been wearing themselves out in both body and soul now work for a double honor. Behold! on this side will be the sorrowful and poor, on that, the rich; on this side, the enemies of the Lord, on that, his friends. Let those who go not put off the journey, but rent their lands and collect money for their expenses; and as soon as winter is over and spring comes, let them eagerly set out on the way with God as their guide."

Excerpts from the "Speech at the Council of Clermont" by Pope Urban II, Fulcher of Chartres version, published in *A Source Book for Mediaeval History*, edited by Oliver J. Thatcher and Edgar McNeal (New York: Charles Scribner's Sons, 1905), 514–17.

Modern myths about the Crusades point to a two-century-long period of unending warfare between Christians and Muslims in the Middle East. However, interactions between Christian and Islamic societies during the medieval and early modern periods were much more complicated than that. Christian and Islamic armies allied together to fight against other Christian and Islamic allies. Long periods spent living in the same places meant that Christians and Muslims, although rarely accepting of each other, had to learn to live together. The results were often societies that alternated between tolerance and oppression. In the excerpts below a writer from the late 1200s describes the different sorts of people whom he views inhabiting the Holy Land.

There are dwelling therein men of every nation under heaven, and each man follows his own rite, and, to tell the truth, our own people, the Latins, are worse than all the other people of the land. The reason of this, I think, is that when any man has been a malefactor, as, for example, a homicide, a robber, a thief, or an adulterer, he crosses the sea as a penitent, or else because he fears for his skin, and therefore dares not stay at home. Wherefore men come thither from all parts—from Germany, Italy, France, England, Spain, Hungary, and all other parts of the world; yet they do but change their climate, not their mind: for when they are there, after they have spent what they brought with them, they have to earn some more, and therefore return again to their vomit, and do worse than they did before. They lodge pilgrims of their own nation in their houses, and these men, if they know not how to take care of themselves, trust them, and lose both their property and their honour. They also breed children, who imitate the crimes of their fathers, and thus bad fathers beget sons worse than themselves, from whom descend most vile grandchildren, who tread upon the holy places with polluted feet. Hence it comes to pass that, because of the sins of the dwellers in the land against God, the land itself, and the places of our redemption, is brought into contempt.

Besides the Latins there are many other races there; for example, the Saracens, who preach Mohammed and keep his law. They call our Lord Jesus Christ the greatest of the prophets, and confess that he was conceived of the Holy Ghost and born of the Virgin Mary. But they deny that he suffered and was buried, but choose to say that he ascended into heaven, and sits at the right hand of the Father, because they admit him to be the Son of God. But they declare that Mohammed sits on God's left hand. They are very unclean, and have as many wives as they can feed; yet, nevertheless, they practice unnatural sins, and have *ephebiae* in every city. Yet they are very hospitable, courteous, and kindly.

Besides these there are the Syrians. The whole land is full of these. They are Christians, but keep no faith with the Latins. They are clothed most wretchedly, and are stingy, giving no alms. They dwell among the Saracens, and for the most part are their servants. In dress they are like the Saracens, except that they are distinguished from them by a woolen girdle.

The Greeks in like manner are Christians, but schismatics, save that a great part of them returned to obedience to the Church at a General Council held by our lord Gregory X. In the Greek church all the prelates are monks, and are men of exceeding austerity of life and wondrous virtue.

The Greeks are exceeding devout, and for the most part greatly honour and revere their Prelates. I have heard one of their Patriarchs say in my presence: "We would willingly live in obedience to the Church of Rome, and venerate it; but I am much surprised at my being ranked below the inferior clergy, such as Archbishops and Bishops. Some Archbishops and Bishops wish to make me a Patrarich, kiss their feet, and do them personal service, which I do not hold myself bound to do, albeit I would willingly do so for the Pope, but for no one else."

There are also Armenians, Georgians, Nestorians, Nubians, Jacobites, Chaldeans, Medes, Persians, Ethiopians, Egyptians, and many other peoples who are Christians. Of those there is an infinite number. Each group of them has its own patriarch and obeys him. Their prelates declare that they would most willingly belong to the church of Rome. Of these the Nestorians, Jacobites, and the like are so named after certain heretics who once were their chiefs.

Moreover, there are in the Holy Land Midianites, who now are called Bedouins and Turcomans, who apply themselves solely to feeding flocks and camels, of which they have exceedingly great numbers. These people have no fixed dwellings, but wherever they learn that there is pasture, thither they go and pitch their tents. They are exceeding warlike, yet only use swords and lances in battle. They do not use arrows, saying that it is base beyond measure to steal away a man's life with an arrow. They are brave in war, but wear only a red shirt, and over it a large flowing mantle, covering their heads only with a cloth. All Syria is full of them, but for the most part they dwell round about the river Jordan, from Lebanon even to the Wilderness of Paran, because there are mountains for sheep and goats, and plains for cattle and camels. The sheep in those parts, and especially the rams, are very big, and have tails of such a size that one tail is as much as three or four men can eat.

Round about the castle of Arachas, beyond Tripoli, up to the castle of Krak des Chevaliers, dwell Saracens called Vannini. Adjoining them are the Saracens called Assassins, who dwell in the mountains beyond Antaradus near the castle of Margat. They have many castles and cities and fertile land, and are said to have forty thousand fighting men. They have one chief, not by hereditary succession, but by personal merit, who is called the Old Man of the Mountains—not because of his age, but of his wisdom. These people are said to be of Persian origin. I have passed through a part of this country. They are obedient even to death, and at their superior's bidding slay anyone soever, and say that thereby they gain paradise, even if they be slain before they have fulfilled their orders. A few years ago they wished to become obedient to the Church of Rome, and to this end sent an ambassador to Acre, who transacted the negotiation to his complete satisfaction, but on his homeward journey was murdered by his escort just before entering his own land, to the loss of the Church as a body, because the others, when they saw that Christians were not be to be trusted, straightway drew back. The boundary between these people's land and that of the Christians is marked by some stones, on which on the side of the Christians are carved crosses, and on that of the Assassins knives. None of the sultans have hitherto been able to subdue them, but they make their own laws and customs and follow them as they choose. They are a terror to all the nations round about because of their exceeding fierceness.

Now, it must be noted as a matter of fact (although some, who like to talk about what they have never seen, declare the contrary) that the whole East beyond the Mediterranean Sea, even unto India and Ethiopia, acknowledges and preaches the name of Christ, save only the Saracens and some Turcomans who dwell in Cappadocia, so that I declare for certain, as I have myself seen and have heard from others who know, that always in every place and kingdom (besides Egypt and Arabia, where Saracens and other followers of Mohammed chiefly dwell), you will find thirty Christians and more for one Saracen. But the truth is that all the Christians beyond the sea are easterners by nation, and although they are

Christians, yet, as they are not much practiced in the use of arms, when they are assailed by the Saracens, Turks, or any other people whatsoever, they yield to them and buy peace and quiet by paying tribute, and the Saracens, or other lords of the land, place their bailiffs and tax-gatherers therein. Hence it arises that their kingdom is said to belong to the Saracens, whereas, as a matter of fact, all the people are Christians save those bailiffs and tax-gatherers and their families, as I have seen with my own eyes in Cilicia and Lesser Armenia, which is subject to the rule of the Tartars [that is, Mongols]. . . . Many, too, are frightened when they are told that in parts beyond seas there dwell Nestorians, Jacobites, Maronites, Georgians, and other sects named after heretics whom the [Roman] church has condemned, where these men are thought to be heretics, and to follow the errors of those after whom they are called. This is by no means true. God forbid! But they are men of simple and devout life; yet I do not deny that there may be fools among them, seeing that even the church of Rome itself is not free from fools. Now, all these aforesaid nations, and many others whom it would take long to write down, have Archbishops, Bishops, Abbots, and other Prelates, even as we ourselves, and call them by the same names, all save the Nestorians, whose chief Prelate is called Iaselich. He is their Pope, and I have learned for certain that his jurisdiction reaches much farther in the East than that of the entire Western Church. The other Prelates of that sect, however, are called Archbishops and Bishops like our own . . .

> Burchard of Mount Sion, excerpts from *A Description of the Holy Land*, translated by Aubrey Stewart (London: Hanover Square, 1896), 102–7.

Long after 1291, people throughout Europe called for a new crusade to be undertaken against the rulers of the east, especially the Ottoman Turks. During the fifteenth century in particular, people wrote many Latin writings to urge rulers to unite together and fight a new crusade. At times, these exhortations focused on liberating the Holy Land, while at other times they focused on retaking Constantinople. The appeals gained increasing urgency after the fall of Constantinople in 1453 and again in the 1480s, when the Ottomans temporarily conquered a small part of southern Italy. The document excerpted below is an example of these calls for a new crusade. It is translated from Latin into English here for the first time.

. . .

I prepared to write about the unfortunate and accursed oppression of the city of Constantinople, from which a message in these recent days so dismayed and afflicted all of us that anyone who does not lead their life afterwards in sorrow and grief must be judged insane or impious and distant and irreverent from our lord Jesus Christ. For Constantinople has fallen into the power of the Turks . . .

But to the point. Constantinople has been seized by a barbarian enemy, a city where our ancestors, by opportunity and force, subdued almost innumerable barbarians. Constantinople is possessed by this vast enemy, whose audacity terrifies pious and prudent Christians, lest it soon oppress them all, lazy and negligent. What, therefore, in these difficult times is to be done before it is too late? What provision? And what can be planned and provided for? After I bring everything together and exhort you to undertake a war, you, most wise princes of the Christian name, will judge what ought to occur according to your prudence and wisdom. Therefore, in the first place, the nature of undertaking the war and of our enemy, their ancestors, and their condition must be pointed out. Then, the fear and impending danger, along with the proposed hope of victory, must be shown. Finally, the leader and commander who should oversee such a war will be proposed.

If we wish to understand the type and condition of the war that we are proposing, it must be considered, serene King, that the war must be waged against an enemy whose ancestors increased their power more because of idleness and inaction in the Christian world than because of their own virtue and power...

. . . I believe that you understand from the preceding narratives, most wise king, the war proposed to your Highness to undertake against this barbaric people. A people who, as they increased their power by the failure, treachery and inactivity of others, they also undermined our own glory, which had been handed down to us through all the generations of our ancestors since the origin of our world itself. Now the greatest danger of disaster is imminent and impending, if we will also be negligent, even as I will show to you a proposed, visible site and certain hope of victory . . .

. . .

But enough about the danger. Now to the topic of my proposal, about which I promised that I would speak: that if a war is undertaken, hope of victory must come . . .

. . . I do not know and I do not see how it can happen that, with the above said things carefully considered, you hesitate and fear. In fact, rather, you should consider them mulled over, certain, and think, with the war undertaken with due observance, order, and quickly, that Christians hold victory in their hands. Now I will stay silent until another time and, if you like, will preserve for another little book the many things which can be said about the even more certain and indisputable victory at mighty Jerusalem, the kingdom for which you hold the title, and of the Holy Land that our Lord Jesus tread upon with his most sacred feet . . .

. . .

You would have easy and quickly, in my judgement, the Republic of Venice with you as an ally in this war. The Venetians are seen to have laid the foundation and prepared for peace because they have always until now cared more than all others for the dominions of Italy and the world. They have sought peace between the quarrelling and contending in war, with diplomats sent at their own expense and even voluntarily. And no one ought to fear that treachery would proceed from this peace, because by the intervention, authority and prayers of the pope at this time, it will seem that the Christian people, the Christian religion, even more our highest, greatest God himself, Jesus Christ, concluded and signed this peace, procured on account of the necessity. It is clear that, with the announcement of these foundations of peace in Italy, all Christian princes and peoples of the world will so heed the pope's admonishments, arguments, and urging that, with matters settled among themselves, they will have popular support to take up arms against the common Turkish enemy. More easily will each one permit themselves to be persuaded to make peace, a peace which fear of an outsider will be a shield and guardian. Often indeed, always in practice and experience it is a fact that where public danger threatens, private enmities cease, and we often read and we often see and we most often have heard that many men frightened by fear of a powerful enemy have offered aid to their most hated enemies: For that reason, most wise Marcus Cato argued against the destruction of Carthage, because he wanted external fear of that city to nourish concord at home among the citizens.

Biondo Flavio, "Ad Alphonsum aragonensem serenissimum regem de expeditione in turchos," in *Scritti inediti e rari*, edited by Bartolomeo Nogara, translated by Brian Maxson (Rome: Tipografia poliglotta vaticana, 1927), 31–51.

Further Reading

Allen, S. J., and Emilie Amt, eds. *The Crusades. A Reader*. 2nd ed. Toronto: University of Toronto Press, 2014.

Andrea, Alfred J., and Andrew Holt, eds. *Seven Myths of the Crusades*. Indianapolis, IN: Hackett, 2015.

Chazan, Robert. *European Jewry and the First Crusade*. Berkeley: University of California Press, 1987.

Christie, Niall. *Muslims and Crusaders*. 2nd ed. London: Routledge, 2020.

Delaney, Carol. "Columbus's Ultimate Goal: Jerusalem." *Comparative Studies in Society and History* 48, no. 2 (April 2006): 260–292.

Harris, Jonathan. *Byzantium and the Crusades*. 2nd ed. London: Bloomsbury, 2014.

Housley, Norman. *Contesting the Crusades*. Malden, MA: Blackwell, 2006.

Housley, Norman. *The Later Crusades, 1274–1580: From Lyons to Alcazar*. Oxford: Oxford University Press, 1992.

Ibn-Munqidh, Usamah. *An Arab-Syrian Gentleman and Warrior in the Period of the Crusades*. Translated by Philip K. Hitti. Princeton, NJ: Princeton University Press, 1987.

Kedar, Benjamin Z., Jonathan Phillips, and Jonathan Riley-Smith, eds. *Crusades*. 18 vols. London: Routledge, 2001–present.

Madden, Thomas F. *The Concise History of the Crusades*. 3rd ed. Lanham, MD: Rowman & Littlefield, 2013.

Madden, Thomas F. "Crusade Myths." *Ignatius Insight*. Found online at http://www.ignatiusinsight.com/features2005/tmadden_crusademyths _feb05.asp (accessed September 23, 2020).

Maxson, Brian Jeffrey. "Claiming Byzantium: Papal Diplomacy, Biondo Flavio, and the Fourth Crusade." *Studi Veneziani* 68 (2013): 31–60.

Phillips, Jonathan. *Holy Warriors*. New York: Random House, 2010.

Riley-Smith, Jonathan. *The Oxford Illustrated History of the Crusades*. Oxford: Oxford University Press, 2001.

Riley-Smith, Jonathan. *What Were the Crusades?* 4th ed. San Francisco: Ignatius Press, 2009.

Riley-Smith, Jonathan. *The Crusades. A History*. 3rd ed. London: Bloomsbury, 2014.

Setton, Kenneth. *A History of the Crusades*. 6 vols. Madison: University of Wisconsin Press, 1969–89.

Tyerman, Christopher. *God's War: A New History of the Crusades*. Cambridge, MA: Belknap, 2009.

Bibliography

Aberth, John, ed. *The Black Death, the Great Mortality of 1348–1350: A Brief History with Documents.* 2nd ed. Boston: Bedford/St. Martin's, 2016.

Abulafia, David. *The Great Sea: A Human History of the Mediterranean.* Oxford: Oxford University Press, 2011.

Anderson, Benedict. *Imagined Communities: Reflections on the Origin and Spread of Nationalism.* Rev. ed. London: Verso, 2006.

Appuhn, Karl. *A Forest on the Sea: Environment Expertise in Renaissance Venice.* Baltimore: Johns Hopkins University Press, 2010.

Atkinson, Niall. *The Noisy Renaissance: Sound, Architecture, and Florentine Urban Life.* University Park: Pennsylvania State University Press, 2017.

Baker, Nicholas Scott. *The Fruit of Liberty: Political Culture in the Florentine Renaissance, 1480–1550.* Cambridge, MA: Harvard University Press, 2013.

Baldassarri, Stefano Ugo, and Arielle Saiber, eds. *Images of Quattrocento Florence: Selected Writings in Literature, History, and Art.* New Haven, CT: Yale University Press, 2000.

Baxandall, Michael. *Painting and Experience in Fifteenth Century Italy: A Primer in the Social History of Pictorial Style.* 2nd ed. Oxford: Oxford University Press, 1988.

Benedict, Philip. *Christ's Churches Purely Reformed. A Social History of Calvinism.* New Haven, CT: Yale University Press, 2002.

Blackburn, Robin. *The Making of New World Slavery: From the Baroque to the Modern, 1492–1800.* London: Verso, 1997.

Blair, Ann. *Too Much to Know. Managing Scholarly Information before the Modern Age.* New Haven, CT: Yale University Press, 2010.

Bossy, John. *Christianity in the West, 1400–1700.* Oxford: Oxford University Press, 1985.

Bourdieu, Pierre, and Louic J. D. Wacquant. *An Invitation to Reflexive Sociology.* Chicago: University of Chicago Press, 1992.

Braudel, Fernand. *The Mediterranean and the Mediterranean World in the Age of Philip II.* Berkeley: University of California Press, 1996.

Brown, Alison. *The Renaissance.* 3rd ed. London: Routledge, 2021.

Bruening, Michael, ed. *A Reformation Sourcebook.* Toronto: University of Toronto Press, 2017.

Burke, Peter. *Popular Culture in Early Modern Europe.* New York: Harper Torchbooks, 1978.

Cameron, Euan. *Enchanted Europe: Superstition, Reason, and Religion, 1250–1750.* Oxford: Oxford University Press, 2011.

Cameron, Euan. *The European Reformation.* Oxford: Oxford University Press, 1991.

Cohen, Richard, Natalie Dohrmann, Elhanan Reiner, and Adam Shear, eds. *Jewish Culture in Early Modern Europe: Essays in Honor of David B. Ruderman.* Pittsburgh, PA: University of Pittsburgh Press, 2014.

Cohen, Thomas V. *Love and Death in Renaissance Italy.* Chicago: University of Chicago Press, 2004.

Collins, James B. *The State in Early Modern France.* Cambridge: Cambridge University Press, 1995.

Collins, James B., and Karen L. Taylor, eds. *Early Modern Europe: Issues and Interpretations.* Malden, MA: Blackwell, 2006.

Crosby, Alfred W., Jr. *The Columbian Exchange: Biological and Cultural Consequences of 1492.* 30th Anniversary ed. Westport, CT: Praeger, 2003.

Davies, Norman. *God's Playground: A History of Poland.* Rev. ed., 2 vols. New York: Columbia University Press, 2005.

Davis, Natalie Zemon. *The Return of Martin Guerre.* Cambridge, MA: Harvard University Press, 1983.

Davis, Natalie Zemon. *Society and Culture in Early Modern France.* Stanford: Stanford University Press, 1975.

Dover, Paul M. *The Information Revolution in Early Modern Europe.* Cambridge: Cambridge University Press, 2021.

Duffy, Eamon. *The Stripping of the Altars: Traditional Religion in England, 1400–1580.* New Haven, CT: Yale University Press, 1992.

Eisenstein, Elizabeth. *The Printing Press as an Agent of Change.* Cambridge: Cambridge University Press, 1980.

Elias, Norbert. *The Civilizing Process.* 2 vols. Oxford: Blackwell, 1978–1982.

Epstein, Steven A. *Speaking of Slavery. Color, Ethnicity, & Human Bondage in Italy.* Ithaca, NY: Cornell University Press, 2001.

Ertman, Thomas. *Birth of the Leviathan: Building States and Regimes in Medieval and Early Modern Europe.* Cambridge: Cambridge University Press, 1997.

Findlen, Paula. *Possessing Nature: Museums, Collecting, and Scientific Culture in Early Modern Italy.* Berkeley: University of California Press, 1994.

Finocchiaro, Maurice A., ed. *The Galileo Affair.* Berkeley: University of California Press, 1989.

Fletcher, Catherine. *The Black Prince of Florence.* Oxford: Oxford University Press, 2016.

Foucault, Michael. *Discipline & Punish: The Birth of the Prison.* Translated by Alan Sheridan. New York: Vintage Books, 1995.

French, Anna, ed. *Early Modern Childhood: An Introduction.* London: Routledge, 2020.

Gaunt, Peter, ed. *The English Civil War: The Essential Readings.* Oxford: Blackwell, 2000.

Ginzburg, Carlo. *The Cheese and the Worms.* Translated by John Tedeschi and Anne Tedeschi. New York: Penguin, 1980.

Goffman, Daniel. *The Ottoman Empire and Early Modern Europe.* Cambridge: Cambridge University Press, 2002.

Goldberg, Edward L. *Jews and Magic in Medici Florence. The Secret World of Benedetto Blanis.* Toronto: University of Toronto Press, 2011.

Grafton, Anthony. *Defenders of the Text: The Traditions of Scholarship in an Age of Science, 1450–1800.* Cambridge, MA: Harvard University Press, 1991.

Greenblatt, Stephen. *The Swerve: How the World Became Modern.* New York: W. W. Norton, 2011.

Greengrass, Mark. *Christendom Destroyed. Europe 1517–1648.* New York: Penguin, 2014.

Gregory, Brad S. *Salvation at Stake: Christian Martyrdom in Early Modern Europe.* Cambridge, MA: Harvard University Press, 1999.

Guy, John. *Tudor England.* Oxford: Oxford University Press, 1990.

Habermas, Jürgen. *The Structural Transformation of the Public Sphere.* Translated by Thomas Burger with Frederick Lawrence. Cambridge, MA: MIT Press, 1989.

Halsall, Paul. *Internet History Sourcebooks Project.* Fordham University. https://sourcebooks.fordham.edu/

Harline, Craig, and Eddy Put. *A Bishop's Tale*. New Haven, CT: Yale University Press, 2000.

Henderson, John. *Florence under Siege: Surviving Plague in an Early Modern City*. New Haven, CT: Yale University Press, 2019.

Hill, Christopher. *The World Turned Upside Down*. New York: Penguin, 1984.

Huppert, George. *After the Black Death: A Social History of Early Modern Europe*. Bloomington: Indiana University Press, 1998.

Jardine, Lisa. *Worldly Goods: A New History of the Renaissance*. New York: W.W. Norton, 1996.

Jurdjevic, Mark. *A Great and Wretched City: Promise and Failure in Machiavelli's Florentine Political Thought*. Cambridge, MA: Harvard University Press, 2014.

Jütte, Robert. *Poverty and Deviance in Early Modern Europe*. Cambridge: Cambridge University Press, 1994.

Kamen, Henry. *Empire. How Spain Became a World Power, 1492–1763*. New York: HaperCollins, 2003.

Kann, Robert A. *A History of the Habsburg Empire, 1526–1918*. Berkeley: University of California Press, 1980.

King, Margaret L. *Women of the Renaissance*. Chicago: University of Chicago Press, 1991.

Kirshner, Julius, ed. *The Origins of the State in Italy, 1300–1600*. Chicago: University of Chicago Press, 1995.

Koenigsberger, H. G., George L. Mosse, and G. Q. Bowler. *Europe in the Sixteenth Century*. 2nd ed. London: Longman, 1989.

Kors, Alan Charles, and Edward Peters, eds. *Witchcraft in Europe, 400–1700. A Documentary History*. Rev. ed. Philadelphia: University of Pennsylvania Press, 2001.

Kümin, Beat, ed. *The European World, 1500–1800: An Introduction to Early Modern History*. 2nd ed. London: Routledge, 2014.

Lazzarini, Isabella. *Communication and Conflict: Italian Diplomacy and the Early Renaissance, 1350–1520*. Oxford: Oxford University Press, 2015.

Levack, Brian. *The Witch-Hunt in Early Modern Europe*. 4th ed. London: Routledge, 2015.

MacCulloch, Diarmaid. *The Reformation: A History*. New York: Penguin, 2003.

Mallett, Michael, and Christine Shaw. *The Italian Wars, 1494–1559*. 2nd ed. London: Routledge, 2019.

Mauss, Marcel. *The Gift: Forms and Functions of Exchange in Archaic Societies*. Translated by Ian Cunninson. London: Cohen & West, 1970.

McGrath, Alistair. *Reformation Thought: An Introduction.* 4th ed. Malden, MA: Wiley-Blackwell, 2012.

Monter, William. *The Rise of Female Kings in Europe, 1300–1800.* New Haven, CT: Yale University Press, 2012.

Mungello, D. E. *The Great Encounter of China and the West, 1500–1800.* Lanham, MD: Rowman & Littlefield, 2012.

Nirenberg, David. *Communities of Violence: Persecution of Minorities in the Middle Ages.* Princeton, NJ: Princeton University Press, 1996.

O'Connell, Monique, and Eric Dursteler. *The Mediterranean World: From the Fall of Rome to the Rise of Napoleon.* Baltimore: Johns Hopkins University Press, 2016.

O'Malley, John W. *Trent and All That.* Cambridge, MA: Harvard University Press, 2000.

Otele, Olivette. *African Europeans: An Untold History.* New York: Basic Books, 2021.

Outram, Dorinda. *The Enlightenment.* Cambridge: Cambridge University Press, 2013.

Ozment, Steven. *The Age of Reform 1250–1550.* New Haven, CT: Yale University Press, 1980.

Pagden, Anthony. *Lords of All the World: Ideologies of Empire in Spain, Britain, and France c.1500–c.1800.* New Haven, CT: Yale University Press, 1995.

Parish, Helen, ed. *Superstition and Magic in Early Modern Europe: A Reader.* London: Bloomsbury, 2015.

Pettegree, Andrew. *The Book in the Renaissance.* New Haven, CT: Yale University Press, 2011.

Pocock, J. G. A. *The Machiavellian Moment: Florentine Political Thought and the Atlantic Republican Tradition.* Princeton, NJ: Princeton University Press, 1975.

Rocke, Michael. *Forbidden Friendships: Homosexuality and Male Culture in Renaissance Florence.* Oxford: Oxford University Press, 1996.

Ross, Sarah Gwyneth. *The Birth of Feminism: Woman as Intellect in Renaissance Italy and England.* Cambridge, MA: Harvard University Press, 2009.

Sandberg, Brian. *War and Conflict in the Early Modern World: 1500–1700.* Cambridge: Polity, 2016.

Scribner, R. W. *For the Sake of Simple Folk.* Oxford: Oxford University Press, 1981.

Shagan, Ethan. *Popular Politics and the English Reformation.* Cambridge: Cambridge University Press, 2003.

Shapin, Steven. *A Social History of Truth. Civility and Science in Seventeenth-Century England*. Chicago: University of Chicago Press, 1994.

Shapin, Steven, and Simon Schaffer. *Leviathan and the Air-Pump: Hobbes, Boyle, and the Experimental Life*. Princeton, NJ: Princeton University Press, 1996.

Skinner, Quentin. *The Foundations of Modern Political Thought*. 2 vols. Cambridge: Cambridge University Press, 1978.

Skinner, Quentin. *Machiavelli: A Very Short Introduction*. 2nd ed. Oxford: Oxford University Press, 2019.

Terpstra, Nicholas, ed. *Lives Uncovered: A Sourcebook of Early Modern Europe*. Toronto: University of Toronto Press, 2019.

Wiesner-Hanks, Merry E. *Early Modern Europe, 1450–1789*. Cambridge: Cambridge University Press, 2006.

Williams, David, ed. *The Enlightenment*. Cambridge: Cambridge University Press, 1999.

Wilson, Peter. *The Thirty Years War: Europe's Tragedy*. Cambridge, MA: Belknap, 2011.

Index

About the Author

Brian Jeffrey Maxson received his doctorate from Northwestern University in 2008. Since then, he has worked at East Tennessee State University, where he also served as Assistant Dean of Graduate Studies during the period 2013–16. He is the author and editor of many different studies on early modern Europe, including the books *The Humanist World of Renaissance Florence* (2014) and *A Short History of Florence and the Florentine Republic* (2023). He has received support for his scholarship from the Massachusetts Historical Society, Villa I Tatti (the Harvard University Center for Italian Renaissance Studies), the Fulbright Program, and other organizations. He is currently serving as an editor for *Renaissance Quarterly*.

9 798216 460527